GRADE 8

TEST PRACTICE
for Common Core

Judith Harmon

and

Nicole Pomaro

D1572789

BARRON'S

About the Authors

Judith Harmon, M. A., is the recently retired chairperson for the Mathematics and Science department at W. T. Clarke M.S., a Blue Ribbon school, in East Meadow, New York. She is a certified teacher of mathematics, physics, and special education for New York State. She also holds a New York State certification for school district and building administration. Judy taught 8th grade mathematics for 20 years. She attended New York State training in the Common Core standards and has spent the last five years providing support and guidance to teachers during the implementation of the new curriculum.

Nicole Pomaro has been teaching seventh and eighth grade English Language Arts at a Blue Ribbon middle school on Long Island for seven years. She has been trained in the implementation of the Common Core standards. She has also recently collaborated with another colleague in the implementation and curriculum development of a Reading and Writing Workshop for eighth graders, which she currently teaches. Ms. Pomaro loves language and literature and strikes to invoke a similar passion in her own students.

Acknowledgments

I would like to thank Tom, Seth, and Jennie for all of their love and support. I would also like to thank the many dedicated teachers and colleagues who have inspired me throughout my career.

— Judy Harmon

I would like to extend my sincerest gratitude to all of my loved ones who make up the strong, encouraging, and enriching foundation upon which I stand, in addition to all of my colleagues, administrators, and friends at MSMS who motivate and inspire me on a daily basis.

— Nicole Pomaro

All inquiries should be addressed to:
Barron's Educational Series, Inc.
250 Wireless Boulevard
Hauppauge, New York 11788
www.barronseduc.com

ISBN: 978-1-4380-0712-0

Library of Congress Control Number: 2015957473

Manufactured by: B11R11
Date of Manufacture: February 2016

PRINTED IN THE UNITED STATES OF AMERICA
9 8 7 6 5 4 3 2 1

CONTENTS

ENGLISH LANGUAGE ARTS

Reading: Literature

Reading: Informational Text

Writing

Language

MATH

The Number System

Expressions and Equations

Functions

Geometry

Statistics and Probability

NOTE TO PARENTS AND EDUCATORS

About Barron's Core Focus Workbooks

Barron's recognizes the need to create products to help students navigate the Common Core State Standards being implemented in schools across America. To meet this need, we have created these grade-specific workbooks that will help bring the Common Core standards to life and will ensure that students are prepared for these national assessments. It is our hope that students can work through these books independently or with the guidance of a parent or teacher.

Barron's Core Focus workbooks are meant to supplement the Common Core teaching that students are receiving in their classrooms. These workbooks, all created by dedicated educators, provide specific practice on the Common Core standards through a variety of exercises and question types, including multiple-choice, short-answer, and extended-response. The questions are organized to build on each other, increasing student understanding from one standard to the next, one step at a time, and they challenge students to apply the standards in different formats. Both the English Language Arts (ELA) and Math sections of the books end with a review test—this is a great way to sum up what the student has learned and reviewed from the exercises throughout.

What is Common Core?

"The standards are designed to be robust and relevant to the real world, reflecting the knowledge and skills that our young people need for success in college and careers."

(2012 Common Core State Standards Initiative)

Simply put, the Common Core is a series of standards that spells out exactly what students are expected to learn in English Language Arts and Mathematics throughout their years in school. These standards are fairly consistent across all grades and are designed so that students, teachers, and parents can understand what students should be learning and achieving at each grade level. Standards are organized to provide a clear understanding of the core concepts and procedures that students should master at each step of the way through school.

Unlike previous standards that were created by individual states, the Common Core is meant to be consistent throughout the country, providing all students with an equal and fair opportunity to learn English Language Arts (ELA) and Math. These standards are also designed to teach students how to apply this knowledge to their everyday lives and experiences.

By sharing the same standards, states can more accurately gauge and compare students' progress and the quality of education received. The ultimate goal of Common Core is to ensure that all students, no matter which state or part of the country they are from, will be equally ready and prepared for college and the workforce.

What is a Standard?

A standard is a skill that should be learned by a student. Standards are organized by *domains*, which are larger groupings of related standards. For instance, in Grade 8 Math, there are five domains: "The Number System," "Expressions and Equations," "Functions," "Geometry," and "Statistics and Probability."

Under the domain "Expressions and Equations," there are eight individual standards which highlight a specific skill or understanding that a student should gain. One standard, **EE.C.8.A**, directs students to "Understand that solutions to a system of two linear equations in two variables correspond to points of intersection of their graphs, because points of intersection satisfy both equations simultaneously." For example, by knowing that every point on a line represents a solution to the equation of that line, a student will also know that when two lines intersect, the point of intersection is a solution to both the equations represented by the lines.

ENGLISH LANGUAGE ARTS

The English Language Arts standards are separated into the different skill sets of Reading, Writing, Language, and Speaking and Listening. The standards build off of one another from grades K–12, and their goal is to provide students with the skills necessary for college-and-career readiness. The Common Core has designated separate reading standards to distinguish between fiction and informational texts. These standards are identified as Reading: Literature and Reading: Informational Text. Most importantly, the reading standards emphasize engaging all students in the reading process. To meet the standards, students are expected to read multiple forms of text types that, in turn, provide deeper literacy experiences for all students. The Common Core also emphasizes the importance of text complexity. "Through extensive reading of stories, dramas, poems, and myths from diverse cultures and different time periods, students gain literary and cultural knowledge as well as familiarity with various text structures and elements." (2012 Common Core State Standards Initiative)

Each of the 6–8 strands is arranged within a College and Career Readiness Anchor Standard. The Anchor Standards are the overarching goals of a K–12 curriculum. These standards remain constant in all grades. Each grade level's strands are built as a scaffold in order to achieve "official" College and Career Readiness Anchor Standards by the end of the grade 12. The College and Career Readiness Anchor Standards for Reading: Literature and Reading: Informational Text focus on identifying key ideas and details, craft and structure, and the integration of knowledge and ideas. To meet the Common Core reading standards, students are expected to read, respond to, and interact with an array of text types of varying complexities. The College and Career Readiness Anchor Standards for Writing focus on text types and purposes, the production and distribution of writing, and research to build and present knowledge. To meet the Common Core writing standards, students are expected to write persuasive, narrative, and informational text. The College and Career Readiness Anchor Standards for Speaking and Listening focus on comprehension, collaboration, and the presentation of knowledge and ideas. The speaking and listening standards focus heavily on students' ability to actively participate, engage, and present academic information in multiple settings. The College and Career Readiness Anchor Standards for Language focus on the conventions of standard English, vocabulary acquisition, and knowledge of language.

The Common Core standards are also designed to help students create digital literature and use technology to communicate ideas and knowledge. The English Language Arts standards are a vision of what it means to be literate in the twenty-first century. These standards foster imperative learning experiences for the twenty-first century learner. "The skills and knowledge captured in the ELA/literacy standards are designed to prepare students for life outside the classroom. They include critical-thinking skills and the ability to closely and attentively read texts in a way that will help them understand and enjoy complex works of literature." (2012 Common Core Initiative)

MATH

The Common Core mathematics standards were developed as a connected progression of learning throughout grades K–12. Ideally, this will enable teachers to close achievement gaps and give students the foundational skills necessary to continue in their learning. The Common Core provides teachers with an opportunity to build a deep and rich understanding of mathematical concepts. Instruction of Common Core mathematics standards encompasses the mathematical practices as well. These practices include skills that math students in every grade are expected to master. The mathematical practices bring rigor and rich learning opportunities to the classroom.

In grade 8, Expressions and Equations is a challenging domain that is taught to students. In grade 7, students studied proportional relationships and their graphic and algebraic representations. In grade 8, students are expected to compare two different proportional relationships represented in different ways. The Common Core standards are related across grade levels as well as across the domains. For example, Function standards share a relationship with Expressions and Equations standards. This connectedness helps students prepare for the real world—remember, we don't use just one skill to balance our checkbook or determine the amount of paint for a room in our home. We have to be able to apply a variety of skills every day, and the goal of the Common Core math standards is to help prepare students for this real-life use of math. The Common Core also supports mathematical understanding of concepts that are developmentally appropriate for students. These standards allow students to build strong number sense in the early grades. In the middle grades (6, 7, and 8), they develop algebraic reasoning and graphing skills along with problem-solving techniques that allow them to relate mathematics to real-world situations. The K–8 Common Core math standards provide students with a solid foundation in the mathematical concepts and skills needed for success in high school and college courses. These standards also foster the development of thinking and problem-solving skills that provide the opportunity for success beyond the classroom.

HOW TO USE THIS BOOK

This test practice workbook is organized by standard—one step at a time—in the order that students will likely see the concepts in the classroom or other learning environment. Each applicable standard is organized in an easy-to-navigate spread(s) providing exposure to the Common Core in the simplest way possible.

In this workbook, students will be able to build skills in multiple formats by answering multiple-choice, short-answer, and extended-response questions. Answers and explanations are included at the end of each section so students, parents, and teachers can easily assess the student's response. These explanations are an important part of the learning process as they provide information on the understanding needed to answer each question, common misconceptions students have, and an explanation of how a student might best approach the question. These explanations will help students not only check the accuracy of their responses but also learn how they can improve their responses. Students using **Barron's Core Focus** workbooks will practice each of the specific content standards as they learn them, and also thoroughly review all the concepts in Math or English Language Arts through the cumulative assessments.

In addition to the practice spreads covering specific standards, each section ends with a comprehensive practice test allowing students to monitor their general progress in either English Language Arts or Math. Answers and explanations provide additional guidance and instruction.

> A complete list of all the grade 8 English Language Arts and Math Common Core standards can be found at the end of this book in Appendices A and B.

FEATURES AND BENEFITS

Barron's Core Focus workbooks provide educators, parents, and students with an opportunity to enhance their knowledge and practice grade-level expectations within the Common Core English Language Arts and Math standards. Each workbook in this series provides questions that specifically correlate to each standard. Every answer explanation provides helpful insight into a student's understanding, identifying common misconceptions and then providing multiple strategies. Each workbook also provides a cumulative assessment for each content area in Math and English Language Arts. Throughout the workbooks, there are tip boxes that contain a variety of information and expose students to vocabulary, tips, and strategies.

- Parents can use this workbook to encourage learning at home. This workbook can be used as guided practice or extra exposure to concepts students may be struggling to master in school.

- Educators can use the workbooks in their classrooms to identify how to assess each standard. These workbooks give teachers insight into what students should be able to do independently in order to master the standard. The detailed answer explanations provide opportunities for teachers to recognize misconceptions students may have about specific standards and how to successfully approach questions applicable to each standard.

- Students can use these workbooks at home to build their knowledge of English Language Arts and Math content. They can practice the content they have learned, are learning, or are going to learn. The workbooks can help prepare students for what's to come and/or as remedial practice for concepts they find challenging. The explanations in the workbooks are extremely valuable to students as they work independently, increasing their awareness of concepts and improving their confidence as they work through each question.

The benefits that **Barron's Core Focus** workbooks will provide students, parents, and educators are endless as the Common Core is implemented in schools across America.

Common Core State Standards Initiative
http://www.corestandards.org/

PARCC
http://www.parcconline.org/

Smarter Balanced Assessment Consortium
www.smarterbalanced.org

ENGLISH LANGUAGE ARTS

The English Language Arts Standards are separated into the different skill sets of Reading, Writing, Language, and Speaking and Listening. The standards build off of one another from grades K–12, and their goal is to provide students with the skills necessary for college-and-career readiness. The Common Core has separate Reading Standards for fiction and informational texts. These standards are identified as Reading: Literature and Reading: Informational Text. In this section, students will practice skills covering a variety of standards. Each section covers a specific standard and provides the student with practice through multiple-choice, short-answer, and extended-response questions.

CITING TEXTUAL EVIDENCE

RL.8.1 Cite the textual evidence that most strongly supports an analysis of what the text says explicitly as well as inferences drawn from the text.

Directions: Read the following excerpt from *The Adventures of Tom Sawyer* by Mark Twain and answer the questions that follow.

Close upon the hour of noon the whole village was suddenly electrified with the ghastly news. No need of the as yet undreamed-of telegraph; the tale flew from man to man, from group to group, from house to house, with little less than telegraphic speed. Of course the schoolmaster gave holiday for that afternoon; the town would have thought
5　strangely of him if he had not.

A gory knife had been found close to the murdered man, and it had been recognized by somebody as belonging to Muff Potter—so the story ran. And it was said that a belated citizen had come upon Potter washing himself in the "branch" about one or two o'clock in the morning, and that Potter had at once sneaked off—suspicious
10　circumstances, especially the washing which was not a habit with Potter. It was also said that the town had been ransacked for this "murderer" (the public are not slow in the matter of sifting evidence and arriving at a verdict), but that he could not be found. Horsemen had departed down all the roads in every direction, and the Sheriff "was confident" that he would be captured before night.

15　All the town was drifting toward the graveyard. Tom's heartbreak vanished and he joined the procession, not because he would not a thousand times rather go anywhere else, but because an awful, unaccountable fascination drew him on. Arrived at the dreadful place, he wormed his small body through the crowd and saw the dismal spectacle. It seemed to him an age since he was there before. Somebody pinched his
20　arm. He turned, and his eyes met Huckleberry's. Then both looked elsewhere at once, and wondered if anybody had noticed anything in their mutual glance. But everybody was talking, and intent upon the grisly spectacle before them.

"Poor fellow!" "Poor young fellow!" "This ought to be a lesson to grave robbers!" "Muff Potter'll hang for this if they catch him!" This was the drift of remark; and the minister
25　said, "It was a judgment; His hand is here."

　- Now Tom shivered from head to heel, for his eye fell upon the stolid[1] face of Injun Joe. At this moment the crowd began to sway and struggle, and voices shouted, "It's him! it's him! he's coming himself!"

"Who? Who?" from twenty voices.

30   "Muff Potter!"

"Hallo, he's stopped!—Look out, he's turning! Don't let him get away!"

People in the branches of the trees over Tom's head said he wasn't trying to get away—he only looked doubtful and perplexed.

"Infernal impudence[2]!" said a bystander; "wanted to come and take a quiet look at his

35   work, I reckon—didn't expect any company."

The crowd fell apart now, and the Sheriff came through, ostentatiously[3] leading Potter by the arm. The poor fellow's face was haggard, and his eyes showed the fear that was upon him. When he stood before the murdered man, he shook as with a palsy[4], and he put his face in his hands and burst into tears.

40   "I didn't do it, friends," he sobbed; "'pon my word and honor I never done it."

"Who's accused you?" shouted a voice.

This shot seemed to carry home. Potter lifted his face and looked around him with a pathetic hopelessness in his eyes. He saw Injun Joe, and exclaimed:

"Oh, Injun Joe, you promised me you'd never—"

45   "Is that your knife?" and it was thrust before him by the Sheriff.

Potter would have fallen if they had not caught him and eased him to the ground. Then he said:

"Something told me 't if I didn't come back and get—" He shuddered; then waved his nerveless hand with a vanquished[5] gesture and said, "Tell 'em, Joe, tell 'em—it ain't any

50   use any more."

Then Huckleberry and Tom stood dumb and staring, and heard the stony-hearted liar reel off his serene statement, they expecting every moment that the clear sky would deliver God's lightnings upon his head, and wondering to see how long the stroke was delayed. And when he had finished and still stood alive and whole, their wavering

55   impulse to break their oath and save the poor betrayed prisoner's life faded and vanished away, for plainly this miscreant[6] had sold himself to Satan and it would be fatal to meddle with the property of such a power as that.

"Why didn't you leave? What did you want to come here for?" somebody said.

"I couldn't help it—I couldn't help it," Potter moaned. "I wanted to run away, but I

60   couldn't seem to come anywhere but here." And he fell to sobbing again.

Injun Joe repeated his statement, just as calmly, a few minutes afterward on the inquest, under oath; and the boys, seeing that the lightnings were still withheld, were confirmed in their belief that Joe had sold himself to the devil. He was now become, to them, the most balefully interesting object they had ever looked upon, and they could not

65   take their fascinated eyes from his face.

---

[1](adj.) showing little or no emotion

[2](n.) rudeness

[3](adv.) in a way that is meant to attract attention, admiration, or envy

[4](n.) a medical condition that causes the body or part of the body to shake uncontrollably

[5](adj.) defeated

[6](n.) a person who does something that is illegal or morally wrong

1. Based on the text, which statement accurately describes the town's reaction to the news of the murdered man?
   - Ⓐ News spread through the town quickly, though no one was much interested.
   - Ⓑ Most of the town heard about it on the news, then quickly ran down to the graveyard to see it for themselves.
   - Ⓒ The whole town was talking about the news, and word traveled rapidly. Even school was canceled that day.
   - Ⓓ Word of the murder traveled rapidly, and many of the townspeople were afraid to leave their homes.

2. Cite two pieces of textual evidence that support your answer to question 1.

   _____

   _____

   _____

   _____

3. Which phrase best describes Muff Potter at this moment in the story?
   - Ⓐ Calm and remorseful
   - Ⓑ Confident and convincing
   - Ⓒ Scared and confused
   - Ⓓ Angry and violent

4. Cite two pieces of textual evidence that support your answer to question 3.

   _____

   _____

   _____

   _____

5. Based on the text, it can be inferred that the townspeople are quick to believe that Muff Potter is the murderer. Which of the following excerpts most strongly supports this inference?

Ⓐ "'I couldn't help it—I couldn't help it,' Potter moaned. 'I wanted to run away, but I couldn't seem to come anywhere but here.' And he fell to sobbing again."

Ⓑ "And when he had finished and still stood alive and whole, their wavering impulse to break their oath and save the poor betrayed prisoner's life faded and vanished away, for plainly this miscreant had sold himself to Satan and it would be fatal to meddle with the property of such a power as that."

Ⓒ "It was also said that the town had been ransacked for this 'murderer' (the public are not slow in the matter of sifting evidence and arriving at a verdict), but that he could not be found."

Ⓓ "People in the branches of the trees over Tom's head said he wasn't trying to get away—he only looked doubtful and perplexed."

6. Based on the text, it can be inferred that Tom and Huck are superstitious, or behave based upon beliefs of the supernatural, nature, or a God. Which of the following excerpts does **not** support this inference?

Ⓐ "Injun Joe repeated his statement, just as calmly, a few minutes afterward on the inquest, under oath; and the boys, seeing that the lightnings were still withheld, were confirmed in their belief that Joe had sold himself to the devil."

Ⓑ "He turned, and his eyes met Huckleberry's. Then both looked elsewhere at once, and wondered if anybody had noticed anything in their mutual glance. But everybody was talking, and intent upon the grisly spectacle before them."

Ⓒ "And when he had finished and still stood alive and whole, their wavering impulse to break their oath and save the poor betrayed prisoner's life faded and vanished away, for plainly this miscreant had sold himself to Satan and it would be fatal to meddle with the property of such a power as that."

Ⓓ "Then Huckleberry and Tom stood dumb and staring, and heard the stony-hearted liar reel off his serene statement, they expecting every moment that the clear sky would deliver God's lightnings upon his head, and wondering to see how long the stroke was delayed."

(Answers are on page 95.)

DETERMINING THEME AND CENTRAL IDEA

RL.8.2 Determine a theme or central idea of a text and analyze its development over the course of the text, including its relationship to the characters, setting, and plot; provide an objective summary of the text.

Directions: Read the following poem by Stephen Vincent Benét and answer the questions that follow.

Nightmare Number Three
by Stephen Vincent Benét

We had expected everything but revolt
And I kind of wonder myself when they started thinking—
But there's no dice in that now.
                        I've heard fellow say
5   They must have planned it for years and maybe they did.
Looking back, you can find little incidents here and there,
Like the concrete-mixer in Jersey eating the wop
Or the roto press that printed 'Fiddle-dee-dee!'
In a three-color process all over Senator Sloop,
10   Just as he was making a speech. The thing about that
Was, how could it walk upstairs? But it was upstairs,
Clicking and mumbling in the Senate Chamber.
They had to knock out the wall to take it away
And the wrecking-crew said it grinned.
15   It was only the best
Machines, of course, the superhuman machines,
The ones we'd built to be better than flesh and bone,
But the cars were in it, of course . . .
                 and they hunted us
20   Like rabbits through the cramped streets on that Bloody Monday,
The Madison Avenue busses leading the charge.
The busses were pretty bad—but I'll not forget
The smash of glass when the Duesenberg left the show-room
And pinned three brokers to the Racquet Club steps
25   Or the long howl of the horns when they saw men run,
When they saw them looking for holes in the solid ground . . .

I guess they were tired of being ridden in
And stopped and started by pygmies for silly ends,
Of wrapping cheap cigarettes and bad chocolate bars
30 Collecting nickels and waving platinum hair
And letting six million people live in a town.
I guess it was that, I guess they got tired of us
And the whole smell of human hands.

                           But it was a shock
35 To climb sixteen flights of stairs to Art Zuckow's office
(Noboby took the elevators twice)
And find him strangled to death in a nest of telephones,
The octopus-tendrils waving over his head,
And a sort of quiet humming filling the air. . . .
40 Do they eat? . . . There was red . . . But I did not stop to look.
I don't know yet how I got to the roof in time
And it's lonely, here on the roof.

                           For a while, I thought
That window-cleaner would make it, and keep me company.
45 But they got him with his own hoist at the sixteenth floor
And dragged him in, with a squeal.
You see, they cooperate. Well, we taught them that
And it's fair enough, I suppose. You see, we built them.
We taught them to think for themselves.
50 It was bound to come. You can see it was bound to come.
And it won't be so bad, in the country. I hate to think
Of the reapers, running wild in the Kansas fields,
And the transport planes like hawks on a chickenyard,
But the horses might help. We might make a deal with the horses.
55 At least, you've more chance, out there.

                           And they need us, too.
They're bound to realize that when they once calm down.
They'll need oil and spare parts and adjustments and tuning up.
Slaves? Well, in a way, you know, we were slaves before.
60 There won't be so much real difference—honest, there won't.
(I wish I hadn't looked into the beauty-parlor
And seen what was happening there.
But those are female machines and a bit high-strung.)
Oh, we'll settle down. We'll arrange it. We'll compromise.
65 It won't make sense to wipe out the whole human race.
Why, I bet if I went to my old Plymouth now
(Of course you'd have to do it the tactful way)
And said, 'Look here! Who got you the swell French horn?'

7

He wouldn't turn me over to those police cars;

70   At least I don't think he would

Oh, it's going to be jake.

There won't be so much real difference—honest, there won't—

And I'd go down in a minute and take my chance—

I'm a good American and I always liked them—

75   Except for one small detail that bothers me

And that's the food proposition. Because, you see,

The concrete-mixer may have made a mistake,

And it looks like just high spirits.

But, if it's got so they like the flavor . . . well . . .

1. To whom is the speaker referring in the line, "I'm a good American and I always liked them—"?

(A) Other Americans

(B) Concrete mixers

(C) Machines

(D) Police cars

2. In order to develop the theme that over-reliance on technology has negative consequences, the poet

(A) lists various examples of the drawbacks of technology.

(B) describes a series of incidents in which technology turned against humans.

(C) identifies the many jobs that have been replaced with machines.

(D) provides comparisons between jobs fulfilled by machines, and humans who can do them better.

3. Which of the following statements *best* summarizes lines 56–71?
   - Ⓐ The speaker fears technology will turn humans into slaves.
   - Ⓑ The speaker believes that all "female" machines should be replaced by "male" machines.
   - Ⓒ The speaker promises not to abuse technology in the future.
   - Ⓓ The speaker has hope that things will eventually get better.

4. According to the speaker, why did the machines start killing humans?
   - Ⓐ They were programmed to.
   - Ⓑ They did not recognize their own strength and never intended to kill.
   - Ⓒ They grew tired of humans.
   - Ⓓ Humans tried to destroy them.

5. Which of the following lines *best* supports the theme that humans have relied too much on technology?
   - Ⓐ "I'm a good American and I always liked them."
   - Ⓑ "It won't make sense to wipe out the whole human race."
   - Ⓒ "Oh, we'll settle down. We'll arrange it. We'll compromise."
   - Ⓓ "Slaves? Well, in a way, you know, we were slaves before."

(Answers are on page 95.)

ANALYZING DIALOGUE AND PLOT

> **RL.8.3** Analyze how particular lines of dialogue or incidents in a story or drama propel the action, reveal aspects of a character, or provoke a decision.

Directions: Read the following excerpt from John Steinbeck's *The Pearl* and answer the questions that follow.

Juana dropped her stone, and she put her arms around Kino and helped him to his feet and supported him into the house. Blood oozed down from his scalp and there was a long deep cut in his cheek from ear to chin, a deep, bleeding sash. And Kino was only half conscious. He shook his head from side to side. His shirt was torn open and

5   his clothes half pulled off. Juana sat him down on his sleeping mat and she wiped the thickening blood from his face with her skirt. She brought him pulque to drink in a little pitcher, and still he shook his head to clear out the darkness.

"Who?" Juana asked.

"I don't know," Kino said. "I didn't see."

10   Now Juana brought her clay pot of water and she washed the cut on his face while he stared dazed ahead of him.

"Kino, my husband," she cried, and his eyes stared past her. "Kino, can you hear me?"

"I hear you," he said dully.

"Kino, this pearl is evil. Let us destroy it before it destroys us. Let us crush it between

15   two stones. Let us—let us throw it back in the sea where it belongs. Kino, it is evil, it is evil!"

And as she spoke the light came back in Kino's eyes so that they glowed fiercely and his muscles hardened and his will hardened.

"No," he said. "I will fight this thing. I will win over it. We will have our chance."

20   His fist pounded the sleeping mat. "No one shall take our good fortune from us," he said. His eyes softened then and he raised a gentle hand to Juana's shoulder. "Believe me," he said. "I am a man." And his face grew crafty.

"In the morning we will take our canoe and we will go over the sea and over the mountains to the capital, you and I. We will not be cheated. I am a man."

25   "Kino," she said huskily, "I am afraid. A man can be killed. Let us throw the pearl back into the sea."

"Hush," he said fiercely. "I am a man. Hush." And she was silent, for his voice was command. "Let us sleep a little," he said. "In the first light we will start. You are not afraid to go with me?"

30   "No, my husband."

His eyes were soft and warm on her then, his hand touched her cheek. "Let us sleep a little," he said.

1. What do the lines of dialogue reveal about the two characters?
   - Ⓐ Kino can be stubborn, while Juana is mostly loyal.
   - Ⓑ Juana is used to making decisions, while Kino is used to following.
   - Ⓒ Both Juana and Kino have difficulty making a decision.
   - Ⓓ Kino is weak, while Juana is strong.

2. Kino repeats the statement "I am a man" in order to
   - Ⓐ convince Juana that he is smarter than her.
   - Ⓑ reassure Juana and get her to understand his motives.
   - Ⓒ make Juana feel inferior so that she has no choice but to follow him.
   - Ⓓ illustrate how much he wants to physically defend the pearl.

3. The events in this passage help to propel the action of the plot because in it Kino is able to
   - Ⓐ change Juana's feelings regarding the pearl.
   - Ⓑ get Juana to destroy the pearl herself.
   - Ⓒ destroy the pearl before heading to the capital.
   - Ⓓ convince Juana to go to the capital with him and the pearl.

4. At the start of the passage, Kino is injured and dazed; shortly in, he becomes firm and "fierce." Kino's strength appears to come from
   - Ⓐ the pulque.
   - Ⓑ Juana's concerns.
   - Ⓒ the pearl.
   - Ⓓ Juana's strength.

5. Lines 17–18 and 27–30 help to reveal
   - Ⓐ the early morning setting.
   - Ⓑ Juana's inability to speak to her husband.
   - Ⓒ how the characters of Kino and Juana affect one another.
   - Ⓓ Kino's uncertainty of the future.

(Answers are on page 95.)

11

WORD MEANING AND FIGURATIVE LANGUAGE

> **RL.8.4** Determine the meaning of words and phrases as they are used in a text, including figurative and connotative meanings; analyze the impact of specific word choices on meaning and tone, including analogies or allusions to other texts.

Directions: Read the following poem and answer the questions that follow.

The Raven
Edgar Allan Poe

I

Once upon a midnight dreary, while I pondered, weak and weary,
Over many a quaint and curious volume of forgotten lore,
While I nodded, nearly napping, suddenly there came a tapping,
As of some one gently rapping, rapping at my chamber door.
5   "'Tis some visitor," I muttered, "tapping at my chamber door—
Only this, and nothing more."

II

Ah, distinctly I remember it was in the bleak December,
And each separate dying ember[1] wrought its ghost upon the floor.
Eagerly I wished the morrow—vainly I had sought to borrow
10   From my books surcease[2] of sorrow—sorrow for the lost Lenore—
For the rare and radiant maiden whom the angels name Lenore—
Nameless here for evermore.

III

And the silken sad uncertain rustling of each purple curtain
Thrilled me—filled me with fantastic terrors never felt before;
15   So that now, to still the beating of my heart, I stood repeating,
"'Tis some visitor entreating entrance at my chamber door—
Some late visitor entreating entrance at my chamber door;—
This it is, and nothing more."

IV

Presently my soul grew stronger; hesitating then no longer,
20   "Sir," said I, "or Madam, truly your forgiveness I implore;
But the fact is I was napping, and so gently you came rapping,
And so faintly you came tapping, tapping at my chamber door,
That I scarce was sure I heard you"—here I opened wide the door;—
Darkness there, and nothing more.

V

25 Deep into that darkness peering, long I stood there wondering, fearing,
Doubting, dreaming dreams no mortals ever dared to dream before;
But the silence was unbroken, and the stillness gave no token,
And the only word there spoken was the whispered word, "Lenore!"
This I whispered, and an echo murmured back the word, "Lenore!"—
30 Merely this, and nothing more.

VI

Back into the chamber turning, all my soul within me burning,
Soon again I heard a tapping somewhat louder than before.
"Surely," said I, "surely that is something at my window lattice:
Let me see, then, what thereat is, and this mystery explore—
35 Let my heart be still a moment and this mystery explore;—
'Tis the wind and nothing more."

VII

Open here I flung the shutter, when, with many a flirt and flutter,
In there stepped a stately raven of the saintly days of yore[3];
Not the least obeisance[4] made he; not a minute stopped or stayed he;
40 But, with mien[5] of lord or lady, perched above my chamber door—
Perched upon a bust of Pallas[6] just above my chamber door—
Perched, and sat, and nothing more.

VIII

Then this ebony bird beguiling[7] my sad fancy into smiling,
By the grave and stern decorum of the countenance[8] it wore.
45 "Though thy crest be shorn and shaven, thou," I said, "art sure no craven,
Ghastly grim and ancient raven wandering from the Nightly shore—
Tell me what thy lordly name is on the Night's Plutonian[9] shore!"
Quoth the Raven, "Nevermore."

IX

Much I marvelled this ungainly[10] fowl to hear discourse[11] so plainly,
50 Though its answer little meaning—little relevancy bore;
For we cannot help agreeing that no living human being
Ever yet was blest with seeing bird above his chamber door—
Bird or beast upon the sculptured bust above his chamber door,
With such name as "Nevermore."

X

55   But the raven, sitting lonely on the placid bust, spoke only
That one word, as if his soul in that one word he did outpour.
Nothing further then he uttered—not a feather then he fluttered—
Till I scarcely more than muttered, "other friends have flown before—
On the morrow he will leave me, as my hopes have flown before."
60   Then the bird said, "Nevermore."

XI

Startled at the stillness broken by reply so aptly[12] spoken,
"Doubtless," said I, "what it utters is its only stock and store,
Caught from some unhappy master whom unmerciful Disaster
Followed fast and followed faster till his songs one burden bore—
65   Till the dirges[13] of his Hope that melancholy burden bore
Of 'Never—nevermore'."

XII

But the Raven still beguiling all my fancy into smiling,
Straight I wheeled a cushioned seat in front of bird, and bust and
door; Then upon the velvet sinking, I betook myself to linking
70   Fancy unto fancy, thinking what this ominous[14] bird of yore—
What this grim, ungainly, ghastly, gaunt and ominous bird of yore
Meant in croaking "Nevermore."

XIII

This I sat engaged in guessing, but no syllable expressing
To the fowl whose fiery eyes now burned into my bosom's core;
75   This and more I sat divining, with my head at ease reclining
On the cushion's velvet lining that the lamplight gloated o'er,
But whose velvet violet lining with the lamplight gloating o'er,
She shall press, ah, nevermore!

XIV

Then methought the air grew denser, perfumed from an unseen censer

80   Swung by Seraphim[15] whose footfalls tinkled on the tufted floor.

"Wretch," I cried, "thy God hath lent thee—by these angels he hath sent thee

Respite[16]—respite and nepenthe[17], from thy memories of Lenore!

Quaff[18], oh quaff this kind nepenthe and forget this lost Lenore!"

Quoth the Raven, "Nevermore."

XV

85   "Prophet!" said I, "thing of evil!—prophet still, if bird or devil!—

Whether Tempter[19] sent, or whether tempest[20] tossed thee here ashore,

Desolate yet all undaunted, on this desert land enchanted—

On this home by horror haunted—tell me truly, I implore—

Is there—is there balm in Gilead[21]?—tell me—tell me, I implore!"

90   Quoth the Raven, "Nevermore."

XVI

"Prophet!" said I, "thing of evil—prophet still, if bird or devil!

By that Heaven that bends above us—by that God we both adore—

Tell this soul with sorrow laden if, within the distant Aidenn[22],

It shall clasp a sainted maiden whom the angels name Lenore—

95   Clasp a rare and radiant maiden whom the angels name Lenore."

Quoth the Raven, "Nevermore."

XVII

"By that word our sign of parting, bird or fiend[23]!" I shrieked, upstarting—

"Get thee back into the tempest and the Night's Plutonian shore!

Leave no black plume[24] as a token of that lie thy soul hath spoken!

100   Leave my loneliness unbroken!—quit the bust above my door!

Take thy beak from out my heart, and take thy form from off my door!"

Quoth the Raven, "Nevermore."

XVIII

And the Raven, never flitting, still is sitting, still is sitting

On the pallid[25] bust of Pallas just above my chamber door;

105   And his eyes have all the seeming of a demon's that is dreaming,

And the lamplight o'er him streaming throws his shadow on the floor;

And my soul from out that shadow that lies floating on the floor

Shall be lifted—nevermore!

---

[1](n.) a smoldering fragment of wood

[2](n.) a pause or stop

[3](n.) time past

[4](n.) a movement of the body that shows respect

[5](n.) an appearance

[6](n.) the Greek Goddess Athena

[7](v.) charming

[8](n.) facial appearance

[9](adj.) pertaining to the classical Underworld

[10](adj.) awkward, ungraceful

[11](n.) conversation

[12](adv.) competently

[13](n.) songs of sadness or grief

[14](adj.) threatening

[15](n.) angels

[16](n.) a period of temporary delay or rest

[17](n.) a potion or drink that makes one forget sorrow

[18](v.) drink

[19](n.) Devil

[20](n.) a violent storm

[21](n.) a biblical reference

[22](n.) the Garden of Eden

[23](n.) a demon or evil spirit

[24](n.) feather tuft

[25](adj.) pale

1. What is the effect of the metaphor used in line 8?
   Ⓐ The comparison of the speaker to dying embers of a fire suggests that the speaker is ill.
   Ⓑ The comparison of the shadows cast by the smoldering pieces of wood to ghosts helps contribute to the dark and mysterious atmosphere of the poem.
   Ⓒ The comparison of the fire to a ghost foreshadows that the speaker will die.
   Ⓓ The comparison of the flickering flames to ghosts indicates the time of year in which the poem is set.

2. In stanza VII, the speaker describes the raven as "with mien of lord or lady." By this description, he most likely means that the raven
   Ⓐ presented itself seriously and obediently.
   Ⓑ called the speaker its servant after entering the chamber.
   Ⓒ appeared formal and commanding of respect.
   Ⓓ exclaimed a formal greeting upon entering the chamber.

3. Which of the following statements *best* summarizes the meaning of the simile used in line 59?
   Ⓐ Because of past experiences, the speaker is hopeful that the raven will soon leave him.
   Ⓑ Because he has been let down in the past, the speaker believes the raven's visit will be short-lived.
   Ⓒ The speaker is relieved by the assumption that the raven will only stay a day, as his presence scares the speaker.
   Ⓓ The affirmation that the bird's visit will be brief, like that of a friend's, causes the speaker to feel comforted.

4. The reference to *Gilead* (line 89) is a biblical **allusion** to a specific location in ancient Palestine where people sought a healing medical ointment (*balm*) to heal their illnesses. Based on this information, which of the following questions is closest in meaning to the phrase, "Is there balm in Gilead?"

> An **allusion** is an indirect reference to something outside of the literary work. In line 89, Poe indirectly references, or alludes to, the Bible.

   Ⓐ "Have you been to Gilead?"

   Ⓑ "Can you take me away?"

   Ⓒ "Do you know if Lenore is safe?"

   Ⓓ "Is there anything to ease my suffering?"

5. Which of the following *best* describes the speaker's tone in stanza XIV?

   Ⓐ Solemn and desperate

   Ⓑ Sentimental and satisfied

   Ⓒ Angry and regretful

   Ⓓ Grateful and amused

6. What words or phrases in stanza XIV help to reveal the tone identified in question 5?

_____

7. How does the repetition of the word "nevermore" contribute to a central message of the poem?

   Ⓐ The use of the word "nevermore" implies that ravens are creatures of imitation.

   Ⓑ The use of the word "nevermore" supports the idea that one may never get over the loss of a loved one.

   Ⓒ The use of the word "nevermore" suggests the final words of Lenore.

   Ⓓ The use of the word "nevermore" emphasizes the negative effect that alcohol can have on a person.

8. Identify three *verbs* that depict what the speaker is doing in stanza I.

_____

9. The three verbs from question 8 help to create an atmosphere of
   Ⓐ surprise.
   Ⓑ relief.
   Ⓒ tranquility.
   Ⓓ excitement.

10. Identify at least three *verbs* that depict what the speaker is doing in stanza V.

_____

11. How does the atmosphere (mood) of stanza V contrast with the atmosphere of stanza I?
    Support your response with details from the poem.

_____

_____

_____

_____

_____

_____

_____

_____

(Answers are on page 96.)

COMPARING AND CONTRASTING STRUCTURE

RL.8.5 Compare and contrast the structure of two or more texts and analyze how the differing structures of each text contributes to its meaning and style.

Directions: Read the two poems. Then, answer the questions that follow.

November
by Alice Cary

The leaves are fading and falling,
   The winds are rough and wild,
The birds have ceased their calling,
   But let me tell you, my child,

Though day by day, as it closes,
   Doth darker and colder grow,
The roots of the bright red roses
   Will keep alive in the snow.

And when the Winter is over,
   The boughs will get new leaves,
The quail come back to the clover,
   And the swallow back to the eaves.

The robin will wear on his bosom
   A vest that is bright and new,
And the loveliest way-side blossom
   Will shine with the sun and dew.

The leaves to-day are whirling,
   The brooks are dry and dumb,
But let me tell you, my darling,
   The Spring will be sure to come.

There must be rough, cold weather,
   And winds and rains so wild;
Not all good things together
   Come to us here, my child.

So, when some dear joy loses
   Its beauteous summer glow,
Think how the roots of the roses
   Are kept alive in the snow.

Fall, leaves, fall
by Emily Brontè

Fall, leaves, fall; die, flowers, away:
Lengthen night and shorten day;
Every leaf speaks bliss to me
Fluttering from the autumn tree.
I shall smile when wreaths of snow
Blossom where the rose should grow;
I shall sing when night's decay
Ushers in a drearier day.

1. Compare and contrast the **structure** and **meaning** of the two poems by completing the following chart:

	"November"	"Fall, leaves, fall"
Number of stanzas		
Rhyme scheme		
Type of poem (sonnet, lyric, narrative, haiku, ballad, epic, elegy, ode, etc.)		
Use of figurative language		
Other poetic techniques (imagery, sound devices such as repetition, alliteration, consonance, and assonance, etc.)		
Speaker Perspective		
Meaning		

2. Which statement best describes how the structure of "November" contributes to its meaning?

   Ⓐ The poem does not have a set rhyme scheme or pattern of sound, which contributes to the feeling of loss.

   Ⓑ Through the use of imagery, personification, and rhyme, the poet creates a feeling of hope.

   Ⓒ By describing a winter's day in several stanzas, the speaker conveys a feeling of solitude.

   Ⓓ Through the use of repetition, rhyme, and onomatopoeia, the poet creates a tone of remorse.

3. Which statement best describes how the structure of "Fall, leaves, fall" contributes to its meaning?

   Ⓐ Through the use of couplets, figurative language, and imagery, the poet reveals a lyrical opinion of winter.

   Ⓑ By using couplets to give examples of fall's beauty, the poet creates a feeling of longing.

   Ⓒ The poem does not have a set rhythm or rhyme, revealing the speaker's conflicting thoughts on the seasons.

   Ⓓ Through the use of rhyme, personification, and simile, the poet creates a tone of anger.

4. How do the structures of the two poems differ?

   Ⓐ "November" has a regular rhythm, while "Fall, leaves, fall" is free verse.

   Ⓑ "November" has no set rhyme scheme, while "Fall, leaves, fall" uses repetition.

   Ⓒ "November" is a sonnet, while "Fall, leaves, fall" is a haiku.

   Ⓓ "November" has an *abab* rhyme scheme, while "Fall, leaves, fall" is written in couplets.

5. How are the structures of the two poems similar?

   Ⓐ Both poems use stanzas to develop meaning.

   Ⓑ Both poems are epic, revealing their meaning through a series of contrasting scenarios.

   Ⓒ Both poems use imagery and onomatopoeia to draw attention to sounds.

   Ⓓ Both poems are lyrical, revealing their meaning through rhyme, figurative language, and a first-person speaker.

6. Which of these statements best compares the use of imagery and figurative language in "November" and "Fall, leaves, fall"?

   (A) Both poems use imagery and figurative language to reveal the speaker's feelings.

   (B) Both poems use imagery and figurative language to convey a feeling of isolation and loss.

   (C) "November" uses imagery to emphasize a sense of loss and hopelessness, while "Fall, leaves, fall" uses figurative language to create the same effect.

   (D) In "November," figurative language is used to describe the setting, while in "Fall, leaves, fall," imagery is used to establish a tone of anger.

7. In a well-developed paragraph, compare and contrast the structure and meaning of "November" to "Fall, leaves, fall," and describe how each poem's structure contributes to its meaning. Use the chart from question 1 to help you.

   _____

   _____

   _____

   _____

   _____

   _____

   _____

   _____

(Answers are on page 97.)

ANALYZING
POINT OF VIEW

RL.8.6 Analyze how differences in the points of view of the characters and the audience or reader (e.g., created through the use of dramatic irony) create such effects as suspense or humor.

Directions: Read the following excerpt from the short story, *The Tell-Tale Heart,* by Edgar Allan Poe, and answer the questions that follow.

And have I not told you that what you mistake for madness is but over-acuteness of the sense?—now, say, there came to my ears a low, dull, quick sound, such as a watch makes when enveloped in cotton. I knew that sound well, too. It was the beating of the old man's heart. It increased my fury, as the beating of a drum stimulates the soldier into
5   courage.

But even yet I refrained and kept still. I scarcely breathed. I held the lantern motionless. I tried how steadily I could maintain the ray upon the eye. Meantime the hellish tattoo of the heart increased. It grew quicker and quicker, and louder and louder every instant. The old man's terror must have been extreme! It grew louder, I say,
10   louder every moment!—do you mark me well I have told you that I am nervous: so I am. And now at the dead hour of the night, amid the dreadful silence of that old house, so strange a noise as this excited me to uncontrollable terror. Yet, for some minutes longer I refrained and stood still. But the beating grew louder, louder! I thought the heart must burst. And now a new anxiety seized me—the sound would be heard by a neighbour!
15   The old man's hour had come! With a loud yell, I threw open the lantern and leaped into the room. He shrieked once—once only. In an instant I dragged him to the floor, and pulled the heavy bed over him. I then smiled gaily, to find the deed so far done. But, for many minutes, the heart beat on with a muffled sound. This, however, did not vex me; it would not be heard through the wall. At length it ceased. The old man was dead. I
20   removed the bed and examined the corpse. Yes, he was stone, stone dead. I placed my hand upon the heart and held it there many minutes. There was no pulsation. He was stone dead. His eye would trouble me no more.

If still you think me mad, you will think so no longer when I describe the wise precautions I took for the concealment of the body. The night waned, and I worked
25   hastily, but in silence. First of all I dismembered the corpse. I cut off the head and the arms and the legs.

I then took up three planks from the flooring of the chamber, and deposited all between the scantlings. I then replaced the boards so cleverly, so cunningly, that no human eye—not even his—could have detected any thing wrong. There was nothing to
30   wash out—no stain of any kind—no blood-spot whatever. I had been too wary for that. A tub had caught all—ha! ha!

When I had made an end of these labors, it was four o'clock—still dark as midnight. As the bell sounded the hour, there came a knocking at the street door. I went down to open it with a light heart,—for what had I now

35 to fear? There entered three men, who introduced themselves, with perfect suavity, as officers of the police. A shriek had been heard by a neighbour during the night; suspicion of foul play had been aroused; information had been lodged at the police office, and they (the officers) had been deputed to search the premises.

I smiled,—for what had I to fear? I bade the gentlemen welcome. The shriek, I said,

40 was my own in a dream. The old man, I mentioned, was absent in the country. I took my visitors all over the house. I bade them search—search well. I led them, at length, to his chamber. I showed them his treasures, secure, undisturbed. In the enthusiasm of my confidence, I brought chairs into the room, and desired them here to rest from their fatigues, while I myself, in the wild audacity of my perfect triumph, placed my own seat

45 upon the very spot beneath which reposed the corpse of the victim.

The officers were satisfied. My manner had convinced them. I was singularly at ease. They sat, and while I answered cheerily, they chatted of familiar things. But, ere long, I felt myself getting pale and wished them gone. My head ached, and I fancied a ringing in my ears: but still they sat and still chatted. The ringing became more distinct:—It

50 continued and became more distinct: I talked more freely to get rid of the feeling: but it continued and gained definiteness—until, at length, I found that the noise was not within my ears.

No doubt I now grew *very* pale;—but I talked more fluently, and with a heightened voice. Yet the sound increased—and what could I do? It was a low, dull, quick sound—

55 much such a sound as a watch makes when enveloped in cotton. I gasped for breath— and yet the officers heard it not. I talked more quickly—more vehemently; but the noise steadily increased. I arose and argued about trifles, in a high key and with violent gesticulations; but the noise steadily increased. Why would they not be gone? I paced the floor to and fro with heavy strides, as if excited to fury by the observations of the

60 men—but the noise steadily increased. Oh God! what could I do? I foamed—I raved—I swore! I swung the chair upon which I had been sitting, and grated it upon the boards, but the noise arose over all and continually increased. It grew louder—louder—louder! And still the men chatted pleasantly, and smiled. Was it possible they heard not? Almighty God!—no, no! They heard!—they suspected!—they knew!—they were making

65 a mockery of my horror!—this I thought, and this I think. But anything was better than this agony! Anything was more tolerable than this derision! I could bear those hypocritical smiles no longer! I felt that I must scream or die! and now—again!—hark! louder! louder! louder! louder!

"Villains!" I shrieked, "dissemble no more! I admit the deed!—tear up the planks! here,

70 here!—It is the beating of his hideous heart!"

1. This passage is told through the perspective of
   - (A) a first-person narrator who has witnessed a murder.
   - (B) an outside narrator describing an occurrence at a nursing home.
   - (C) a first-person narrator who has committed murder.
   - (D) an outside narrator describing a murder.

2. The behavior of the police officers helps add suspense to the passage because it
   - (A) encourages the narrator to show them the body of the old man.
   - (B) causes the reader to question whether or not the officers suspect the narrator.
   - (C) causes the narrator to run away from them.
   - (D) persuades the reader that the narrator was interrogated.

3. By the end of the passage, what is the reader aware of that the narrator is not?
   - (A) The old man is still alive.
   - (B) The old man's heart is not beating under the floor boards.
   - (C) The police are making a mockery of the narrator.
   - (D) The police are only pretending not to hear the heartbeat.

> **Dramatic Irony** exists when the reader is aware of something that the characters in the story are not.

4. The murderer's internal struggle at the end of the passage is made more dramatic by the use of
   - (A) first-person narration and irony.
   - (B) third-person omniscient narration.
   - (C) third-person narration and metaphor.
   - (D) second-person narration and hyperbole.

27

5. More than likely, the sound that the narrator hears in lines 53–68 is
   Ⓐ made up.
   Ⓑ his own heartbeat.
   Ⓒ the heartbeat of one of the police officers.
   Ⓓ the police officer's watch.

6. How would the story be different if it were told in **third-person omniscient** point of view?

_____

_____

_____

_____

_____

_____

_____

_____

_____

_____

(Answers are on page 98.)

CITING EVIDENCE IN INFORMATIONAL TEXT

RI.8.1 Cite the textual evidence that most strongly supports an analysis of what the text says explicitly as well as inferences drawn from the text.

Directions: Read the following excerpt from Samuel Langhorne Clemens's (Mark Twain's) obituary, published in the *New York Times* on April 22, 1910.

Mark Twain Is Dead at 74

Danbury, Conn., April 21—Samuel Langhorne Clemens, "Mark Twain," died at 22 minutes after 6 tonight. Beside him on the bed lay a beloved book—it was Carlyle's "French Revolution"—and near the book his glasses, pushed away with a weary sigh a few hours before. Too weak to speak clearly, "Give me my glasses," he had written on
5   a piece of paper. He had received them, put them down, and sunk into unconsciousness from which he glided almost imperceptibly into death. He was in his seventy-fifth year.

For some time, his daughter Clara and her husband, Ossip Cabrilowitsch, and the humorist's biographer, Albert Bigelow Paine, had been by the bed waiting for the end, which Drs. Quintard and Halsey had seen to be a matter of minutes. The patient felt
10   absolutely no pain at the end and the moment of his death was scarcely noticeable.

Death came, however, while his favorite niece, Mrs. E. E. Looms, and her husband, who is Vice President of the Delaware, Lackawanna and Western Railway, and a nephew, Jervis Langdon, were on the way to the railroad station. They had left the house much encouraged by the fact that the sick man had recognized them, and took a train for
15   New York ignorant of what happened later.

Hopes Aroused Yesterday

Although the end had been foreseen by the doctors and would not have been a shock at any time, the apparently strong rally of this morning had given basis for the hope that it would be postponed for several days. Mr. Clemens awoke at about 4 o'clock this morning after a few hours of the first natural sleep he has had for several days, and the
20   nurses could see by the brightness of his eyes that his vitality had been considerably restored. He was able to raise his arms above his head and clasp them behind his neck with the first evidence of physical comfort he had given for a long time.

His strength seemed to increase enough to allow him to enjoy the sunrise, the first signs of which he could see out of the windows in the three sides of the room where he
25   lay. The increasing sunlight seemed to bring ease to him, and by the time the family was about he was strong enough to sit up in bed and overjoyed them by recognizing all of them and speaking a few words to each. This was the first time that his mental powers

had been fully his for nearly two days, with the exception of a few minutes early last evening, when he addressed a few sentences to his daughter.

Calls for His Book

30   For two hours he lay in bed enjoying the feeling of this return of strength. Then he made a movement asked in a faint voice for the copy of Carlyle's "French Revolution," which he has always had near him for the last year, and which he has read and re-read and brooded over.

The book was handed to him, and he lifted it up as if to read. Then a smile faintly
35   illuminated his face when he realized that he was trying to read without his glasses. He tried to say, "Give me my glasses," but his voice failed, and the nurses bending over him could not understand. He motioned for a sheet of paper and a pencil, and wrote what he could not say.

With his glasses on he read a little and then slowly put the book down with a sigh.
40   Soon he appeared to become drowsy and settled on his pillow. Gradually he sank and settled into a lethargy. Dr. Halsey appreciated that he could have been roused, but considered it better for him to rest. At 3 o'clock he went into complete unconsciousness.

Later Dr. Quintard, who had arrived from New York, held a consultation with Dr. Halsey, and it was decided that death was near. The family was called and gathered
45   about the bedside watching in a silence which was long unbroken. It was the end. At twenty-two minutes past 6, with the sunlight just turning red as it stole into the window in perfect silence he breathed his last.

Died of a Broken Heart

The people of Redding, Bethel, and Danbury listened when they were told that the doctors said Mark Twain was dying of angina pectoris. But they say among themselves
50   that he died of a broken heart. And this is a verdict not of popular sentiment alone. Albert Bigelow Paine, his biographer to be and literary executor, who has been constantly with him, said that for the last year at least Mr. Clemens had been weary of life. When Richard Watson Gilder died, he said: "How fortunate he is. No good fortune of that kind ever comes to me."

55   The man who has stood to the public for the greatest humorist this country has produced has in private life suffered overwhelming sorrows. The loss of an only son in infancy, a daughter in her teens and one in middle life, and finally of a wife who was a constant and sympathetic companion, has preyed upon his mind. The recent loss of his daughter Jean, who was closest to him in later years when her sister was abroad
60   studying, was the final blow. On the heels of this came the first symptoms of the disease which was surely to be fatal and one of whose accompaniments is mental depression. Mr. Paine says that all heart went out of him and his work when his daughter Jean died. He has practically written nothing since he summoned his energies to write a last chapter memorial of her for his autobiography.

65   He told his biographer that the past Winter in Bermuda was gay but not happy. Bermuda is always gay in Winter and Mark Twain was a central figure in the gayety. He was staying at the home of William H. Allen. Even in Bermuda, however, Mr. Clemens found himself unable to write and finally relied on Mr. Allen's fifteen-year-old daughter, Helen, to write the few letters he cared to send.

70   His health failed rapidly and finally Mr. Allen wrote to Albert Bigelow Paine that his friend was in a most serious condition. Mr. Paine immediately cabled to Mrs. Cabrilowitsch, his surviving daughter, who was in Europe, and started himself on April 2 for Bermuda, embarking with the humorist for the return to New York immediately after his arrival. On the trip over Mark Twain became very much worse and finally realized his condition.

75   "It's a losing game," he said to his companion. "I'll never get home alive."

      Mr. Clemens did manage to summon his strength, however, and in spite of being so weak that he had to be carried down the gangplank he survived the journey to his beautiful place at Redding. The first symptom of angina pectoris came last June when he went to Baltimore to address a young ladies school. In his room at the hotel he was

80   suddenly taken with a terrible gripping at the heart. It soon passed away, however, and he was able to make an address with no inconvenience. The pains however, soon returned with more frequency and steadily grew worse until they became a constant torture.

      One of the last acts of Mark Twain was to write out a check for $6,000 for the library in which the literary coterie[1] settled near Redding have been interested for a year; fairs,

85   musicales, and sociables having been held in order to raise the necessary amount. The library is to be a memorial to Jean Clemens, and will be built on a site about half a mile from Stormfield at ... Cross Roads.

---

[1](n.) an intimate and often exclusive group of persons with a unifying common interest or purpose

1. Which of the following statements is valid, according to the information provided in the obituary excerpt?

   (A) Samuel L. Clemens, otherwise known as Mark Twain, died while alone at his private home in Connecticut.

   (B) Samuel L. Clemens was vibrant and alert up until the last moments of his life.

   (C) Samuel L. Clemens, though widely known for his humor, suffered a great amount of heartache in his personal life.

   (D) Though mainly known as a dark, morbid figure, Samuel L. Clemens, otherwise known as Mark Twain, was a lively and comical man.

2. Cite two pieces of textual evidence that support your answer to question 1.

   _____

   _____

   _____

   _____

   _____

   _____

   _____

   _____

   _____

   _____

   _____

3. This obituary was written
   - (A) on the day that Samuel L. Clemens passed away.
   - (B) on the one year anniversary of Samuel L. Clemens's death.
   - (C) shortly before the actual death of Samuel L. Clemens.
   - (D) one hundred years after the death of Samuel L. Clemens.

4. According to the section titled "Hopes Aroused Yesterday," what happened to Samuel L. Clemens shortly before he passed away? Use *two* details from the obituary to support your response.

_____

_____

_____

_____

_____

_____

_____

_____

_____

_____

_____

5. Which of the following statements is a valid claim that could be made based upon the information provided in the obituary?

    Ⓐ Mark Twain lived a lonely and heartbreaking life.

    Ⓑ Though many knew him as a humorous writer, Samuel L. Clemens, otherwise known as Mark Twain, is mostly remembered for his contribution to a library near Redding, New York.

    Ⓒ Samuel L. Clemens, otherwise known as Mark Twain, was a widely popular and adored figure in American history.

    Ⓓ Though many knew him as a serious writer, Mark Twain is mostly remembered for his tragic life.

6. Which of the following quotations from the text *best* helps to support the claim identified in question 5?

    Ⓐ "For some time, his daughter Clara and her husband, Ossip Cabrilowitsch, and the humorist's biographer, Albert Bigelow Paine, had been by the bed waiting for the end, which Drs. Quintard and Halsey had seen to be a matter of minutes."

    Ⓑ "Mr. Clemens did manage to summon his strength, however, and in spite of being so weak that he had to be carried down the gangplank he survived the journey to his beautiful place at Redding."

    Ⓒ "Death came, however, while his favorite niece, Mrs. E. E. Looms, and her husband, who is Vice President of the Delaware, Lackawanna and Western Railway, and a nephew, Jervis Langdon, were on the way to the railroad station."

    Ⓓ "The man who has stood to the public for the greatest humorist this country has produced has in private life suffered overwhelming sorrows."

(Answers are on page 99.)

DETERMINING CENTRAL IDEA

RI.8.2 Determine a central idea of a text and analyze its development over the course of the text, including its relationship to supporting ideas; provide an objective summary of the text.

Directions: Read the following article from *National Geographic Creative* and answer the questions that follow.

Marine Pollution

1   The oceans are so vast and deep that until fairly recently, it was widely assumed that no matter how much trash and chemicals humans dumped into them, the effects would be negligible. Proponents of dumping in the oceans even had a catchphrase: "The solution to pollution is dilution."

2   Today, we need look no further than the New Jersey-size dead zone that forms each summer in the Mississippi River Delta, or the thousand-mile-wide swath of decomposing plastic in the northern Pacific Ocean to see that this "dilution" policy has helped place a once flourishing ocean ecosystem on the brink of collapse.

Pollution's Many Forms

3   There is evidence that the oceans have suffered at the hands of mankind for millennia, as far back as Roman times. But recent studies show that degradation, particularly of shoreline areas, has accelerated dramatically in the past three centuries as industrial discharge and runoff from farms and coastal cities has increased.

4   Pollution is the introduction of harmful contaminants that are outside the norm for a given ecosystem. Common man-made pollutants that reach the ocean include pesticides, herbicides, chemical fertilizers, detergents, oil, sewage, plastics, and other solids. Many of these pollutants collect at the ocean's depths, where they are consumed by small marine organisms and introduced into the global food chain. Scientists are even discovering that pharmaceuticals ingested by humans but not fully processed by our bodies are eventually ending up in the fish we eat.

5   Many ocean pollutants are released into the environment far upstream from coastlines. Nitrogen-rich fertilizers applied by farmers inland, for example, end up in local streams, rivers, and groundwater and are eventually deposited in estuaries, bays, and deltas. These excess nutrients can spawn massive blooms of algae that rob the water of oxygen, leaving areas where little or no marine life can exist. Scientists have counted some 400 such dead zones around the world.

6   Solid waste like bags, foam, and other items dumped into the oceans from land or by ships at sea are frequently consumed, with often fatal effects, by marine mammals, fish, and birds that mistake it for food. Discarded fishing nets drift for years, ensnaring fish and mammals. In certain regions, ocean currents corral trillions of decomposing plastic items and other trash into gigantic, swirling garbage patches. One in the North Pacific, known as the Pacific Trash Vortex, is estimated to be the size of Texas. A new, massive patch was discovered in the Atlantic Ocean in early 2010.

Noise Pollution

7   Pollution is not always physical. In large bodies of water, sound waves can carry undiminished for miles. The increased presence of loud or persistent sounds from ships, sonar devices, oil rigs, and even from natural sources like earthquakes can disrupt the migration, communication, hunting, and reproduction patterns of many marine animals, particularly aquatic mammals like whales and dolphins.

End of the "Dilution" Era

8   Humans are beginning to see the shortsightedness of the "dilution" philosophy. Many national laws as well as international protocols now forbid dumping of harmful materials into the ocean, although enforcement can often be spotty. Marine sanctuaries are being created to maintain pristine ocean ecosystems. And isolated efforts to restore estuaries and bays have met with some success.

Reprinted with permission from *National Geographic Creative.*

1. Which quotation expresses the central idea of the article?
    - Ⓐ "Pollution is not always physical."
    - Ⓑ "Solid waste like bags, foam, and other items dumped into the oceans from land or by ships at sea are frequently consumed, with often fatal effects, by marine mammals, fish, and birds that mistake it for food."
    - Ⓒ "Common man-made pollutants that reach the ocean include pesticides, herbicides, chemical fertilizers, detergents, oil, sewage, plastics, and other solids."
    - Ⓓ "Today, we need look no further than the New Jersey-size dead zone that forms each summer in the Mississippi River Delta, or the thousand-mile-wide swath of decomposing plastic in the northern Pacific Ocean to see that this 'dilution' policy has helped place a once flourishing ocean ecosystem on the brink of collapse."

2. The author develops the central idea of the article by
   Ⓐ analyzing investigative data to find the cause of ocean pollution.
   Ⓑ summarizing scientific opinions to show the effects of dilution.
   Ⓒ providing examples of pollutants and the various effects of dilution.
   Ⓓ debating conflicting views of dilution and its effects on the marine world.

3. The mention of the "New Jersey-size dead zone" in the Mississippi River and the "thousand-mile-wide" stretch of decomposing plastic in the Pacific Ocean in paragraph two contributes to the central idea of the article by
   Ⓐ providing the reader with a visual of pollution.
   Ⓑ highlighting the severity of ocean pollution.
   Ⓒ calling attention to New Jersey's growing issue with pollution.
   Ⓓ identifying the West Coast as one of the largest contributors to ocean pollution.

4. Which of the following sentences would be best to include in a summary of this article?
   Ⓐ Humans should have known all along that dilution was not the solution to pollution.
   Ⓑ Ocean pollution is caused by a wide variety of things.
   Ⓒ Humans are beginning to recognize that "diluting" pollution into our planet's water supply has devastating effects.
   Ⓓ Farmers are single-handedly responsible for the devastating effects caused by dumping pollutants in the oceans.

5. Which of the following best summarizes the section titled "Pollution's Many Forms"?

Ⓐ Over the past three centuries there's been an increase in the amount of pollutants dumped into our planet's oceans. The effects of this are noticeable, and the growing number of plastics, foam, pesticides, oil, and chemicals poured into the ocean will one day have devastating results.

Ⓑ The increase in the amount of pollutants, such as plastics, pesticides, oil, foam, fertilizers, and sewage, over the past three hundred years has wreaked havoc on our planet's marine life. Scientists predict that marine mammals, fish, and birds will start to die off as a result of pollutant consumption, and the effects of the increase will span world-wide.

Ⓒ The increase in the amount of pollutants over the past three centuries has had devastating effects on our planet's ocean environments. Not only have pollutants, such as plastics, sewage, fertilizers, pesticides, pharmaceuticals, oil, etc., produced dead zones and massive garbage patches in oceans around the world, they have also been the cause of death for many marine mammals, fish, and birds after they have been mistaken for food and consumed.

Ⓓ As the amount of pollutants in oceans increases, solid pollutants such as plastic bags, foam, and other discarded items become the planet's biggest threat. Garbage patches the size of Texas are making their way across oceans around the world.

(Answers are on page 100.)

ANALYZING COMPARISONS, ANALOGIES, AND CATEGORIES

RI.8.3 Analyze how a text makes connections among and distinctions between individuals, ideas, or events (e.g., through comparisons, analogies, or categories).

Directions: The following speech, titled "Tribute to a Dog," was delivered to a jury by one-time U.S. Senator George Graham Vest while he was practicing law in Missouri in 1855. Read the speech. Then, answer the questions that follow.

1   Gentlemen of the Jury: The best friend a man has in the world may turn against him and become his enemy. His son or daughter that he has reared with loving care may prove ungrateful. Those who are nearest and dearest to us, those whom we trust with our happiness and our good name may become traitors to their faith. The money that a man has, he may lose. It flies away from him, perhaps when he needs it most. A man's reputation may be sacrificed in a moment of ill-considered action. The people who are prone to fall on their knees to do us honor when success is with us, may be the first to throw the stone of malice when failure settles its cloud upon our heads.

2   The one absolutely unselfish friend that man can have in this selfish world, the one that never deserts him, the one that never proves ungrateful or treacherous is his dog. A man's dog stands by him in prosperity and in poverty, in health and in sickness. He will sleep on the cold ground, where the wintry winds blow and the snow drives fiercely, if only he may be near his master's side. He will kiss the hand that has no food to offer. He will lick the wounds and sores that come in encounters with the roughness of the world. He guards the sleep of his pauper master as if he were a prince. When all other friends desert, he remains. When riches take wings, and reputation falls to pieces, he is as constant in his love as the sun in its journey through the heavens.

3   If fortune drives the master forth, an outcast in the world, friendless and homeless, the faithful dog asks no higher privilege than that of accompanying him, to guard him against danger, to fight against his enemies. And when the last scene of all comes, and death takes his master in its embrace and his body is laid away in the cold ground, no matter if all other friends pursue their way, there by the graveside will the noble dog be found, his head between his paws, his eyes sad, but open in alert watchfulness, faithful and true even in death.

1. How does the speaker distinguish dogs from people?
   Ⓐ Dogs are depicted as mostly loyal while people are depicted as mostly evil.
   Ⓑ People are depicted as consistent while dogs are depicted as unstable.
   Ⓒ Dogs are depicted as companions while people are depicted as dishonest.
   Ⓓ People are depicted as inconsistent while dogs are depicted as constant.

2. Explain *how* the speaker depicts the idea chosen in question 1. Use details from the speech in your response.

_____

_____

_____

3. Vest compares a dog to all of the following *except*
- Ⓐ those whom someone may trust with his or her happiness.
- Ⓑ those who would risk their lives for someone else.
- Ⓒ a son or daughter who has been raised with love.
- Ⓓ the sun in its journey through the heavens.

4. The speaker illustrates how unselfish a dog is through all of the following *except*
- Ⓐ describing the world as selfish.
- Ⓑ providing examples of how a dog will suffer for the sake of its master.
- Ⓒ describing the ways in which a dog will give of itself without expecting anything in return.
- Ⓓ contrasting dogs and other pets that are more selfish.

5. What is the connection among all of the details in paragraph 2?
- Ⓐ They describe a dog's many positive attributes.
- Ⓑ They provide reasons for dogs' unselfish behavior.
- Ⓒ They help to explain the few times when dogs act selfishly.
- Ⓓ They provide examples to support the world as selfish.

6. The speaker depicts a dog as the most loyal companion a person can have. Describe the comparisons and descriptions that the speaker uses throughout the speech in order to depict a dog as such. Use an additional sheet of paper if necessary.

_____

_____

_____

_____

_____

7. According to the speaker, a dog is all of the following *except*
- Ⓐ the one absolutely unselfish friend a man can have.
- Ⓑ the one to remain when all others have left.
- Ⓒ the one to stand by only in prosperity.
- Ⓓ the one to never prove ungrateful.

(Answers are on page 100.)

WORD MEANING AND FIGURATIVE LANGUAGE IN INFORMATIONAL TEXT

RI.8.4 Determine the meaning of words and phrases as they are used in a text, including figurative, connotative, and technical meanings; analyze the impact of specific word choices on meaning and tone, including analogies or allusions to other texts.

Directions: The following speech was given by famous women's rights activist Susan B. Anthony in 1873 after she was arrested for casting an illegal vote in the presidential election of 1872. Read the speech, and answer the questions that follow.

1   Friends and fellow citizens: I stand before you tonight under indictment for the alleged crime of having voted at the last presidential election, without having a lawful right to vote. It shall be my work this evening to prove to you that in thus voting, I not only committed no crime, but, instead, simply exercised my citizen's rights, guaranteed to me and all United States citizens by the National Constitution, beyond the power of any state to deny.

2   The preamble of the Federal Constitution says:

"We, the people of the United States, in order to form a more perfect union, establish justice, insure domestic tranquility, provide for the common defense, promote the general welfare, and secure the blessings of liberty to ourselves and our posterity[1], do ordain[2] and establish this Constitution for the United States of America."

3   It was we, the people; not we, the white male citizens; nor yet we, the male citizens; but we, the whole people, who formed the Union. And we formed it, not to give the blessings of liberty, but to secure them; not to the half of ourselves and the half of our posterity, but to the whole people—women as well as men. And it is a downright mockery to talk to women of their enjoyment of the blessings of liberty while they are denied the use of the only means of securing them provided by this democratic-republican government—the ballot.

4   For any state to make sex a qualification that must ever result in the disfranchisement[3] of one entire half of the people, is to pass a bill of attainder, or, an ex post facto law, and is therefore a violation of the supreme law of the land. By it the blessings of liberty are forever withheld from women and their female posterity.

5   To them this government has no just powers derived from the consent of the governed. To them this government is not a democracy. It is not a republic. It is an odious[4] aristocracy[5]; a hateful oligarchy[6] of sex; the most hateful aristocracy ever established on the face of the globe; an oligarchy of wealth, where the rich govern the poor. An oligarchy of learning, where the educated govern the ignorant, or even an oligarchy of race, where the Saxon[7] rules the African, might be endured; but this oligarchy of sex, which makes father, brothers, husband, sons, the oligarchs over the mother and sisters, the wife and

daughters, of every household—which ordains all men sovereigns[8], all women subjects, carries dissension[9], discord, and rebellion into every home of the nation.

6   Webster, Worcester, and Bouvier all define a citizen to be a person in the United States, entitled to vote and hold office.

7   The only question left to be settled now is: Are women persons? And I hardly believe any of our opponents will have the hardihood to say they are not. Being persons, then, women are citizens; and no state has a right to make any law, or to enforce any old law, that shall abridge their privileges or immunities. Hence, every discrimination against women in the constitutions and laws of the several states is today null and void, precisely as is every one against Negroes.

_____

[1](n.) future generations

[2](v.) to establish or order by appointment, decree, or law

[3](n.) the act of preventing a person or group of persons from voting

[4](adj.) causing hatred or strong dislike

[5](n.) government by the best individuals or by a small privileged class

[6](n.) a government in which a small group exercises control, especially for corrupt and selfish purposes

[7](n.) a member of the Germanic people who entered and conquered England in the fifth century A.D.

[8](n.) an acknowledged leader

[9](n.) disagreement

1. Which of the following quotes does **not** best contribute to the overall formal or serious tone of the speech?
    Ⓐ "Friends and fellow citizens: I stand before you tonight under indictment for the alleged crime of having voted at the last presidential election, without having a lawful right to vote."
    Ⓑ "Webster, Worcester, and Bouvier all define a citizen to be a person in the United States, entitled to vote and hold office."
    Ⓒ "It was we, the people; not we, the white male citizens; nor yet we, the male citizens; but we, the whole people, who formed the Union."
    Ⓓ "Being persons, then, women are citizens; and no state has a right to make any law, or to enforce any old law, that shall abridge their privileges or immunities."

2. How does the repetition of the words *we* and *people* in paragraph 3 contribute to the meaning of that paragraph?
    Ⓐ The use of the words "we" and "people," and their reference to the Constitution, help to emphasize Anthony's point that American citizens are not merely white males.
    Ⓑ The use of the words "we" and "people" help to further warn American citizens of the dangers in placing their future in the hands of white males only.
    Ⓒ The use of the words "we" and "people" help to explain the origins of the American government in contrast to that of other governments.
    Ⓓ The use of the words "we" and "people" help to call attention to the virtues of the American government.

41

3. Which statement best explains why the speaker used the phrases *odious aristocracy*, *hateful oligarchy*, *hateful aristocracy*, and *oligarchy of wealth*, as well as the words *subjects*, *dissension*, *discord*, and *rebellion* in paragraph 5?

    (A) To warn Americans of the dangers of aristocracies and oligarchies

    (B) To explain the contrast between America's government and those of other countries

    (C) To emphasize the negative effects of women and African Americans being denied the right to vote

    (D) To draw attention to the corrupt ruling forces of the American government

---

Connotation vs. Denotation

Denotation refers to a word's technical meaning; for example, the word *odor's* denotation is "a particular smell."

Connotation refers to the **feelings** or implications that are attached to a word; for example, the word *odor* tends to have a *negative* connotation, while the word *fragrance*, though similar in denotation, tends to have a *positive* connotation.

---

4. The **connotations** of the words and phrases listed in question 3 are mostly

    (A) positive.

    (B) negative.

    (C) neutral.

    (D) Both A and B

5. What is the meaning of the word *alleged* as it is used in paragraph 1?

    (A) Definite

    (B) Observed

    (C) Dangerous

    (D) Supposed

6. As used in paragraph 6, *Webster*, *Worcester*, and *Bouvier* most likely refer to

    (A) dictionaries.

    (B) lawyers.

    (C) laws.

    (D) government documents.

7. Which of the following words is closest in meaning to the phrase *null and void*, as it is used in paragraph 7?

(A) Unbearable

(B) Powerful

(C) Invalid

(D) Illegal

Directions: Read the following description of Susan B. Anthony, found on *www.historynet.com*, before answering questions 8 and 9.

Susan B. Anthony was one of the driving forces of the women's suffrage movement, a staunch equal rights advocate, and social activist. She devoted her life to not only fighting for women's equality, but for the equality of all people. She was deeply self-conscious of her looks and speaking abilities, but because her Quaker upbringing

5   had placed her on equal footing with the male members of the family and encouraged her to express herself, she overcame these fears to more effectively fight for equal rights.

8. Which of the following words or phrases is closest in meaning to the phrase *driving forces*, as used in line 1?

(A) Key motivators

(B) Creators

(C) Strongest supporters

(D) Main operators

9. Which of the following phrases is closest in meaning to the phrase *on equal footing*, as used in line 5?

(A) At the same height

(B) At the same weight

(C) Of the same distance

(D) Of the same rank or position

(Answers are on page 101.)

43

ANALYZING THE STRUCTURE OF PARAGRAPHS

RI.8.5 Analyze in detail the structure of a specific paragraph in a text, including the role of particular sentences in developing and refining a key concept.

Directions: Read the following excerpt from *Black Boy*, an autobiography by Richard Wright, and answer the questions that follow.

1   I knew what was wrong with me, but I could not correct it. The words and actions of white people were baffling signs to me. I was living in a culture and not a civilization and I could learn how that culture worked only by living with it. Misreading the reactions of whites around me made me say and do the wrong things. In my dealings with whites I was conscious of the entirety of my relations with them, and they were conscious only of what was happening at a given moment. I had to keep remembering what others took for granted; I had to think out what others felt.

2   I had begun coping with the white world too late. I could not make subservience an automatic part of my behavior. I had to feel and think out each tiny item of racial experience in the light of the whole race problem, and to each item I brought the whole of my life. While standing there before a white man I had to figure out how to perform each act and how to say each word. I could not help it. I could not grin. In the past I had always said too much, now I found that it was difficult to say anything at all. I could not react as the world in which I lived expected me to; that world was too baffling, too uncertain.

3   I was idle for weeks. The summer waned. Hope for school was now definitely gone. Autumn came and many of the boys who held jobs returned to school. Jobs were now numerous. I heard that hallboys were needed at one of the hotels, the hotel in which Ned's brother had lost his life. Should I go there? Would I, too, make a fatal slip? But I had to earn money. I applied and was accepted to mop long white tiled hallways that stretched around the entire perimeter of the office floors of the building. I reported each night at ten, got a huge pail of water, a bushel of soap flakes and, with a gang of moppers, I worked. All the boys were Negroes and I was happy; at least I could talk, joke, laugh, sing, say what I pleased.

4   I began to marvel at how smoothly the black boys acted out the roles that the white race had mapped out for them. Most of them were not conscious of living a special, separate, stunted way of life. Yet I knew that in some period of their growing up—a period that they had no doubt forgotten—there had been developed in them a delicate, sensitive controlling mechanism that shut off their minds and emotions from all that the white race had said was taboo[1]. Although they lived in an America where in theory there existed equality of opportunity, they knew unerringly[2] what to aspire to and what not to aspire to. Had a black boy announced that he aspired to be a writer, he would have been unhesitatingly called

crazy by his pals. Or had a black boy spoken of yearning to get a seat on the New York Stock Exchange, his friends—in the boy's own interest—would have reported his odd ambition to the white boss.

---

[1](adj.) not acceptable to talk about or do
[2](adv.) without error, unfailingly

1. How do the sentences in paragraph 1 help to develop a key concept of the passage?
   - Ⓐ The sentences outline the difficulties that the narrator had in dealing with white people.
   - Ⓑ The sentences compare and contrast the black and white cultures.
   - Ⓒ The sentences explain the differences in opinion between blacks and whites.
   - Ⓓ The sentences describe the narrator's childhood in an all-white community.

2. Which statement *best* expresses a key concept of paragraph 4?
   - Ⓐ Richard, like most boys his age, challenged the "way of life" placed before him.
   - Ⓑ Many blacks were accepting of the limitations placed upon them by whites.
   - Ⓒ Opportunities for black females were even harder to come by than opportunities for black males.
   - Ⓓ Many blacks were not conscious of the limitations placed upon them by whites.

3. How do the sentences in paragraph 3 help to develop the key concept of that paragraph?
   - Ⓐ They describe the types of jobs that blacks in the early 1900s were able to uphold.
   - Ⓑ They describe the dangers blacks faced in obtaining a job.
   - Ⓒ They describe the ways in which blacks found comfort in their jobs.
   - Ⓓ They describe the circumstances surrounding Richard's job opportunity.

4. How do the sentences in paragraph 2 help to develop a key concept of the passage?
   - Ⓐ They describe the reasons why it was difficult for Richard to find a job.
   - Ⓑ They describe the struggles Richard faced trying to get by in a white-dominated society.
   - Ⓒ They describe the demands whites often placed on blacks.
   - Ⓓ They describe the ways in which whites were able to dominate blacks in basic social interactions.

(Answers are on page 102.)

DETERMINING POINT OF VIEW OR AUTHOR'S PURPOSE

RI.8.6 Determine an author's point of view or purpose in a text and analyze how the author acknowledges and responds to conflicting evidence or viewpoints.

Directions: Read the following speech entitled "All Together Now," presented by keynote speaker Barbara Jordan at the Democratic Convention of 1992.

1   When I look at race relations today I can see that some positive changes have come about. But much remains to be done, and the answer does not lie in more legislation. We have the legislation we need; we have laws. Frankly, I don't believe that the task of bringing us all together can be accomplished by government. What we need now is soul force—the efforts of people working on a small scale to build a truly tolerant, harmonious society. And parents can do a great deal to create that tolerant society.

2   We all know that race relations in America have had a very rocky history. Think about the 1960s when Dr. Martin Luther King Jr. was in his heyday and there were marches and protests against segregation and discrimination. The movement culminated in 1963 with the March on Washington.

3   Following that event, race relations reached an all-time peak. President Lyndon B. Johnson pushed through the Civil Rights Act of 1964, which remains the fundamental piece of civil rights legislation in this century. The Voting Rights Act of 1965 ensured that everyone in our country could vote. At last, black people and white people seemed to live together in peace.

4   But that is not what happened. By the 1990s the good feelings had diminished. Today the nation seems to be suffering from compassion fatigue, and issues such as race relations and civil rights have never regained momentum.

5   Those issues, however, remain crucial. As our society becomes more diverse, people of all races and backgrounds will have to learn to live together. If we don't think this is important, all we have to do is look at the situation in Bosnia[1] today.

6   How do we create a harmonious society out of so many kinds of people? The key is tolerance—the one value that is indispensable in creating community.

7   If we are concerned about community, if it is important to us that people not feel excluded, then we have to do something. Each of us can decide to have one friend of a different race or background in our mix of friends. If we do this, we'll be working together to push things forward.

8   One thing is clear to me: We, as human beings, must be willing to accept people who are different from ourselves. I must be willing to accept people who don't look as I do and don't talk as I do. It is crucial that I am open to their feelings, their inner reality.

9   What can parents do? We can put our faith in the young people as a positive force. I have yet to find a racist baby. Babies come into the world as blank as slates and, with their beautiful innocence, see others not as different but as enjoyable companions. Children learn ideas and attitudes from the adults who nurture them. I absolutely believe that children do not adopt prejudices unless they absorb them from their parents or teachers.

46

10   The best way to get this country faithful to the American dream of tolerance and equality is to start small. Parents can actively encourage their children to be in the company of people who are of other racial and ethnic backgrounds. If a child thinks, "Well, that person's color is not the same as mine, but she must be okay because she likes to play with the same things I like to play with," that child will grow up with a broader view of humanity.

11   I'm an incurable optimist. For the rest of the time that I have left on this planet I want to bring people together. You might think of this as a labor of love. Now, I know that love means different things to different people. But what I mean is this: I care about you because you are a fellow human being and I find it okay in my mind, in my heart, to simply say to you, I love you. And maybe that would encourage you to love me in return.

12   It is possible for all of us to work on this—at home, in our schools, at our jobs. It is possible to work on human relationships in every area of our lives.

---

[1]From 1992–1995, a war raged between different ethnic groups in Bosnia, resulting in a death toll of over 100,000. This event is known in history as the Bosnian Genocide.

1.   According to keynote speaker Barbara Jordan, how did the 1990s differ from the past in terms of race relations?
   Ⓐ   In the past, there seemed to be more compassion for people than there was in the 1990s.
   Ⓑ   In the past, parents were more active in teaching their children tolerance than they were in the 1990s.
   Ⓒ   More legislation regulating race relations existed in the 1960s than in the 1990s.
   Ⓓ   Fewer issues regarding race relations existed in the past than they did in the 1990s.

2.   Why does the speaker reference Bosnia in her speech?
   Ⓐ   To stress the importance of granting all American citizens the right to vote
   Ⓑ   To support the idea that religious differences can tear a country apart
   Ⓒ   To warn Americans of what could happen when there is a lack of harmony
   Ⓓ   To persuade America to help other countries

3.   In paragraph 11, how does the speaker respond to people's various definitions of love?
   Ⓐ   She politely explains why her viewpoint is right.
   Ⓑ   She acknowledges the differences and clarifies her own feelings.
   Ⓒ   She encourages people to change their definitions of love.
   Ⓓ   She promotes a single, common definition of love that everyone should share.

4.   What is the speaker's point of view regarding the 1960s?
   Ⓐ   She feels that a great amount of progress in human relations is owed to the political activists of that time.
   Ⓑ   She believes that decade to be a disgraceful time in American history.
   Ⓒ   Though she acknowledges the milestones of the 60s, she believes there is still much to be done as far as bringing American citizens together.
   Ⓓ   She believes the 1960s to be the motivation the nation needed in upholding a harmonious future.

(Answers are on page 102.)

ARGUMENT WRITING

W.8.1 Write arguments to support claims with clear reasons and relevant evidence.

Supporting Claims with Logical Reasoning and Relevant Evidence

1. Which of the following details would be *most* beneficial to include when supporting the following claim?

   Texting while driving is incredibly dangerous.

   Ⓐ As of January 2014, 90 percent of adults own a cell phone.

   Ⓑ Approximately 62 percent of smartphone owners have used their phone in the past year to look up information about a health condition.

   Ⓒ According to a recent survey, approximately 78 percent of eighth-grade students have cell phones.

   Ⓓ Texting while driving increases your chances of crashing by up to 23 percent.

2. What can be done to strengthen the claim made in question 1?

   Ⓐ Add the phrase "I think" to the beginning of the claim.

   Ⓑ Include in the claim examples showing that texting while driving is sometimes necessary.

   Ⓒ Provide two or three reasons at the end of the claim to support why texting while driving is dangerous.

   Ⓓ Change the word "incredibly" to "very."

Providing Evidence from Credible Sources

3. Study the following Internet source descriptions. Which of the following sites would be *least* credible to use in researching information regarding the dangers of texting while driving?

   Ⓐ The Federal Communications Commission's Guide to The Dangers of Texting While Driving, found at *www.fcc.gov*

   Ⓑ A list of statistics on cell phone use while driving, provided by the Edwin Snyden and Associates Law Firm, representing injured people, found at *www.edwinsnyden.com*

   Ⓒ The National Safety Council's report on Distracted Driving, found at *www.nsc.org*

   Ⓓ The U.S. Department of Transportation's 2013 publication of its Summary of Statistical Findings of Distracted Driving in 2011, found at *www.nhtsa.gov*

Providing a Concluding Statement

4. Which statement below would function **most** effectively as a closing sentence for an argument against texting while driving?

   Ⓐ Overall, the multitude of dangers that cell phone use creates should encourage people to stop using them.

   Ⓑ In December of 2012, more than 171 billion text messages were sent or received in the United States.

   Ⓒ Approximately 31 percent of U.S. drivers between the ages of eighteen and sixty-four have reported that they have sent text messages or e-mails while driving.

   Ⓓ Distraction, injury, and death are only a few examples of why texting while driving should be avoided at all times.

5. State officials are considering lengthening the school day to eight hours instead of six and a half. Write an essay in which you argue *either* for or against this idea. Before you begin writing, search the Internet for information to back up your argument. Support your argument with at least **three** reasons. Use an additional sheet of paper if necessary.

_____

_____

_____

_____

_____

_____

_____

_____

_____

_____

_____

_____

_____

_____

(Answers are on page 102.)

INFORMATIVE WRITING

W.8.2 Write informative/explanatory texts to examine a topic and convey ideas, concepts, and information through the selection, organization, and analysis of relevant content.

1. Write an essay explaining the steps in the scientific method. Make sure to provide definitions of key terms, such as **hypothesis**, and provide examples of each of the steps. Provide a graphic that depicts the steps of the scientific method to go along with your essay.

   _____

   _____

   _____

   _____

   _____

   _____

   _____

   _____

   _____

2. Use your history textbook or the Internet to find information regarding Japan's attack on Pearl Harbor (*http://www.history.com/topics/world-war-ii/pearl-harbor* is a good resource). In your own words, explain what happened at Pearl Harbor and why it marked a turning point in World War II.

   _____

   _____

   _____

   _____

   _____

   _____

   _____

   _____

3. Choose a favorite character from a book you have read. Write an essay explaining who this character is and at least three reasons why he or she is your favorite. In your response, be sure to include the title and author of the book in which your character appears.

_____

_____

_____

_____

_____

_____

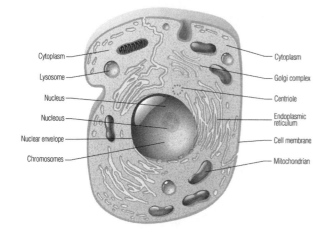

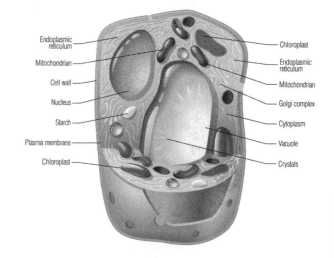

4. Study the preceding image of an animal cell and a plant cell. Then, write an essay comparing and contrasting the two cells. Where possible, explain the functions of the cell parts that you mention. Use a science textbook or the Internet to help you.

_____

_____

_____

_____

_____

_____

_____

(Answers are on page 104.)

NARRATIVE WRITING

W.8.3 Write narratives to develop real or imagined experiences or events using effective technique, relevant descriptive details, and well-structured event sequences.

1. You are asked to describe the scenery in the following image to someone who is unable to see it. How would you describe what you see? Be as specific as you can in your description. Use precise words and phrases, telling details, and sensory language so that the other person is able to fully visualize the image in his or her mind.

_____

_____

_____

_____

_____

_____

_____

_____

_____

2. After much begging on your end, your older sibling (or best friend) finally agrees to lend you his or her _____ (fill in the blank with something of great emotional or monetary value). You promise to be as careful as possible, but the inevitable happens: his or her item is destroyed while in your possession. Describe the chain of events that led to the item's destruction.

_____

_____

_____

_____

_____

_____

_____

3. Describe the event that led to the posting of the following sign in the school cafeteria:

> **ATTENTION:**
> AS OF MAY 1, 2015,
> **GUMMY BEARS**
> ARE
> **NO LONGER ALLOWED**
> IN THE CAFETERIA.
> THANK YOU!

_____

_____

_____

_____

_____

_____

_____

_____

_____

4. A man is caught trying to sneak his pet lizard into the movie theater during a showing of *Jurassic World*. Write the **dialogue** that occurs between the man and the theater attendant.

Read your dialogue aloud. Dialogue should sound natural; reading it aloud while writing will help you achieve this effect.

_____

_____

_____

_____

_____

_____

_____

_____

5. Write a story that conveys the following theme: Over-reliance on technology can have negative effects.

_____

_____

_____

_____

_____

_____

_____

_____

6. Write a story that goes along with the image in question 1. You may use your response from question 1 in the description of your story's setting.

_____

_____

_____

_____

_____

_____

_____

_____

_____

_____

_____

_____

_____

_____

_____

_____

_____

(Answers are on page 105.)

CONSIDERING TASK, AUDIENCE, AND PURPOSE

> **W.8.4** Produce clear and coherent writing in which the development, organization, and style are appropriate to task, purpose, and audience.

1. Your class would like to go on a field trip, and you have been asked to write a letter to your principal, asking for his or her permission to do so. Write a **formal letter** explaining where your class would like to go, why this location is relevant, and why the trip would be beneficial to students.

    _____

    _____

    _____

    _____

    _____

    _____

    _____

    _____

2. You have been asked to entertain a group of elementary school students by reading your own creative writing. Write a series of text messages that might take place between a dog and his owner. You will read these text messages aloud to the elementary students.

    _____

    _____

    _____

    _____

    _____

    _____

    _____

3. It's the first day of eighth grade. Write a **friendly letter** to your English teacher introducing yourself. In your letter describe your family, your hobbies, your experience in seventh grade, and any strengths and weaknesses that you have as far as English class is concerned. Close your letter with a positive statement about the upcoming year.

_____

_____

_____

_____

_____

_____

4. Write an **e-mail** to your teacher asking for an extension on tonight's homework. In your e-mail, be sure to include valid reasons for the extension.

_____

_____

_____

_____

_____

_____

5. Refer back to the passage from *The Adventures of Tom Sawyer*, found on pages 2 and 3 of the workbook. Write a **journal entry** through the perspective of Muff Potter. Make sure that you describe the scene, and include Muff Potter's feelings.

_____

_____

_____

_____

_____

_____

_____

(Answers are on page 107.)

GRAMMAR AND USAGE— GERUNDS, PARTICIPLES, AND INFINITIVES

L.8.1 Demonstrate command of the conventions of standard English grammar and usage when writing or speaking.

L.8.1.A Explain the function of verbals (gerunds, participles, infinitives) in general and their function in particular sentences.

Directions: Based upon its function in the sentence provided for questions 1–6, identify each underlined **verbal** as a/an

- Ⓐ **gerund**
- Ⓑ **participle**
- Ⓒ **infinitive**

> **Gerunds vs. Present Participles**
>
> Though both gerunds and present participles end in *-ing*, gerunds act as **nouns**, and present participles act as **adjectives**, modifying a noun or pronoun.

1. In addition to helping you remain physically fit, <u>running</u> may help relieve stress.

   _____

2. <u>To laugh</u> at the child's mistake seemed cruel.

   _____

3. Amazingly, the man climbed out of the <u>burning</u> vehicle unharmed.

   _____

4. The monument, after it was <u>destroyed</u>, was never rebuilt.

   _____

5. Everyone wanted <u>to leave</u>, but Debra convinced us to stay.

   _____

6. <u>Driving</u> while intoxicated may result in arrest, injury, or even death.

   _____

Directions: For questions 7 and 8, choose the letter of the correct answer.

7. What is the function of the word *running* in the sentence provided in question 1?
   - Ⓐ *Running* acts as an **adjective** to describe the pronoun *you*.
   - Ⓑ *Running* acts as an **adverb** to describe the adverb *physically*.
   - Ⓒ *Running* acts as a **noun,** suggested as a stress reliever.
   - Ⓓ *Running* acts as a **verb** to show what the subject *you* is doing in the sentence.

8. What is the function of the word *burning* in the sentence provided in question 3?
   - Ⓐ *Burning* acts as a **noun**, modifying the noun *vehicle*.
   - Ⓑ *Burning* acts as an **adverb**, modifying the adverb *amazingly*.
   - Ⓒ *Burning* acts as a **verb**, showing what the subject *the man* is doing in the sentence.
   - Ⓓ *Burning* acts as an **adjective**, modifying the noun *vehicle*.

(Answers are on page 107.)

GRAMMAR AND USAGE— ACTIVE AND PASSIVE VOICE

L.8.1 Demonstrate command of the conventions of standard English grammar and usage when writing or speaking.

L.8.1.B Form and use verbs in the active and passive voice.

In **active voice,** the subject of the sentence **performs** the action. In **passive voice,** the subject of the sentence **receives** the action.

Directions: Answer questions 1 and 2 on **active** and **passive** voice.

1. Which of the following statements is written in the **active** voice?
   - (A) The rules were followed by most of the students.
   - (B) After everyone left, the dishes were washed by Greg.
   - (C) Danielle accidentally threw away the tickets to the concert.
   - (D) The bill was signed by the president on August 13, 1927.

Passive voice often includes the use of the verb "**to be**" and all its various forms.

2. Convert the following sentence into the **active** voice.

   The necklace was given to Gabrielle by Garrett.

   _____

   _____

Directions: Make the following passive sentences in questions 3 and 4 clearer and less wordy by rewriting them in the **active** voice.

3. Several vases were broken when the table was bumped into by Tom.

   _____

   _____

4. It was found by the specialists that the report was inconclusive.

_____

_____

Directions: Review the following information on **passive** voice. Then, answer questions 5 and 6.

> Writing in the **passive** voice is sometimes necessary and appropriate. Use the passive voice when:
>
> - **The subject performing the action is unknown**
>   _My car has been stolen!_
> - **The subject performing the action is irrelevant**
>   _The house was built in 1968._
> - **Your intention is to be vague**
>   _Mistakes were made._
> - **You are speaking of a general truth**
>   _Life is meant to be lived._
> - **Your intention is to emphasize the person or thing acted _on_**
>   _Passive voice continues to be used more frequently by young adults._

5. Which one of the following statements uses the **passive** voice _most_ effectively?
- Ⓐ The alarm was sounded by the fire department.
- Ⓑ Last year, an estimated 312,000 people were injured in alcohol-related crashes.
- Ⓒ The baton was passed by George in the final relay event.
- Ⓓ Mistakes were made on the exam by both Danielle and Josh.

6. Which of the following effective statements uses the **active** voice?
- Ⓐ The suspects were taken into custody and questioned by the police.
- Ⓑ The Nobel Peace Prize was awarded to Martin Luther King Jr.
- Ⓒ Pistachio nuts are grown in Iran.
- Ⓓ The burglar fled the scene before the cops arrived.

(Answers are on page 108.)

COMMAS, DASHES, AND ELLIPSES

L.8.2 Demonstrate command of the conventions of standard English capitalization, punctuation, and spelling when writing.

L.8.2.A Use punctuation (comma, ellipsis, dash) to indicate a pause or break.

L.8.2.B Use an ellipsis to indicate an omission.

Directions: Read sentences 1–4, and add commas where necessary. Then choose the correct option for questions 5 and 6.

1. Diana like many girls her age loves listening to music and attending concerts.

2. While shopping Rick remembered he still needed to pick up the dog stop at the post office and put air in his tires.

3. She read the book over his shoulder for a while then said "What fun are you anyway?"

4. Though he died the following morning former president Abraham Lincoln was shot on April 14 1865 in Washington D.C.

5. Which of the following sentences is punctuated correctly?
   - (A) Thousands of animals, like the one in this photograph are abandoned each year.
   - (B) Thousands of animals—like the one in this photograph are abandoned each year.
   - (C) Thousands of animals—like the one in this photograph—are abandoned each year.
   - (D) Thousands of animals like the one in this photograph, are abandoned each year.

6. Which of the following sentences is punctuated correctly?
   - (A) "You're not going to believe what I have to—Watch out!"
   - (B) "You're not going to believe what I have to: Watch out!"
   - (C) "You're not going to believe what I have to, Watch out!"
   - (D) "You're not going to believe, what I have to Watch out!"

The Ellipsis and the Dash

Use an **ellipsis [...]**:

- to indicate the trailing off of a thought

  If only I had… oh, it doesn't matter now.

- to indicate hesitation

  Well, what I mean is… I don't really… the thing is…

- to indicate an omission, or in quoting material that you wish to abbreviate

  When the poet writes, "Where on the deck my captain lies…," he means…

Use a **dash [—]**:

- to replace a pair of parentheses

  When the teacher discovered the typos—all 12 of them—she suggested the student retype the paper.

- in place of a colon, particularly at the end of a sentence

  After months of deliberating, the jury final reached a verdict—guilty.

- to indicate a break in thought

  Don't step on the—Look out!

- in place of commas, to enhance readability

  When she was finished—nearly three months later—no one was around to admire her work.

7. Add the necessary punctuation to the following sentence in order to show a break in thought.

   I wish you would tell me when you oh, never mind.

8. Add the necessary punctuation to the following sentence in order to offset information that is not essential to the meaning of the rest of the sentence.

   Many people like my parents, for instance were against the new building project.

9. Rewrite the following sentence by omitting text and using an ellipsis.

   We were warned by the Assistant Principal not to run in the halls.

10. Rewrite the following sentence by omitting text and using an ellipsis.

    Try as she may—and she tried with all her might—she would not be able to stop him.

    > When omitting information, you want to be sure *not* to omit anything **necessary** or **important**.

(Answers are on page 108.)

DETERMINING THE MEANING OF UNKNOWN AND MULTIPLE-MEANING WORDS OR PHRASES

> **L.8.4** Determine or clarify the meaning of unknown and multiple-meaning words or phrases based on grade 8 reading and content, choosing flexibly from a range of strategies.
>
> **L.8.4.A** Use context (e.g., the overall meaning of a sentence or paragraph; a word's position or function in a sentence) as a clue to the meaning of a word or phrase.
>
> **L.8.4.B** Use common, grade-appropriate Greek or Latin affixes and roots as clues to the meaning of a word.

Directions: Use **context clues** to determine the meaning of the bold-faced word in questions 1–3. In each passage, circle the context clues that helped to identify the word's meaning.

1. "The day my son Laurie started kindergarten he **renounced** corduroy overalls and began wearing blue jeans with a belt; I watched him go off the first morning with the older girl next door, seeing clearly that an era of my life was ended, my sweet-voiced nursery-school tot being replaced by a long-trousered, swaggering character who forgot to stop at the corner and wave good-bye to me."

    from *Charles,* by Shirley Jackson

    Ⓐ Wore
    Ⓑ Gave up
    Ⓒ Clothes
    Ⓓ Stripped

2. "But we loved with a love that was more than love—
        I and my Annabel Lee—
    With a love that the wingèd **seraphs** of Heaven
        Coveted her and me."

    from *Annabel Lee,* by Edgar Allan Poe

    Ⓐ Messengers
    Ⓑ Rulers
    Ⓒ Angels
    Ⓓ Birds

3. "He felt that the stars had been **pulverized** by the sound of the black jets and that in the morning the earth would be covered with their dust like a strange snow."

from *Fahrenheit 451*, by Ray Bradbury

    Ⓐ Demolished

    Ⓑ Extinguished

    Ⓒ Burnt

    Ⓓ Blown away

4. Study the different definitions of the word *long*:

> **long** (adj.) :
>
> 1) extending for a considerable distance
>
> 2) having a specified length
>
> 3) having the capacity to reach, extend, or travel a considerable distance
>
> 4) extending over a considerable time

Which definition best fits the word *long* as it is used in the following passage?

"I'm about to leave when I remember the importance of sustaining the star-crossed lover routine and I lean over and give Peeta a **long**, lingering kiss. I imagine the teary sighs emanating from the Capitol and pretend to brush away a tear of my own. Then I squeeze through the opening in the rocks out into the night."

from *The Hunger Games*, by Suzanne Collins

    Ⓐ Definition 1

    Ⓑ Definition 2

    Ⓒ Definition 3

    Ⓓ Definition 4

5. Study the different definitions of the word *hard*:

> **hard** (adj.) :
> 1) not easily penetrated
> 2) difficult to bear or endure
> 3) intense in force, manner, or degree
> 4) lacking consideration, compassion, or gentleness

Which definition best fits the word *hard* as used in the following sentence?

"Yet in his **hard** face there was character, pride, and a savage defiance of the world."

from *The Outsiders*, by S.E. Hinton

Ⓐ Definition 1
Ⓑ Definition 2
Ⓒ Definition 3
Ⓓ Definition 4

Greek and Latin Word Roots

Root	Meaning
ambi, amphi	both, on both sides, around
bene	good, well
cert	sure
crypto	hidden, secret

Directions: For questions 6–9, use the chart above to help you determine the meaning of the bold-faced word.

6. He tried to **ascertain** whether or not the photo had been manipulated.

   Meaning: _____

7. Because Timothy is **ambidextrous**, he was still able to take notes when he broke his left hand.

   Meaning: _____

8. The software will **encrypt** the message before it is sent.

   Meaning: _____

9. The **benevolent** man donated his lottery winnings to charity.

   Meaning: _____

(Answers are on page 109.)

FIGURATIVE LANGUAGE, WORD RELATIONSHIPS, AND NUANCES IN WORD MEANINGS

L.8.5 Demonstrate understanding of figurative language, word relationships, and nuances in word meanings.

L.8.5.A Interpret figures of speech (e.g., verbal irony, puns) in context.

L.8.5.B Use the relationship between particular words to better understand each of the words.

Directions: Use the following poem to answer questions 1–5.

> Asleep inside my head there is a song.
> It wakes while I am resting in my bed.
> It sings its tune of mystery all night long.
> When morning comes again the song has fled.
>
> 5   While driving on the road I take to school,
> I'm startled by the music that I hear;
> Too quick, the words are fading now, you fool,
> The song was being whispered in my ear.
>
> My hearing's blocked, the muse[1] has thwarted me.
> 10   The poem inside refuses to break free.
> The song that once was whispered by the breeze,
> Is pantomimed[2] by leaves that fall from trees.

_____

[1](n.) inspiration
[2](v.) acted out silently

1. The word *song* in line 1 means
   Ⓐ a composition of words and music.
   Ⓑ an unwritten poem.
   Ⓒ a prayer.
   Ⓓ a melody.

2. As used in the poem, the word *wakes* in line 2 most nearly means
   Ⓐ dies.
   Ⓑ trails made by a boat driving through water.
   Ⓒ comes to the speaker's conscious mind.
   Ⓓ get out of bed.

3. In line 6, the word *music* means
   Ⓐ what the speaker hears on the radio.
   Ⓑ a written score for piano.
   Ⓒ drum beats.
   Ⓓ poetic ideas.

4. The word *Asleep* in line 1 is an example of
   Ⓐ personification.
   Ⓑ onomatopoeia.
   Ⓒ verbal irony.
   Ⓓ simile.

5. Line 8 contains
   Ⓐ a simile.
   Ⓑ a pun.
   Ⓒ a metaphor.
   Ⓓ onomatopoeia.

Directions: For questions 6–10, read each statement and answer the question that follows.

6. In William Shakespeare's play, *Romeo and Juliet*, Romeo and Juliet's love would have been forbidden by their parents. This only fueled the fire of their love.

   The phrase *fueled the fire* as used above means
   Ⓐ made them stop loving each other.
   Ⓑ caused them to think twice about being in love.
   Ⓒ gave them something to think about.
   Ⓓ caused them to love each other more.

7. The pair climbed the heights of love in the moment of their first kiss.

   The phrase *climbed the heights of love* as used above means
   Ⓐ became very passionate.
   Ⓑ went mountaineering.
   Ⓒ lost interest in each other.
   Ⓓ became better people.

8. After watching Romeo make a fool of himself over love, one of his friends remarked that Romeo was "getting schooled."

   Romeo's friend most likely meant that Romeo was
   Ⓐ getting smarter.
   Ⓑ likely to learn from his mistake.
   Ⓒ leaving for college soon.
   Ⓓ likely to be very happy.

9. When Shakespeare introduces his two antagonistic families in *Romeo and Juliet*, he describes them as two households that are "alike in dignity." Based on this description, the reader may think that the two families are both honorable and dignified, only to discover later in the play that the families are violently competitive and undignified.

According to the statement above, Shakespeare's initial description of the two families is an example of

Ⓐ a pun.

Ⓑ a simile.

Ⓒ a metaphor.

Ⓓ verbal irony.

10. Read the following scenario from William Shakespeare's play, *Hamlet*. In the play, Hamlet's father was murdered. Claudius is Hamlet's stepfather (and uncle).

Hamlet is annoyed by Claudius's constant referral to him as his "son," so when Claudius asks him, "How is it that the clouds still hang over you?"—meaning why is he still mourning for his father—Hamlet responds, "Not so, my lord, I am too much in the sun."

In the scenario above, a pun is found

Ⓐ in lines 1 and 3 together.

Ⓑ in line 2.

Ⓒ in lines 2 and 3 together.

Ⓓ in line 3 only.

(Answers are on page 109.)

DENOTATION AND CONNOTATION

L.8.5 Demonstrate understanding of figurative language, word relationships, and nuances in word meanings.

L.8.5.C Distinguish among the connotations (associations) of words with similar denotations (definitions) (e.g., bullheaded, willful, firm, persistent, resolute).

Directions: Each of the following groups of words have similar **denotations**, but differ in their **connotations.** First, decide which of the words is the general denotation for the group and circle it. Then, rank the words in order from *most negative* connotation to *most positive* connotation.

For an explanation of **denotation** and **connotation,** see page 42.

Example: **Group A:** slim, gaunt, (thin), bony, slender

Ranked from most negative to most positive: **gaunt, bony, thin, slim, slender**

Group 1: strong, stubborn, pigheaded, dogged, determined

Ranked: _____

Group 2: surprised, amazed, astonished, shocked, dumbfounded

Ranked: _____

Group 3: pretty, beautiful, lovely, stunning, attractive

Ranked: _____

Group 4: absorbed, obsessed, focused, engaged, interested

Ranked: _____

Directions: For questions 1–4, identify each word as having a positive, negative, or neutral connotation.

1. foreign, strange, exotic

    positive: _____

    negative: _____

    neutral: _____

2. young, youthful, childish

   positive: _____

   negative: _____

   neutral: _____

3. lazy, inactive, laid-back

   positive: _____

   negative: _____

   neutral: _____

4. curious, interested, nosy

   positive: _____

   negative: _____

   neutral: _____

5. List as many words as you can think of that mean about the same as the word *said*, but have negative connotations.

   _____

   _____

   _____

   _____

   _____

6. List as many words as you can think of that mean about the same as the word *said*, but have positive connotations.

   _____

   _____

   _____

   _____

   _____

(Answers are on page 110.)

ENGLISH LANGUAGE ARTS PRACTICE TEST

My Name: _____

Today's Date: _____

Directions: Read the following excerpt from Ray Bradbury's *Fahrenheit 451*. Then, answer questions 1–5.

Mildred shrieked with laughter in the hall.

Montag went to his bedroom closet and flipped through his file-wallet to the heading: FUTURE INVESTIGATIONS (?). Faber's name was there. He hadn't turned it in and he hadn't erased it.

He dialed the call on a secondary phone. The phone on the far end of the line called Faber's name a dozen times before the professor answered in a faint voice. Montag identified himself and was met with a lengthy silence. "Yes, Mr. Montag?"

"Professor Faber, I have a rather odd question to ask. How many copies of the Bible are left in this country?"

"I don't know what you're talking about!"

"I want to know if there are *any* copies left at all."

"This is some sort of trap! I can't talk to just anyone on the phone!"

"How many copies of Shakespeare and Plato?"

"None! You know as well as I do. None!"

Faber hung up.

Montag put down the phone. None. A thing he knew of course from the firehouse listings. But somehow he had wanted to hear it from Faber himself.

In the hall Mildred's face was suffused[1] with excitement. "Well, the ladies are coming over!"

Montag showed her a book. "This is the Old and New Testament, and…"

"Don't start that again!"

"It might be the last copy in this part of the world."

"You've got to hand it back tonight, don't you? Captain Beatty *knows* you got it, doesn't he?"

"I don't think he knows *which* book I stole. But how do I choose a substitute? Do I turn in Mr. Jefferson? Mr. Thoreau? Which is least valuable? If I pick a substitute and Beatty does know which book I stole, he'll guess we've an entire library here!"

Mildred's mouth twitched. "See what you're *doing*? You'll ruin us! Who's more important, me or that Bible?" She was beginning to shriek now, sitting there like a wax doll melting in its own heat.

He could hear Beatty's voice. "Sit down, Montag. Watch. Delicately, like the petals of a flower. Light the first page, light the second page. Each becomes a black butterfly. Beautiful, eh? Light the third page from the second and so on, chain smoking, chapter by chapter, all the silly things the words mean, all the false promises, all the second-hand notions and time-worn philosophies." There sat Beatty, perspiring gently, the floor littered with swarms of black moths that had died in a single storm.

Mildred stopped screaming as quickly as she started. Montag was not listening. "There's only one thing to do," he said. "Sometime before tonight when I give the book to Beatty, I've got to have a duplicate made."

"You'll be here for the White Clown[2] tonight, and the ladies coming over?" cried Mildred.

Montag stopped at the door, with his back turned. "Millie?"

A silence. "What?"

"Millie? Does the White Clown love you?"

No answer.

"Millie, does—" He licked his lips. "Does your 'family'[3] love you, love you very much, love you with all their heart and soul, Millie?"

He felt her blinking slowly at the back of his neck. "Why'd you ask a silly question like that?"

He felt he wanted to cry, but nothing would happen to his eyes or his mouth.

"If you see that dog[4] outside," said Mildred, "give him a kick for me."

He hesitated, listening at the door. He opened it and stepped out.

The rain had stopped and the sun was setting in the clear sky. The street and the lawn and the porch were empty. He let his breath go in a great sigh.

He slammed the door.

_____

[1](v.) flushed or spread over

[2]White Clown refers to a TV show, considered a comedy, in which cartoon clowns did violent things such as chop off each other's limbs.

[3]Montag is referring to another television show that Mildred enjoys watching, in which she gets to "participate" by reciting lines on certain cues.

[4]Mildred is referring to a mechanical hound that is programmed to find books and kill people.

1. Read the following sentence from the passage:

   "She was beginning to shriek now, sitting there like a wax doll melting in its own heat."

   In addition to illustrating how upset Mildred is, this simile helps to
   Ⓐ establish setting by identifying how warm Montag's house is.
   Ⓑ reveal aspects of Mildred's character by likening her to something non-living.
   Ⓒ foreshadow later events by suggesting that Mildred is hiding a collection of dolls.
   Ⓓ reveal aspects of Montag's character by referencing his dislike of dolls.

2. Who are Mr. Jefferson and Mr. Thoreau?
   Ⓐ Other men who are hiding books
   Ⓑ Montag's uncles
   Ⓒ The president and vice president in the story
   Ⓓ Authors of other books that Montag has hidden

3. Provide textual evidence that supports your answer to question 2.

_____

_____

_____

4. Why does Montag ask Mildred if the White Clown loves her?

Ⓐ   He's curious.

Ⓑ   He himself is amused with the White Clown and jealous of Mildred.

Ⓒ   He's trying to remind her of who and what is important.

Ⓓ   He wants to know if Mildred plans on running away with the White Clown.

5. Towards the end of the passage, why might Montag want to cry?

Ⓐ   He feels bad for upsetting Mildred.

Ⓑ   He realizes Mildred is unable to recognize her disconnect from real human relationships.

Ⓒ   He's afraid of the mechanical hound waiting outside.

Ⓓ   He is insulted by Mildred's question.

Directions: Read the following excerpt from Maya Angelou's autobiography, *I Know Why the Caged Bird Sings,* and answer questions 6–11.

1   For nearly a year, I sopped around the house, the Store, the school and the church, like an old biscuit, dirty and inedible. Then I met, or rather got to know, the lady who threw me my first lifeline.

2   Mrs. Bertha Flowers was the aristocrat of Black Stamps. She had the grace of control to appear warm in the coldest weather, and on the Arkansas summer days it seemed she had a private breeze which swirled around, cooling her. She was thin without the taut look of wiry people, and her printed voile dresses and flowered hats were as right for her as denim overalls for a farmer. She was our side's answer to the richest white woman in town.

3   Her skin was a rich black that would have peeled like a plum if snagged, but then no one would have thought of getting close enough to Mrs. Flowers to ruffle her dress, let alone snag her skin. She didn't encourage familiarity. She wore gloves too.

4   I don't think I ever saw Mrs. Flowers laugh, but she smiled often. A slow widening of her thin black lips to show even, small white teeth, then the slow effortless closing. When she chose to smile on me, I always wanted to thank her. The action was so graceful and inclusively benign.

5   She was one of the few gentlewomen I have ever known, and has remained throughout my life the measure of what a human being can be…

6   One summer afternoon, sweet-milk fresh in my memory, she stopped at the Store to buy provisions. Another Negro woman of her health and age would have been expected to carry the paper sacks home in one hand, but Momma said, "Sister Flowers, I'll send Bailey up to your house with these things."

7   She smiled that slow dragging smile, "Thank you, Mrs. Henderson. I'd prefer Marguerite, though." My name was beautiful when she said it. "I've been meaning to talk to her, anyway." They gave each other age-group looks.

8   Momma said, "Well, that's all right then. Sister, go and change your dress. You going to Sister Flowers's…"

9   There was a little path beside the rocky road, and Mrs. Flowers walked in front swinging her arms and picking her way over the stones.

10 She said, without turning her head, to me, "I hear you're doing very good school work, Marguerite, but that it's all written. The teachers report that they have trouble getting you to talk in class." We passed the triangular farm on our left and the path widened to allow us to walk together. I hung back in the separate unasked and unanswerable questions.

11 "Come and walk along with me, Marguerite." I couldn't have refused even if I wanted to. She pronounced my name so nicely. Or more correctly, she spoke each word with such clarity that I was certain a foreigner who didn't understand English could have understood her.

12 "Now no one is going to make you talk—possibly no one can. But bear in mind, language is man's way of communicating with his fellow man and it is language alone which separates him from the lower animals." That was a totally new idea to me, and I would need time to think about it.

13 "Your grandmother says you read a lot. Every chance you get. That's good, but not good enough. Words mean more than what is set down on paper. It takes the human voice to infuse them with the shades of deeper meaning."

14 I memorized the part about the human voice infusing words. It seemed so valid and poetic.

15 She said she was going to give me some books and that I not only must read them, I must read them aloud. She suggested that I try to make a sentence sound in as many different ways as possible.

16 "I'll accept no excuse if you return a book to me that has been badly handled." My imagination boggled at the punishment I would deserve if in fact I did abuse a book of Mrs. Flowers'. Death would be too kind and brief

…

17 Childhood's logic never asks to be proved (all conclusions are absolute). I didn't question why Mrs. Flowers had singled me out for attention, nor did it occur to me that Momma might have asked her to give me a little talking to. All I cared about was that she had made tea cookies for me and read to me from her favorite book. It was enough to prove that she liked me.

6. In your own words, explain the meaning of the phrase *threw me my first lifeline* from the second sentence of the excerpt.

_____

_____

_____

7. Based upon the description provided by the narrator, which of the following set of words could be used to describe Mrs. Flowers?
   - Ⓐ Bold and disrespectful
   - Ⓑ Comfortable and laid-back
   - Ⓒ Graceful and proper
   - Ⓓ Cold and thin

8. Provide evidence from the text that supports your answer to question 7.

_____

_____

_____

9. Which of the following lines from the passage best supports the inference that Marguerite was in awe of Mrs. Flowers?
   - Ⓐ "She said, without turning her head, to me, 'I hear you're doing very good school work, Marguerite, but that it's all written.'"
   - Ⓑ "We passed the triangular farm on our left and the path widened to allow us to walk together."
   - Ⓒ "Her skin was a rich black that would have peeled like a plum if snagged, but then no one would have thought of getting close enough to Mrs. Flowers to ruffle her dress, let alone snag her skin."
   - Ⓓ "When she chose to smile on me, I always wanted to thank her."

10. Which quotation expresses the central idea of the passage?
   - Ⓐ "For nearly a year, I sopped around the house, the Store, the school and the church, like an old biscuit, dirty and inedible."
   - Ⓑ "She was one of the few gentlewomen I have ever known, and has remained throughout my life the measure of what a human being can be…"
   - Ⓒ "Then I met, or rather got to know, the lady who threw me my first lifeline."
   - Ⓓ "One summer afternoon, sweet-milk fresh in my memory, she stopped at the Store to buy provisions."

78

11. What does the use of the phrase *sweet-milk fresh* in paragraph 6 help the reader to understand about Marguerite's memory?
   Ⓐ She has negative feelings about that day, though she remembers it vividly.
   Ⓑ She has positive feelings about the day and remembers it clearly.
   Ⓒ She has neutral feelings about the day and remembers it clearly.
   Ⓓ Though the memory is faint in her mind, she remembers the positive feelings associated with it.

Directions: Use the following poem to answer questions 12–18.

On a Night of Snow
by Elizabeth Coatsworth

Cat, if you go outdoors you must walk in the snow.
You will come back with little white shoes on your feet,
Little white slippers of snow that have heels of sleet.
Stay by the fire, my Cat. Lie still, do not go.
5 See how the flames are leaping and hissing low,
I will bring you a saucer of milk like a Marguerite[1],
So white and smooth, so spherical and sweet—
Stay with me, Cat. Outdoors the wild winds blow.

Outdoors the wild winds blow, Mistress, and dark is the night.
10 Strange voices cry in the trees, intoning[2] strange lore[3];
And more than cats move, lit by our eyes' green light,
On silent feet where the meadow grasses hang hoar[4]—
Mistress, there are portents[5] abroad of magic and might,
And things that are yet to be done. Open the door!

_____
[1](n.) a daisy
[2](v.) singing or chanting
[3](n.) knowledge
[4](adj.) white or grey
[5](n.) signs of warning

12. Which of the following best summarizes the poem?
   Ⓐ On a winter's day, a Mistress tries to convince her cat to stay inside.
   Ⓑ On a winter's evening, a cat begs his Mistress to let him back inside.
   Ⓒ A woman describes her encounter with a cat on a cold winter's evening.
   Ⓓ The poem describes a conversation between a cat and its owner on a cold winter's night.

13. How would you describe the speaker's tone in stanza one? Include details from the poem to support your response.

_____

_____

_____

_____

_____

_____

14. The Mistress thinks that compared to outdoors, indoors is
    Ⓐ less dangerous.
    Ⓑ more comfortable.
    Ⓒ more exciting.
    Ⓓ less adventurous.

15. The cat thinks that compared to indoors, outdoors is
    Ⓐ much colder.
    Ⓑ filled with danger.
    Ⓒ filled with adventure.
    Ⓓ much calmer.

16. Which of the following best describes the cat in the poem?
    Ⓐ Fearful
    Ⓑ Content
    Ⓒ Desperate
    Ⓓ Dangerous

17. Which of the following best describes the Mistress in the poem?
    Ⓐ Angry
    Ⓑ Protective
    Ⓒ Demanding
    Ⓓ Cruel

18. Which of the following is true of the Mistress?
    Ⓐ She allows her cat to go outside.
    Ⓑ She demands that her cat stay inside by the fire.
    Ⓒ She suggests that her cat only go outside for a little while.
    Ⓓ She desires that her cat stay inside.

Directions: Use the following article on the Hopi tribe, from Grolier Online, to answer questions 19–24.

Hopi

1   Unlike most Native Americans, the Hopi people have lived in the same place for nearly a thousand years. One of their settlements, Old Oraibi, may be the oldest continuously inhabited place in the United States, established around 1100. The harsh landscape and remote location of their homeland may have kept out possible invaders. The Hopi lived on the high, flat-topped rock mesas of northeastern Arizona, and still inhabit that region today.

2   The Hopi name comes from the word Hopituh, which in the Hopi language means "peaceful ones." True to their name, Hopi have always been known for their cooperation and peaceful, religious spirit. Traditional Hopi believe that all parts of a person's life— religion, work, art, and nature—remain tied together. They call this approach to life the Hopi Way.

Origins

3   The Hopi trace their ancestry to the ancient Anasazi people—cliff dwellers and desert farmers who lived near the Grand Canyon in northeastern Arizona over 20,000 years ago until they mysteriously disappeared. Like the Anasazi, the Hopi farmed the dry desert and used natural springs to water their crops. They built their villages, or pueblos, on rocky tablelands carved out of the Colorado Plateau between the Colorado River and the Rio Grande.

4   The Hopi made the walls and buildings of their pueblos from stone and clay bricks, which they cemented together with mud. The men laid the stone and bricks, and the women covered the outside with a brownish-red plaster made of wet clay. Traditionally, the finished pueblos had neither doors nor windows. People entered their homes through openings in the roofs. In the village plazas, the Hopi dug *kivas*, underground rooms with stone walls, which they used for chapels and clubhouses. A *sipapu*, or stone-lined hole in the floor, represented the entrance to the cave world from which their ancestors had come.

5   The Hopi skillfully farmed the desert, growing squash, beans, cotton, and tobacco. Their favorite crop was corn, for which they developed more than 50 recipes. The Hopi also raised turkeys and gathered wild plants for food. In addition to farming, women made clay bowls decorated with geometric designs and wove beautiful baskets from plants. Hopi men wove cotton to make blankets and clothing, and the women dyed the cloth in bright colors.

6   Chiefs, who were also shamans, or medicine men, governed the Hopi tribes. Groups of related families, called clans, directed their own religious ceremonies and, together, made important decisions about their village.

7   The Hopi enjoyed religious ceremonies throughout the year, with many dances and other rituals dedicated to bringing rain for their crops. In particular, the Hopi believed in guardian spirits, called *kachinas*. Hopi men acted the part of kachinas in the tribe's dances, wearing painted masks made of wood, feathers, and other materials. The most dramatic of these dances, the snake dance, required the kachina dancer to perform with

a live snake wrapped around his body. Dancers also handed out wooden kachina dolls to village children.

Friendship and Conflict

8   In 1540, the Spanish explorers Pedro de Tobar and Juan de Padilla became the first Europeans to meet the Hopi. Over the next century, more Spanish settlers moved to the region, and Spanish missionaries forced the Hopi to convert to Christianity. When the missionaries ordered an end to kachina worship, the Hopi rebelled. Along with neighboring tribes, they launched the Pueblo Rebellion of 1680. They destroyed many Spanish missions and returned to their traditional religious practices.

9   In the mid-1800s, Hopi first came into contact with citizens of the United States. American missionaries, like the Spanish, tried to force the Hopi from their traditional religious practices. In 1882, the U.S. government recognized the Hopi's rights to their own lifestyle and land by establishing the Hopi Reservation, which included the Hopi's historic pueblos and the land surrounding them. Today, their 500-square-mile (1,300-square-kilometer) reservation stands inside a much larger Navajo reservation.

Modern Life

10   Most Hopi today live in modern homes on their northeastern Arizona reservation. Yet, in many ways, they remain close to tradition. Kachina dances continue to play an important role in cultural life, and many Hopi live off the land as farmers and sheep ranchers. Hopi craftspeople still produce basketry, pottery, weaving, and kachina dolls, which they sell to tourists as well as to shops and art galleries throughout the Southwest and around the world. The Hopi have also become world-famous as fine silversmiths.

19. According to the section titled "Origins," what can be inferred about the Hopi people?
   Ⓐ The Hopi are religious people.
   Ⓑ The Hopi rely on neighboring tribes for much of their food supply.
   Ⓒ Hopi medicine men are regarded as outcasts.
   Ⓓ The Hopi men do most of the work on a day-to-day basis.

20. Provide evidence from the passage that supports your answer to question 19.

_____

_____

_____

_____

21. According to the article, how were the Hopi different from most Native American tribes?
    Ⓐ Other Native Americans lived off of the land, while the Hopi relied on importing goods.
    Ⓑ The Hopi are known for being peaceful, while other Native Americans are mostly violent.
    Ⓒ The Hopi people have inhabited the same place for almost one thousand years.
    Ⓓ The Hopi did not conduct a religious ceremony dedicated to their crops.

22. In paragraph 8, the sentences help to develop a key concept by describing
    Ⓐ the reasons for the end of the kachina worship.
    Ⓑ the circumstances surrounding the Pueblo Rebellion of 1680.
    Ⓒ how the Hopi embraced Christianity.
    Ⓓ the effects the Spanish missionaries had on the Hopi culture.

23. What is the meaning of the word *reservation*, as used in paragraph 9?
    Ⓐ An arrangement to have something held for use at a later time
    Ⓑ A feeling of doubt or uncertainty
    Ⓒ An area of land kept separate
    Ⓓ A limited condition

24. Compare and contrast the modern life of the Hopi to the traditional life of the Hopi. What has changed since the introduction of foreign settlers in the 1500s? What has remained the same? Use details from the article in your response.

    _____

    _____

    _____

    _____

    _____

    _____

    _____

    _____

O Captain! My Captain!
by Walt Whitman

O Captain! my Captain! our fearful trip is done,
The ship has weather'd every rack, the prize we sought is won,
The port is near, the bells I hear, the people all exulting,
While follow eyes the steady keel, the vessel grim and daring;
5   But O heart! heart! heart!
          O the bleeding drops of red,
         Where on the deck my Captain lies,
           Fallen cold and dead.

O Captain! my Captain! rise up and hear the bells;
10 Rise up—for you the flag is flung—for you the bugle trills,
For you bouquets and ribbon'd wreaths—for you the shores a-crowding,
For you they call, the swaying mass, their eager faces turning;
           Here Captain! dear father!
           This arm beneath your head!
15   It is some dream that on the deck,
           You've fallen cold and dead.

My Captain does not answer, his lips are pale and still,
My father does not feel my arm, he has no pulse nor will,
The ship is anchor'd safe and sound, its voyage closed and done,
20 From fearful trip the victor ship comes in with object won;
           Exult O shores, and ring O bells!
           But I with mournful tread,
           Walk the deck my Captain lies,
           Fallen cold and dead.

25. Which of the following words best describes the speaker in the poem?
    Ⓐ Hopeful
    Ⓑ Heartbroken
    Ⓒ Confused
    Ⓓ Excited

26. What adjectives would you use to describe the captain in the poem? Use details from the poem to support your response.

    _____

    _____

    _____

    _____

    _____

    _____

27. Which of the following best describes the speaker's **tone** in lines 1–4?
    Ⓐ Celebratory
    Ⓑ Mournful
    Ⓒ Proud
    Ⓓ Uncertain

28. What words or phrases help to reveal the tone identified in question 27?

    _____

    _____

    _____

29. Which of the following statements best summarizes lines 13–16?
    Ⓐ The speaker shall never forget his Captain.
    Ⓑ The captain was like a father to the speaker.
    Ⓒ The speaker cannot believe the captain is dead.
    Ⓓ The speaker asks for help to lift the captain.

Directions: Read the following passage from *To Kill a Mockingbird*, by Harper Lee, and answer questions 30–34.

He answered [the phone], then went to the hat rack in the hall. "I'm going down to Mrs. Dubose's for a while," he said. "I won't be long."

But Atticus stayed away until long past my bedtime. When he returned he was carrying a candy box. Atticus sat down in the livingroom and put the box on the floor beside his chair.

"What'd she want?" asked Jem.

We had not seen Mrs. Dubose for over a month. She was never on the porch any more when we passed.

"She's dead, son," said Atticus. "She died a few minutes ago."

"Oh," said Jem. "Well."

"Well is right," said Atticus. "She's not suffering any more. She was sick for a long time. Son, didn't you know what her fits were?"

Jem shook his head.

"Mrs. Dubose was a morphine addict," said Atticus. "She took it as a pain-killer for years. The doctor put her on it. She'd have spent the rest of her life on it and died without so much agony, but she was too contrary—"

"Sir?" said Jem.

Atticus said, "Just before your escapade she called me to make her will. Dr. Reynolds told her she had only a few months left. Her business affairs were in perfect order but she said, 'There's still one thing out of order.' "

"What was that?" Jem was perplexed.

"She said she was going to leave this world beholden to nothing and nobody. Jem, when you're as sick as she was, it's all right to take anything to make it easier, but it wasn't all right for her. She said she meant to break herself of it before she died, and that's what she did."

Jem said, "You mean that's what her fits were?"

"Yes, that's what they were. Most of the time you were reading to her I doubt if she heard a word you said. Her whole mind and body were concentrated on that alarm clock. If you hadn't fallen into her hands, I'd have made you go to read to her anyway. It may have been some distraction. There was another reason—"

"Did she die free?" asked Jem.

"As the mountain air," said Atticus. "She was conscious to the last, almost. Conscious," he smiled, "and cantankerous[1]. She still disapproved heartily of my doings, and said I'd probably spend the rest of my life bailing you out of jail. She had Jessie fix you this box—"

Atticus reached down and picked up the candy box. He handed it to Jem.

Jem opened the box. Inside, surrounded by wads of damp cotton, was a white, waxy, perfect camellia[2]. It was a Snow-on-the-Mountain[3].

Jem's eyes nearly popped out of his head. "Old hell-devil, old hell-devil!" he screamed, flinging it down. "Why can't she leave me alone?"

In a flash Atticus was up and standing over him. Jem buried his face in Atticus's shirt front. "Sh-h," he said. "I think that was her way of telling you—everything's all right now, Jem, everything's all right. You know, she was a great lady."

"A lady?" Jem raised his head. His face was scarlet. "After all those things she said about you, a lady?"

"She was. She had her own views about things, a lot different from mine, maybe…son, I told you that if you hadn't lost your head I'd have made you go read to her. I wanted you to see something about her—I wanted you to see what real courage is, instead of getting the idea that courage is a man with a gun in his hand. It's when you know you're licked before you begin but you begin anyway and you see it through no matter what. You rarely win, but sometimes you do. Mrs. Dubose won, all ninety-eight pounds of her. According to her views, she died beholden to nothing and nobody. She was the bravest person I ever knew."

Jem picked up the candy box and threw it in the fire. He picked up the camellia, and when I went off to bed I saw him fingering the wide petals. Atticus was reading the paper.

_____

[1](adj.) cranky, argumentative
[2](n.) a white flower
[3](n.) a type of plant, grown in North America, with white-edged leaves and white flowers

30. Why did Mrs. Dubose want to break her morphine addiction before she died?
   Ⓐ It was making her sicker.
   Ⓑ She did not want to die dependent on anything or anyone.
   Ⓒ She felt it was illegal.
   Ⓓ She was embarrassed and did not want anyone to know of her addiction.

31. What is the meaning of the word *licked* as used in the following excerpt?

   "It's when you know you're licked before you begin but you begin anyway and you see it through no matter what."

   Ⓐ Touched
   Ⓑ Broken
   Ⓒ Slapped
   Ⓓ Defeated

32. Read the following excerpt.

   "Mrs. Dubose was a morphine addict," said Atticus. "She took it as a pain-killer for years. The doctor put her on it. She'd have spent the rest of her life on it and died without so much agony, but she was too contrary—"
   "Sir?" said Jem.

   What does Jem's question reveal about his response to Atticus's statements?
   Ⓐ He wants Atticus to stop talking.
   Ⓑ He's confused.
   Ⓒ He's trying to get Atticus's attention.
   Ⓓ He wants to remind Atticus that he respects him.

33. Which of the following would *not* accurately describe Mrs. Dubose?

Ⓐ Courageous

Ⓑ Disrespectful

Ⓒ Dignified

Ⓓ Stubborn

34. In your own words, explain what message the passage is trying to convey about **courage.** Then, explain how the character of Mrs. Dubose helps to reveal this message.

_____

_____

_____

_____

_____

_____

_____

_____

_____

_____

_____

_____

Directions: Read the following poem. Then, answer questions 35–38. For question 38, you will need to refer back to the previous passage from *To Kill a Mockingbird*.

Courage
by Edgar Guest

Courage isn't a brilliant dash,
A daring deed in a moment's flash;
It isn't an instantaneous thing
Born of despair with a sudden spring.
5   It isn't a creature of flickered hope
Or the final tug at a slipping rope;
But it's something deep in the soul of man
That is working always to serve some plan.

Courage isn't the last resort
10   In the work of life or the game of sport;
It isn't a thing that a man can call
At some future time when he's apt to fall;
If he hasn't it now, he will have it not
When the strain is great and the pace is hot.
15   For who would strive for a distant goal
Must always have courage within his soul.

Courage isn't a dazzling light
That flashes and passes away from sight;
It's a slow, unwavering, ingrained trait
20   With the patience to work and the strength to wait.
It's part of a man when his skies are blue,
It's part of him when he has work to do.
The brave man never is freed of it.
He has it when there is no need of it.

25   Courage was never designed for show;
It isn't a thing that can come and go;
It's written in victory and defeat
And every trial a man may meet.
It's part of his hours, his days, and his years,
30   Back of his smiles and behind his tears.
Courage is more than a daring deed:
It's the breath of life and a strong man's creed.

35. With which of the following statements might the speaker of the poem agree?
 (A) Courage requires action.
 (B) Even a courageous person is sometimes weak.
 (C) Courage comes from deep inside a person.
 (D) Courage only appears in moments of despair.

36. According to the speaker, which of the following does **not** define courage?
 (A) Something never designed for show
 (B) Something written in victory and defeat
 (C) A daring action that happens spur of the moment
 (D) The breath of life

37. All of the following lines from the poem help to support the idea that courage is not something temporary **except**:
 (A) "Courage isn't a brilliant dash,"
 (B) "It isn't a thing that can come and go;"
 (C) "It's part of his hours, his days, and his years,"
 (D) "Courage was never designed for show;"

38. Write an **informative essay** that addresses the following prompt:

Explain how the excerpt from *To Kill a Mockingbird* and the poem *Courage* are similar in their definitions of courage. Use details from both the passage and the poem in your response.

_____

_____

_____

_____

_____

_____

_____

_____

_____

_____

_____

_____

_____

_____

_____

_____

_____

Directions: For questions 39–42, choose the letter of the best answer.

39. What is the function of the word *sleeping* in the following sentence?

    My cat's favorite activity is sleeping.

    Ⓐ *Sleeping* acts as an adjective to describe the noun *activity*.
    Ⓑ *Sleeping* acts as an adverb to describe the verb *is*.
    Ⓒ *Sleeping* acts as a verb to show what the subject, *cat,* is doing in the sentence.
    Ⓓ *Sleeping* acts as a noun, identifying the cat's favorite activity.

40. Which of the following sentences uses the active voice?
    Ⓐ The stockings were hung by the chimney with care.
    Ⓑ The children were nestled all snug in their beds.
    Ⓒ I sprang from my bed to see what was the matter.
    Ⓓ A miniature sleigh could be observed.

41. Which of the following sentences is punctuated correctly?
    Ⓐ Not a creature, was stirring, not even a mouse.
    Ⓑ Away to the window I flew like a flash tore open the shutters, and threw up the sash.
    Ⓒ And then, in a twinkling, I heard on the roof the prancing and pawing of each little hoof.
    Ⓓ I laughed when I saw him in spite of, myself.

42. Which of the following sentences is punctuated correctly?
    Ⓐ His eyes—how they twinkled!
    Ⓑ The beard—on his chin was as white as—the snow.
    Ⓒ His—eyes—how they twinkled!
    Ⓓ The beard on—his chin was as white as the snow.

Directions: For questions 43 and 44, circle the word with the ***most*** positive connotation.

43. self-confident, conceited, self-centered, boastful

44. old, aged, elderly, ancient

Directions: Use the following passage to answer questions 45–49.

One dark October night, I stopped by the local funeral parlor to pick up flowers that the parlor was donating to the hospital in which I worked. When I arrived, I went around to the side entrance, the spot designated for flower drop-off and removal. I found the door already open, so—as I'm friendly with the parlor's owner—I walked inside to gather the flowers, closing the door behind me.

Once inside, however, I noticed that everything was dark. Immediately terrified, I tried to make light of the situation. "Things seem pretty dead around here," I thought to myself, and chuckled nervously at my own joke.

Suddenly, I heard a crash from somewhere in the distance, followed by a long, high-pitched lament. Before I knew what was happening, the ground reached up to meet me.

45. Explain the pun used in paragraph 2.

_____

_____

_____

_____

_____

46. Which of the following statements means about the same as "I tried to make light of the situation"?
   Ⓐ I tried to find a light switch.
   Ⓑ I tried to make the situation less serious or scary.
   Ⓒ I tried to distract myself by thinking about something else.
   Ⓓ I tried not to make much noise.

47. When the narrator says, "the ground reached up to meet me," she means that
   Ⓐ the ground was alive.
   Ⓑ there was an earthquake.
   Ⓒ she fainted.
   Ⓓ she had stepped on someone.

48. What is the meaning of the word *lament*, as used in the passage?
   Ⓐ Siren
   Ⓑ Rumble
   Ⓒ Alarm
   Ⓓ Wail

49. Write a narrative that picks up where this excerpt leaves off. Continue in first-person perspective and develop events of the plot.

_____

_____

_____

_____

_____

_____

_____

_____

Directions: For question 50, refer back to George Graham Vest's "Tribute to a Dog" speech on page 38 of the workbook.

50. According to his speech, Vest believed that there is no creature that is more loyal to a human than a dog. Do you agree with Vest's views? Write an argument essay that explains at least three reasons why you agree or disagree. Use details from the speech in your response.

_____

_____

_____

_____

_____

_____

_____

_____

_____

(Answers are on page 110.)

ENGLISH LANGUAGE ARTS ANSWERS EXPLAINED

Reading: Literature

Citing Textual Evidence (RL.8.1), page 2

1. **C** The first paragraph of the excerpt describes the town's reaction to the murder. Twain mentions there was no need for the "as yet undreamed-of telegraph," as "the tale flew from man to man, from group to group, from house to house, with little less than telegraphic speed." Additionally, the school-master gives "holiday" for the day (line 4). There is no mention of "the news" (choice B), and line 15 states, "All the town was drifting toward the grave-yard," which disproves choices A and D.

2. **Any and all of lines 1–5 would support answer choice C in question 1, in addition to line 15, which disproves answer choices A and D.** *See the answer explanation to question 1 for more information.*

3. **C** Line 33 describes Muff Potter as "doubtful and perplexed." Line 37 describes Potter as a "poor fellow" whose face was "haggard" and whose "eyes showed…fear."

4. **See the answer explanation provided for question 3.** Additional lines include lines 38–39, 42–43, and 46–50.

5. **C** Though the knife found at the scene of the murder was only thought to be Potter's, the excerpt in choice C explains how the townspeople, "not slow [to arrive] at a verdict," spread word quickly and "ransacked" the town looking for Potter, the "murderer." Use of the verb *ransacked* implies that great, almost desperate effort was used in searching for him. The townspeople most likely would not have looked so hard if they did not believe Potter to be the murderer.

6. **B** The references to the "lightnings," "Satan," and "God" in choices A, C, and D help to support the inference that both Tom and Huck are superstitious. They act, or refrain from acting, based upon fear that stems from a belief in the supernatural. In choice B, although Tom and Huck glance nervously around them, they do so not because they are superstitious; they merely wonder if anyone notices them look at one another for fear that they may be associated with the crime at hand.

Determining Theme and Central Idea (RL.8.2), page 6

1. **C** With the exception of line 13, the speaker uses the pronoun *they* throughout the poem to reference machines. This is first revealed in lines 15 and 16: "It was only the best/ Machines, of course, the superhuman machines." His reference to *them* in line 74 refers to the same subject—machines.

2. **B** The reference to a *revolt* in the first line of the poem implies that someone (or something) rebelled—or turned—against something or some-one else. Lines 7–14, 20–26, 34–40, 44–46, and 61–63 all describe incidents in which technology, or specific machines, attacked humans.

3. **D** Lines 57, 58, 60, 64, 65, and 71 suggest that the speaker has hope that the machines will "calm down," and relations between humans and technology will return to the way they were—or even better.

4. **C** The speaker suggests the reasons for the machines' revolt in lines 27–33. In lines 32 and 33 the speaker states, "I guess it was that, I guess they got tired of us /And the whole smell of human hands."

5. **D** The line referenced in choice D suggests that humans were "slaves" to machines or technology. This implies that humans had surrendered them-selves, or submitted in a way, to technology, proving their over-reliance.

Analyzing Dialogue and Plot (RL.8.3), page 10

1. **A** Though Juana warns Kino of the dangers of the pearl, already-wounded Kino dismisses her, proclaiming, "I am a man" and "I will win..." These

95

responses back the idea that Kino can be stubborn. Juana's loyalty is shown through the way in which she tends to Kino and his wounds, through her concession to go with him to the capital, and by her response of "No, my husband" when Kino asks her if she is afraid to go with him (line 30).

2. **B** Each time Kino exclaims that "[he is] a man" (lines 22, 24, and 27), it is preceded by Juana's concerns. By stating that he is a man, he appears to be reassuring Juana that all will work out. He also reaffirms that he "will win" and they "will not be cheated." He will not back down in wanting to go to the capital, and he uses "I am a man" as his reason.

3. **D** There is not enough evidence to go so far as to say that Juana changes her feelings regarding the pearl and the "evil" she believes it to possess. In line 30, Juana does give in to Kino's commands and states that she is not afraid to go with him to the capital; whether or not she is truthful remains unknown. This, then, makes choice D the best answer.

4. **B** Immediately after Juana voices her concerns about the pearl (lines 14–16), Steinbeck writes, "And as she spoke the light came back in Kino's eyes so that they glowed fiercely and his muscles hardened and his will hardened." Prior to line 14, Kino had responded "dully" to Juana, and his eyes stared past her. Kino again responds "fiercely" in line 27, after Juana voices her fears a second time.

5. **C** In both excerpts, the characters of Juana and Kino are responding to one another. Lines 17–18 show the effect that Juana's concerns have on Kino. Lines 27–30 show the effect that Kino's words have on Juana: "And she was silent, for his voice was command."

Word Meaning and Figurative Language (RL.8.4), page 12

1. **B** The metaphor, "And each separate dying ember wrought its ghost upon the floor" compares the shadows cast by the smoldering pieces of wood to ghosts. The setting has already been described as a "midnight dreary" in "bleak December," which suggests early on an overall dark and mysterious, or suspenseful, mood.

2. **C** Comparing the raven's appearance to that of a lord or lady implies that the bird presents itself as important and formal. Stanza VII also states, "Not the least obeisance made he; not a minute stopped or stayed he;" revealing that the raven showed no sign of respect to the speaker upon entering the room. This implies that the raven found itself to be above the speaker in terms of status, therefore commanding respect. Later descriptions of the raven (*grave, stern, grim, ungainly, ghastly, gaunt, ominous,* etc.) also support the formality of the bird's appearance.

3. **B** The speaker's remark that the raven, like other "friends" and "hopes," will soon leave indicates that the speaker has been let down, or disappointed, in the past. "On the morrow he will leave me" illustrates the speaker's belief that the bird's visit will be brief.

4. **D** Throughout the poem, the speaker appears plagued with the memory of his lost love, Lenore. He looks to the raven for answers (stanzas VII, XV and XVI) and begs to "forget" the lost Lenore (stanza XIV). Like those seeking the balm of Gilead to make them feel better, the speaker is looking for something that will ease his sadness and suffering.

5. **A** The use of the word "then" in line 79 suggests a sudden change in tone and mood. The speaker's description of the sudden dense air is serious. He uses the word *cried*—not *yelled* or *shouted*—and repeats the need for a rest from his memories of Lenore (line 82). That, as well as the repetition of his need to drink to make him forget ("Quaff, oh quaff"), makes the speaker sound desperate for relief.

6. **Possible answers**: "Air grew denser," "unseen censer," "Wretch," "cried," "Respite—respite and nepenthe, from thy memories of Lenore!," "Quaff, oh quaff this kind nepenthe," and "forget this lost Lenore!" All of these words and phrases help to reveal a solemn and desperate tone.

7. **B** In stanza II, the speaker identifies a source of sorrow: the loss of Lenore. He states that he hopes to "borrow" from his books a "surcease" of this sorrow. In stanza V, it's Lenore's name that the speaker whispers questioningly into the hall, implying that she's the first name on the speaker's mind. The speaker later references the fact that others have left him—"'other friends have flown before—/On the

96

morrow he will leave me, as my hopes have flown before'" (stanza X), and cries for relief from Lenore's memory (stanza XIV). He goes on to beg the raven for answers in stanzas XV and XVI, and once again calls attention to his sorrow, referring to himself as a "soul with sorrow laden" in stanza XVI. These details suggest that the speaker is having extreme difficulty getting over Lenore, and the raven's only response of "Nevermore" offers no comfort or relief. Poe ends the poem with this word, and the image of the speaker's heavy, sorrow-laden soul "floating on the floor." The speaker's ceaseless turmoil over the loss of Lenore supports the idea that one may never get over the loss of a loved one.

8. In stanza I, Poe uses the verbs **pondered**, **nodded**, and **muttered**, to describe what the speaker is doing.

9. **C** Through the use of the verbs "pondered" and "nodded" while the speaker is "nearly napping," the reader feels a sense of peace and calm. "Muttered" also suggests a soft reply.

10. In stanza V, Poe uses the verbs **peering**, **stood**, **wondering**, **fearing**, **doubting, dreaming**, and **whispered** to describe what the speaker is doing.

11. There exists a slight shift in the mood between stanza I and stanza V. Though the poem starts with a more relaxing atmosphere, created by the use of the verbs *pondered, nodded,* and *muttered* in stanza I, the mood seems to turn more mysterious, or suspenseful, in stanza V. The use of the verbs *peering, fearing*, and *whispered* in stanza V help to create this sudden mysterious mood, which continues through stanzas VI and VII, as well.

Comparing and Contrasting Structure (RL.8.5), page 20

1.

	"November"	"Fall, leaves, fall"
Number of stanzas	seven	one
Rhyme scheme	abab, cdcd	aabbccdd - couplets
Type of poem (sonnet, lyric, narrative, haiku, ballad, epic, elegy, ode, etc.)	lyric	lyric
Use of figurative language	personification: "*The robin will wear on his bosom/ A vest that is bright and new*" "*when some dear joy loses/its beauteous summer glow*"	personification: "*Every leaf speaks bliss to me*"; "*when night's decay/Ushers in a drearier day.*" metaphor: "*wreaths of snow;*" "*night's decay*"
Other poetic techniques (imagery, sound devices such as repetition, alliteration, consonance, and assonance, etc.)	imagery	imagery
Speaker Perspective	first-person perspective	first-person perspective
Meaning	Answers will vary. Possible answers include: Life goes on continuously. Hold on to hope when all seems lost.	Answers will vary. Possible answers include: Winter is dreary and wonderful. Fall is the messenger of winter.

2. **B** Each stanza of the poem uses imagery and a set rhyme scheme to present instances where something negative will eventually give way to something positive, thus conveying a feeling of hope. Stanza IV also contains personification. *See the answer chart for question 1 for further clarification.*

3. **A** The poem, a lyric comprised entirely of couplets, reveals the speaker's feelings on winter. The images and figurative language in lines 3–8 reveal the speaker's feelings, as well ("Every leaf speaks bliss to me," "I shall smile when wreaths of snow…," "I shall sing when night's decay…").

4. **D** Every other line in each of the seven stanzas of "November" rhymes, yielding a set rhyme scheme of *abab.* "Fall, leaves, fall," on the other hand, is comprised of couplets: every two lines rhyme with each other.

5. **D** *See the answer chart for question 1 for clarification.*

6. **A** In addition to rhyme scheme and a first-person point of view, both poems use imagery and figurative language to reveal the speaker's feelings. In "November," stanza VI seems to summarize the speaker's feelings ("There must be rough, cold weather, / And winds and rains so wild; / Not all good things together / Come to us here, my child"), though the same idea of hope despite loss or hardships is alluded to in each of the stanzas. In "Fall, leaves, fall," the speaker's love for dreary winter—and, consequently, the season that ushers it in (fall)—is revealed.

7. **Answers will vary.**

   Sample Response: The poems "November" and "Fall, leaves, fall" have some similarities in their structures, though they differ in their meanings. "November" is a lyric poem that contains seven stanzas, follows an *abab* rhyme scheme, and uses a first-person speaker, figurative language, and imagery to reveal the theme that hope should be held on to, even when all seems lost. "Fall, leaves, fall," though containing only one stanza and following an *aabb* rhyme scheme, is also a lyric poem that uses figurative language and imagery to reveal meaning. The meaning of "Fall, leaves, fall"—that winter is dreary and wonderful—is revealed through the poet's use of personification in line

3 ("Every leaf speaks bliss to me"), and imagery in lines 5 and 6 ("I shall smile when wreaths of snow / Blossom where the rose should grow"). "November's" message that hope should be held on to, even when all seems lost, is revealed through the imagery and first-person speaker of stanzas V ("The leaves to-day are whirling,/ The brooks are dry and dumb, / But let me tell you, my darling, / The Spring will be sure to come") and VII ("So, when some dear joy loses / Its beauteous summer glow, / Think how the roots of the roses / Are kept alive in the snow").

Analyzing Point of View (RL.8.6), page 24

1. **C** In first-person narration, the narrator is also the main character of the story. Throughout the passage, the narrator uses the pronouns "I," "me," and "my" when describing the events of the story, which proves he is a part of the story's action. In lines 15–22, the narrator reveals how he murdered the old man.

2. **B** Though the narrator's perception cannot be fully trusted (as he is mentally unstable), the police officers appear to respond casually to the narrator. In line 46, the narrator describes them as "satisfied." Later on, the officers chat "pleasantly" and do not respond when the narrator becomes hysterical at the end of the passage. The fact remains, however, that they do not leave, causing both the narrator and the reader to question their motives. This uncertainty helps builds suspense in the story.

3. **B** Lines 19–26 describe both the death and the dismemberment of the old man's body. It would be impossible, then, for the man's heart to still be beating beneath the floor boards. The fact that the narrator murdered the old man proves his inability to rationalize information. While the reader most likely realizes that the sound (if any) cannot be the man's heartbeat, the narrator obviously does not.

4. **A** The narrator describes his *own* turmoil in the last two paragraphs of the passage ("Oh God! what could I do? I foamed—I raved—I swore!... I could bear those hypocritical smiles no longer! I felt that I must scream or die!"), proving it to be first-person narration. This perspective allows the reader to experience firsthand the narrator's struggle, which

creates a more dramatic effect. The narrator, unlike the reader, is not aware of the impossibility of the old man's heart beating and believes it to be getting louder and louder. The irony of the reader being aware of something that a character in the story is not also adds drama and suspense to the story.

5. **B** Textual evidence supports that the sound the narrator hears is his own heartbeat. In lines 53–54, the narrator begins to talk "more fluently, and with a heightened voice," as if he's shouting. In lines 54–55 he describes the sound as "a low, dull, quick sound—much such a sound as a watch makes when enveloped in cotton," a comparison he also uses in lines 2–3 to describe the beating of the old man's heart. The narrator appears to become even more frantic in lines 55–68; he gasps for breath, speaks more "vehemently," arises, argues—"in a high key and with violent gesticulations," paces the floor "with heavy strides," and swings a chair. It is probable, in this state, that the narrator would have an elevated heartbeat.

6. **Answers will vary.** If the story was told through a third-person omniscient narrator, a narrator "out-side" the story's action would reveal the thoughts and actions of *all* characters, providing the reader with much more information than first-person per-spective. For example, whether or not the officers suspected the narrator or heard the same noise as the narrator at the end of the passage would be revealed. Insight into the old man's thoughts would be revealed, as well. Because the reader is left to wonder much less, third-person omniscient perspec-tive would make the story less suspenseful.

Reading: Informational Text

Citing Evidence in Informational Text (RI.8.1), page 28

1. **C** The section titled "Died of a Broken Heart" describes the heartaches that Clemens endured due to the loss of an infant son, a teenage daughter, a middle-aged daughter, and a wife: "The man who has stood to the public for the greatest humorist this country has produced has in private life suffered overwhelming sorrows." These details support the

statement posed in choice C. Choices A, B, and D can all be disproved by specific evidence within the text.

2. **Answers will vary.** *See the answer explanation for question 1 for more information.* Answers may provide textual evidence that supports the statement in choice C, *or* evidence that helps to disprove the other choices.

3. **A** Lines 1 and 2 state that Samuel Langhorne Clemens "died at 22 minutes after 6 *tonight*." Additionally, lines 18–19 describes Clemens waking at four o'clock "this morning.*"*

4. **Answers will vary** but should look similar to the following sample response. Student responses should contain the student's own words and analy-sis together with details from the text.

   Sample Response: Shortly before passing away, Samuel L. Clemens's health appeared to improve. Hours before his death, Clemens was able to sleep on his own and awoke bright, alert, and stronger than he had been in days. Lines 19–21 state that "the nurses could see by the brightness of his eyes that his vitality had been considerably restored." He even enjoyed a sunrise, which "seemed to bring ease to him, and by the time the family was about he was strong enough to sit up in bed and overjoyed them by recognizing all of them and speaking a few words to each" (lines 25–27). His apparent improve-ment had given his family hope that his death would be postponed.

5. **C** Though it can be said that Clemens/Twain had a heartbreaking life, evidence in the obituary contra-dicts that he was "lonely," which eliminates choice A. The mention of Clemens being "mostly remem-bered for this tragic life" cannot be supported with adequate evidence from the obituary either, which eliminates choice D. Because Clemens/Twain is described as "the greatest humorist this country has produced" (lines 55–56), the claim that he was a widely popular and adored figure in American history appears most valid.

6. **D** Choice D (lines 55–56) describes the public's perception of Twain as "the greatest humorist this country has produced." This description helps best to support the claim that Twain was widely popular and adored.

Determining Central Idea (RI.8.2), page 34

1. **D** The article describes the various negative effects dilution has had on the world's oceans. Choices A, B, and C all serve as supporting details to support the central idea identified in choice D.

2. **C** The article provides examples of the various pollutants, including liquid, solid, and noise pollutants, as well as the effects that these pollutants—through being dumped in an effort to "dilute" them—has had on ocean environments.

3. **B** The mention of the "New Jersey-size dead zone" and the "thousand-mild-wide" stretch of decomposing plastic help to show the astronomical effects that pollution/dilution has had on the world's oceans, as their descriptions imply such a grand scale of pollution.

4. **C** Though choice B is objective and accurate, it remains somewhat vague. Choices A and D contain an opinion, which should be left out of summaries. Because a main idea of the article centers around dilution and the effects it has had, the sentence in choice C should be found in a summary of the article.

5. **C** The summary provided in choice C is the only accurate summary provided. Choices A, B, and D each contain a detail or details that is/are false, according to information provided in the section. Information provided in the section titled "Pollutant's Many Forms" disproves that the effects of ocean pollutants are noticeable (choice A), supports that marine life has *already* started to die as a result of pollution (choice B), and does not contain enough evidence to support that solid pollutants, solely, are becoming the planet's biggest threat (choice D).

Analyzing Comparisons, Analogies, and Categories (RI.8.3), page 38

1. **D** In paragraph 2, Vest describes a dog as the one to remain "when all other friends desert" and "constant in his love as the sun in its journey through the heavens." People, on the other hand, are described as those who may "turn against [a man] and become his enemy," "prove ungrateful," "become traitors," and "be the first to throw the stone of malice when failure settles its cloud upon our heads" (paragraph 1). While it appears that people can change, dogs remain constant.

2. **Answers will vary.** Supporting details can be found in the answer explanation for question 1.

   Sample response: In his speech to the jury, George Graham Vest depicts people as inconsistent and dogs as constant. In paragraph 2, Vest states that dogs will remain "when all other friends desert." A person can always trust that a dog is "constant in his love as the sun in its journey through the heavens." Vest believes that people are much more inconsistent. Their loyalty wanes quickly depending on the situation. He describes people as those who may "turn against [a man] and become his enemy." He explains that people will stick with those who are successful, but they will then "be the first to throw the stone of malice when failure settles its clouds upon our heads" (paragraph 1). While it appears through Vest's speech that people can change, dogs do not. They will always remain loyal.

3. **B** Vest does not mention, in any paragraph, someone or something risking their life for another. In paragraph 1, Vest mentions both the people with whom one would trust his or her happiness, as well as the son or daughter who would prove ungrateful after being raised with loving care, as examples of those whom a dog proves better than. The last line of paragraph 2 compares a dog to the sun in its journey through the heavens.

4. **D** Paragraph 2 makes mention of "this selfish world," and it also provides an example of how a dog may suffer for the sake of his master ("He will sleep on the cold ground, where the wintry winds blow and the snow drives fiercely, if only he may be near his master's side"). Paragraphs 2 and 3 both describe the ways in which a dog will give of itself without expecting anything in return: "He will kiss the hand that has no food to offer...If fortune drives the master forth, an outcast in the world, friendless and homeless, the faithful dog asks no higher privilege than that of accompanying him…faithful and true even in death." Nowhere in the speech does Vest provide examples of other pets.

5. **A** Each sentence in paragraph 2 describes a positive action of a dog, from being one that "never proves ungrateful or treacherous" to one who remains "constant in his love" when riches have taken "wings" and reputation has fallen "to pieces."

6. **Answers will vary.**

   Sample response: The speaker depicts a dog as the most loyal companion a person can have. In paragraph 1, Vest describes instances in which a person may prove unfaithful or disloyal. For example, he states that even a best friend may turn against a person. In paragraph 2, Vest provides examples of how a dog's behaviors contrast with those of a human. He describes a dog as "the one absolutely unselfish friend that man can have in this selfish world, the one that never deserts him, the one that never proves ungrateful or treacherous…" Vest also depicts a dog as loyal in paragraph 3 when he describes a dog as "faithful" and states, "no matter if all other friends pursue their way, there by the graveside will the noble dog be found…faithful and true even in death."

7. **C** Choice C is disproven by the sentence, "A man's dog stands by him in prosperity and in poverty, in health and in sickness" (paragraph 2).

Word Meaning and Figurative Language in Informational Text (RI.8.4), page 40

1. **B** In choice A, a formal, serious tone is established through the use of the phrases "fellow citizens" and "under indictment for the alleged crime." In choice C, the repetition and emphasis of the word "we" suggests a firm, formal tone. In choice D, a serious tone is depicted in the phrase "and no state has a right to make any law, or to enforce any old law." The sentence in choice B, both in and out of context, does not contain any words or phrases that would specifically suggest a formal or serious tone.

2. **A** The words "we" and "people" allude to the Preamble of the American Constitution, which is quoted in paragraph 2. In paragraph 3, Anthony firmly states, "And we formed it, not to give the blessings of liberty, but to secure them; not to the half of ourselves and the half of our posterity, but to the whole people—women as well as men." By this she means that white males are not the sole citizens of the United States.

3. **C** The words and phrases mentioned all have negative connotations. Anthony uses these words to illustrate the negative effects of denying both women and African Americans the right to vote. In paragraph 5, she states, "or even an oligarchy of race, where the Saxon rules the African," and "but this oligarchy of sex…carries dissension, discord, and rebellion into every home of the nation" in order to highlight the present situation in America and its negative effects.

4. **B** Each word's denotation (official meaning), and the context in which it is used, suggests connotations or feelings of something bad or negative.

5. **D** In paragraph 1, Anthony states that she stands before the crowd "under indictment for the alleged crime of having voted at the last presidential election." By that, she means that she has been accused of a crime, despite the fact that she does not believe that it should be a crime for women to vote in an election. The word *supposed* could be substituted for the word *alleged* because, while others have accused her of committing a crime, she does not believe that she is guilty of any offense.

6. **A** *Webster*, *Worcester*, and *Bouvier* were all famous dictionaries at the time that this speech was given. To answer this question, refer back to how this phrase is used in the speech. In paragraph 6, Anthony states that "Webster, Worcester, and Bouvier all define a citizen to be a person in the United States, entitled to vote and hold office." The key word here is *define*. This word suggests that this phrase must refer to sources of definitions, which are dictionaries.

7. **C** In paragraph 7, Anthony states that "every discrimination against women in the constitutions and laws of the several states is today null and void, precisely as is every one against Negroes." By saying that these discriminatory practices are *null and void*, she means that they are *invalid* or without any merit. Previously, she explains that no state has the right to make any laws that restrict the basic privileges that should be awarded to all citizens, regardless of gender or race. Thus, any practices that continue to limit these privileges are baseless and illogical.

8. **A** This description states that "Susan B. Anthony was one of the driving forces of the women's suffrage movement." This means that she was one of the key individuals who helped maintain the momentum of this movement in order to keep it going, attract more followers, and ultimately enact change. Her words, particularly those in this speech, motivated individuals to listen to her calls for equality and take the steps necessary to make that happen.

9. **D** This description states that Anthony's "Quaker upbringing had placed her on equal footing with the male members of the family." In this context, "on equal footing" means "of the same rank or position." There is nothing in this description to suggest that her height, weight, or any sort of distance factor are

being compared to that of her male family members. Instead, this phrase means that she achieved equal standing in comparison to her male family members. She was not treated any differently, or held to a lower position or standard, simply because she was a woman. As the description suggests, it was likely the fact that she was considered an equal in her family that inspired her to fight for equality for all citizens.

Analyzing the Structure of Paragraphs (RI.8.5), page 44

1. **A** Most of the passage describes Richard's internal and external struggle in getting by in a society where he was expected to act subservient. The sentences in paragraph 1 outline his constant struggle in interacting with whites.

2. **D** Paragraph 4 states, "Most of them were not conscious of living a special, separate, stunted way of life." Other sentences of the paragraph provide examples of what blacks did almost subconsciously to further submit to the limitations that were placed upon them.

3. **D** The sentences in paragraph 3 are specific to Richard's experience in obtaining a job and what this experience was like for him.

4. **B** Paragraph 2 further develops a key concept of Richard's constant struggle to exist in a world where he had to submit to others. The sentences provide examples of some of the things Richard had to think about while interacting with whites in a way that he was "supposed" to.

Determining Point of View or Author's Purpose (RI.8.6), page 46

1. **A** In paragraph 4, Jordan states that "Today, the nation seems to be suffering from compassion fatigue."

2. **C** The footnote explains the unfortunate events in Bosnia during the 1990s. The speaker's reference to these events serves as a warning of what could happen when people of a nation are unable to coexist. Tolerance and living together harmoniously are concepts that the speaker stresses throughout the speech.

3. **B** Paragraph 11 states, "Now, I know that love means different things to different people. But what

I mean is this: I care about you because you are a fellow human being and I find it okay in my mind, in my heart, to simply say to you, I love you." These sentences best support that the speaker acknowledges differences in opinions but clarifies her own.

4. **C** Paragraphs 2 and 3 refer to specific events and accomplishments that took place in the 1960s. These events are alluded to first in paragraph 1: "When I look at race relations today, I can see that some positive changes have come about." Jordan goes on to say, however, that "much remains to be done," and that living together in peace is "not what happened" (paragraphs 1 and 4). These details help to support choice C.

Writing

Argument Writing (W.8.1), page 48

1. **D** Choices A, B, and C do not contain information that's relevant to the claim presented.

2. **C** Adding specific reasons or examples to your claim can strengthen your argument by making it more specific.

3. **B** Though the information provided at the law firm's website could be fair and accurate, .com indicates a commercial site, meaning money is usually the incentive behind the information that is provided. Sites that are .org or .gov are generally more credible than those of .com, as they are non-profit and tend to have less of a bias. Additionally, choices A, C, and D describe very formal organizations that have a high probability of being regulated.

4. **D** Closing statements should reflect and reiterate what is mentioned in the original claim. Choice A is too vague and does not reflect an argument specifically posed at texting while driving. Though answer choices B and C are related to the topic of the claim, they would both function better as supporting details. Choice D suggests that texting while driving should be avoided at all times and would more effectively reiterate a claim posing an argument against texting while driving.

5. **Answers will vary.** Use the following *Rubric for Argument Writing* to assess your response. Because the question asks for three specific reasons, it would be a good idea to include an introduction, three body paragraphs, and a conclusion in your essay.

Rubric for Argument Writing

	Exceeding Standards	Meeting Standards	Approaching Standards	Not Meeting Standards
Claim	A strong, specific, logical claim is made, with mention of an opposing claim.	A clear claim is made, with mention of an opposing claim.	An attempt at a claim is made, but it is vague or unspecific. No mention of an opposing claim is made.	No claim is made. The writer has presented both sides with no definitive position on the topic presented. A claim is made that does not flow logically from the task presented.
Support of Claim	A thorough amount of logical, accurate reasoning and relevant evidence from credible sources is provided. The writer demonstrates a deep understanding of the topic.	An adequate amount of logical, accurate reasoning and relevant evidence from credible sources is provided. The writer demonstrates a basic understanding of the topic.	Not enough evidence to support the claim is presented. Some irrelevant or inaccurate information is provided, possibly from an unreliable source.	Evidence is not presented logically and/or strays from the claim. No information is provided to support the claim.
Cohesion/ Organization	Evidence to support the claim is organized logically and effectively throughout the entirety of the work. Transition statements are used that enhance readability and strengthen the argument presented.	Evidence to support the claim is organized logically and effectively throughout the entirety of the work. Appropriate transition statements are used between paragraphs or to connect ideas.	Some attempt at organization is made but is not consistent throughout the work.	No attempt at organization is made. Information provided does not logically flow from the task presented.
Style	A formal style is established and maintained. The writer demonstrates full command of the conventions of English grammar and usage, with little to no errors.	A formal style is established and maintained. The writer abides by the conventions of English grammar and usage, with very few errors.	A formal style fails to be maintained. The writing contains errors in the conventions of English grammar and usage that may interfere with comprehension.	The writing lacks a formal style. The writer demonstrates little to no control of the conventions of English grammar and usage.
Concluding Statement	A strong, clear, developed concluding statement is provided that accurately reflects the argument presented.	A clear concluding statement is provided that accurately reflects the argument presented.	A concluding statement is provided, but it does not reflect the argument presented.	No concluding statement is provided.

The following rubric should be used to assess answers to questions 1–4.

Rubric for Informational Writing

	Exceeding Standards	Meeting Standards	Approaching Standards	Not Meeting Standards
Introduction of Topic	The topic is introduced clearly, along with a thorough description of what is to follow, including various categories, graphics, and/or multimedia that are related to the topic and used in the response.	A clear topic is introduced, along with a brief description of what is to follow, including any categories, graphics, and/or multimedia used in the response.	Partially orients reader to the topic within the introduction and previews what is to follow.	No introduction is provided.\n\nAn introduction is presented that does not orient the reader to the topic at all.
Development	The topic is thoroughly developed through the use of relevant, well-chosen facts, definitions, concrete details, and quotations from a wide variety of credible sources.\n\nThe writer demonstrates a deep understanding of the topic.	An adequate amount of relevant, well-chosen facts, definitions, concrete details, and quotations is provided through a variety of credible sources.\n\nThe writer demonstrates a basic understanding of the topic.	Minimal evidence to support the topic is provided.\n\nSome irrelevant or inaccurate information is provided, possibly from an unreliable source.	Evidence is not presented logically and/or strays from the topic.\n\nNo sources have been used or cited.\n\nNo information is provided to support the topic.
Presentation/ Organization	Evidence to develop the topic is organized logically and effectively throughout the entirety of the work. Well-developed paragraphs and transition statements are used that enhance readability and strengthen the argument presented.\n\nA variety of techniques are used to organize ideas, concepts, and information related to the topic.	Evidence to develop the topic is organized logically and effectively throughout the entirety of the work. Paragraphs create cohesion, and appropriate transition statements are used between paragraphs or to connect ideas.\n\nUses a variety of techniques to organize ideas, concepts, and information related to the topic.	Some attempt at organization is made but is not consistent throughout the work.\n\nSome techniques are used to organize ideas, concepts, and information related to the topic.	No attempt at organization is made.\n\nInformation provided does not logically flow from the topic presented.\n\nFails to develop the topic with body paragraphs.\n\nIncludes little or no organization techniques.

	Exceeding Standards	Meeting Standards	Approaching Standards	Not Meeting Standards
Style	A formal style is established and maintained. The writer demonstrates full command of the conventions of English grammar and usage, with little to no errors.	A formal style is established and maintained. The writer abides by the conventions of English grammar and usage, with very few errors.	A formal style fails to be maintained. The writing contains errors in the conventions of English grammar and usage that may interfere with comprehension.	The writing lacks a formal style. The writer demonstrates little to no control of the conventions of English grammar and usage.
Concluding Statement	A strong, clear, developed concluding statement is provided that accurately reflects the information or explanation presented.	A clear concluding statement is provided that accurately reflects the information or explanation presented.	A concluding statement is provided, but it does not reflect the information or explanation presented.	No concluding statement is provided.

Narrative Writing (W.8.3), page 52

The following rubric should be used to assess answers to the prompts for questions 1–6.

Rubric for Narrative Writing

	Exceeding Standards	Meeting Standards	Approaching Standards	Not Meeting Standards
Introduction	The context—including the narrator, characters, and setting—is introduced in a logical, descriptive manner, using vivid language that highly engages the reader.	The context—including the narrator, characters, and setting—is introduced in a logical manner that engages the reader.	Some elements of the context are introduced in a manner that may or may not engage the reader.	No introduction to the context is presented. The context of the introduction is unclear or illogical.
Narrative Techniques	The writer uses a wide variety of narrative techniques, such as dialogue, pacing, description, and reflection to deeply develop experiences, events, and/or characters.	The writer uses some variety of narrative techniques, such as dialogue, pacing, description, and reflection to develop experiences, events, and/or characters.	Few narrative techniques—such as dialogue, pacing, description, and reflection—are used. Characters and/or events are underdeveloped.	No narrative techniques—such as dialogue, pacing, description, and reflection—are used. Characters and/or events are mostly undeveloped.

	Exceeding Standards	Meeting Standards	Approaching Standards	Not Meeting Standards
Transition of Ideas	A wide variety of highly effective transition words, phrases, and clauses are used to convey sequence, signal shifts from one time frame or setting to another, and show the relationships among experiences and events. The transition between events, details, and/or experiences is virtually flawless.	A variety of effective transition words, phrases, and clauses are used to convey sequence, signal shifts from one time frame or setting to another, and show the relationships among experiences and events. The transition between events, details, and/or experiences is clear and easy to follow.	Some transition words, phrases, and clauses are used. Some confusion or inconsistency exists in the order of events or the way in which information is presented.	No transition words, phrases, and clauses are used. Events, details, and/or experiences do not flow logically. Much confusion exists in the order of events or the way in which information is presented.
Language	Action is vividly captured and experiences or events are effectively conveyed through the use of precise words and phrases, many relevant descriptive details, and sensory language.	The writer uses precise words and phrases, relevant descriptive details, and sensory language to capture action and convey experiences or events.	Some vague words or phrases are used in an attempt to capture action and/or convey experiences or events. Not enough descriptive details or sensory language is provided. Action or experiences or events are underdeveloped.	Minimal attempt is made to capture action and/or convey experiences or events. Action and experiences or events are underdeveloped.
Conclusion	A highly-developed and effective conclusion that follows logically from and reflects on the narrated experience or event is provided.	An effective conclusion that follows logically from and reflects on the narrated experience or event is provided.	A conclusion that somewhat follows or reflects on the narrated experience or event is provided.	No concluding statement is provided. A conclusion that does not follow or reflect on the narrated experience or event is provided.

Considering Task, Audience, and Purpose (W.8.4), page 56

1. For the task provided, it is important that you maintain a respectful, professional tone at all times, and follow the format for a *formal* or *business letter*, described below.

   Business or Formal Letter Format:
   ✔ Sender's name and address is provided at the top, *right-hand* corner of the letter.
   ✔ Date is provided, written out, at the top, *right-hand* corner of the letter, aligned with the sender's information and spaced one line below.
   ✔ Recipient's name and address is provided to the *left* of the page, spaced one line beneath the date.
   ✔ A formal salutation, followed by a colon, is provided to the *left* of the page, following the recipient's information and spaced one line below.
   ✔ Body paragraphs are not indented. One line is skipped between each, instead.
   ✔ A closing and a signature—containing your first and last name—are provided at the end of the letter, to the right of the page, aligned with the sender's information and the date.

2. The writing style for this particular task would take a more *playful* and *informal* approach. What are some things that a dog would say, if given a voice? Keep in mind, in addressing his owner, the dog would be addressing someone who cares and provides for him; more than likely, the tone would be one of respect and/or adoration. The use of innocent humor or exciting details could be effective in entertaining elementary school students.

3. This task requires the production of a *friendly letter*, which is informal in style and follows the format described below.

   Friendly Letter Format:
   ✔ Sender's name and address is provided at the top, *right-hand* corner of the page.
   ✔ Date is provided at the top, *right-hand* corner of the letter, aligned with the sender's information and spaced one line below.
   ✔ An informal salutation or greeting, followed by a comma, is provided to the *left* of the page, following the date and spaced one line below.
   ✔ Body paragraphs are indented.

   ✔ An informal closing and a signature (first name only is acceptable) are provided at the end of the letter, to the left of the page, not indented.

4. An e-mail is an electronic letter. In this instance, you should follow the same guidelines as a friendly letter, but keep in mind you are addressing your teacher; though your e-mail can be more informal than other forms of writing, such as a business letter, essay, or speech, for example, it should maintain *some* formality, and a respectful tone. You are also attempting to be persuasive, so you should provide strong, valid reasons as support.

5. Journal entries are *informal* and employ the use of first-person pronouns, such as *I*, *me*, *mine*, *my*, *we*, *us*, etc. In the scene provided from *The Adventures of Tom Sawyer* on pages 2 and 3 of the workbook, the character of Muff Potter comes across as scared and confused. These feelings should be addressed in the journal entry, along with accurate and specific details from the passage.

Language

Grammar and Usage—Gerunds, Participles, and Infinitives (L.8.1, L.8.1.A), page 58

1. **A** In the sentence provided, the verbal *running* acts as a noun, suggested as something to alleviate stress.

2. **C** An infinitive is a verbal consisting of the word "to," plus a verb. In the sentence provided, the word *to* is followed by the verb *laugh*. Here, the verbal *to laugh* functions as the subject of the sentence.

3. **B** In the sentence provided, the verbal *burning* acts as an adjective, modifying the noun *vehicle*.

4. **B** In the sentence provided, the verbal *destroyed* acts as an adjective, modifying the pronoun *it*.

5. **C** An infinitive is a verbal consisting of the word "to," plus a verb. In the sentence provided, the word *to* is followed by the verb *leave*. Here, the verbal *to leave* functions as the direct object of the sentence.

6. **A** In the sentence provided, the verbal *driving* acts as a noun, as it is the *subject* of the sentence. Think of it as, "[Doing *this*] while intoxicated may result in arrest, injury, or even death."

7. **C** In the sentence, "In addition to helping you remain physically fit, running may help relieve stress," *running* is acting as a thing that provides stress relief, making *running* function as a noun.

8. **D** In the sentence, "Amazingly, the man climbed out of the burning vehicle unharmed," *burning* modifies the noun *vehicle*, making it function as an adjective.

Grammar and Usage—Active and Passive Voice (L.8.1, L.8.1.B), page 60

1. **C** In choice C, the subject of the sentence, *Danielle*, performs the action (*threw*). In choices A, B, and D, the subjects (*rules, dishes*, and *bill*) receive the action.

2. The active voice would read, "**Garrett gave the necklace to Gabrielle**." *Garrett* is the one performing the action in this sentence, so his name should come first.

3. Depending on meaning or emphasis, both "**Tom bumped into the table and broke several vases**." and "**Tom broke several vases when he bumped into the table**." are acceptable.

4. "**The specialists found the report inconclusive**." would be the best way to phrase this sentence.

5. **B** Choices A, C, and D appear awkward. Each would sound clearer in the active voice. Choice B is appropriate and effective if and when the emphasis is meant to be placed on the amount of people injured.

6. **D** Though choices A, B, and C function as clear and acceptable sentences, they are written in the passive voice. Choice D is the only sentence where the subject (*The burglar*) is performing the action (*fled*).

Commas, Dashes, and Ellipses (L.8.2, L.8.2.A, L.8.2.B), page 62

1. Use a pair of commas in the middle of a sentence to set off clauses, phrases, or words that are not essential to the meaning of the sentence. Correct: **Diana, like many girls her age, loves listening to music and attending concerts.**

2. Use commas before introductory clauses, phrases, or words, and to separate items written in a series. Correct: **While shopping, Rick remem-bered he still needed to pick up the dog, stop at the post office, and put air in his tires.**

3. Use a comma to set off quoted elements and near the end of a sentence to indicate a distinct pause or shift. Correct: **She read the book over his shoulder for a while, then said, "What fun are you, anyway?"**

4. Use commas before introductory clauses, phrases, or words, and to set off all geographical names, items in dates, and titles in names. Correct: **Though he died the following morning, former president Abraham Lincoln was shot on April 14, 1865 in Washington, D.C.**

5. **C** Dashes can be used to set off parenthetical material that you want to emphasize but that is not necessary in forming the complete sentence. In the sentence provided, "Thousands of animals" is clearly the subject, as indicated by the verb *are*. The phrase, "like the one in this photograph" is added information that is not necessary to the forming of the sentence, but nonetheless intended to be emphasized to the reader. This phrase could be placed in parentheses, as well.

6. **A** While intending to tell a story, it's clear that the speaker was interrupted and had to change his or her thought in order to relay a warning (*Watch out!*). In writing dialogue, the dash is used to show breaks in thought and shifts in tone.

7. Both an ellipsis […] and a dash [—] can show a break in thought. In the sentence provided, the break in thought occurs after the word *you*; therefore, the sentence should be written as "**I wish you would tell me when you—oh, never mind**." *or* "**I wish you would tell me when…oh, never mind**."

8. The phrase "like my parents, for instance" is information that is not essential to the meaning of the sentence; therefore, the sentence should be written as, "**Many people—like my parents, for instance—were against the new building project**." Though a pair of commas could also be used to offset information that is not essential to the sentence, the additional comma before *for instance* in this sentence makes the use of dashes a better choice.

9. Answers should not omit the main clause "We were warned." Possible answers include "**We were**

warned...not to run in the halls." and "We were warned by the Assistant Principal..."

10. In the given sentence, the phrase "and she tried with all her might" is unnecessary to the meaning of the sentence and therefore could be omitted. The sentence could then be written as "**Try as she may...she would not be able to stop him.**"

Determining the Meaning of Unknown and Multiple-Meaning Words or Phrases (L.8.4, L.8.4.A, L.8.4.B), page 64

1. **B** Context clues include **began wearing blue jeans**, **replaced**, and **long-trousered**.

2. **C** Context clues include **wingèd** and **Heaven**.

3. **A** Context clues include **sound of the black jets**, **covered**, **dust**, and **snow**.

4. **D** The use of the word *lingering* after the word *long* in the excerpt suggests that the kiss lasted a considerable amount of time.

5. **D** The description *savage defiance of the world* suggests that his face is hard in a sense of lacking gentleness or compassion.

6. ascertain: (v.) **to learn or find out; to make certain**

7. ambidextrous: (adj.) **able to use both hands equally well**

8. encrypt: (v.) **to change from one form to another, especially to hide meaning**

9. benevolent: (adj.) **kind and generous; marked by a desire to do good things**

Figurative Language, Word Relationships, and Nuances in Word Meanings (L.8.5, L.8.5.A, L.8.5.B), page 68

1. **B** Although the speaker uses the word *song*, which is an extended metaphor in the poem, the speaker refers in line 10 to the *poem* that refuses to break free. Songs and poems are closely related, but here the speaker is talking about the elusive inspiration for poetry, and how it comes to us when we are relaxed and open to creative ideas.

2. **C** Although the word *wake* can sometimes mean the definitions provided in choices A, B, and D, here the speaker is hoping to *wake*—or call to mind—the poem (as made explicit in line 10) inside her head.

3. **D** Although line 6 uses the word *music*, line 7 includes the phrase "words are fading," suggesting that what is elusive is something that contains words; of the four choices presented, only poetic ideas would contain words.

4. **A** Since songs are not living things, they cannot literally be *asleep*. The poet is giving human characteristics to the *song* or *poem*. That is called personification.

5. **C** Since no one is actually whispering, this is a metaphor for the speaker/poet's faint, incomplete perception of the poetic idea, as a whisper is often a faint, incomplete sound.

6. **D** Fuel added to a fire makes it stronger, in the same way that forbidden love seems more appealing.

7. **A** Since they are kissing, the phrase is clearly not about mountaineering, or literally climbing mountains. Additionally, the feeling is of increased interest and at a high level, so it would be the opposite of losing interest. "Becoming better people" doesn't happen in a moment, so this would not be an appropriate choice. "Heights of love" would most appropriately be interpreted as great passion.

8. **B** "Getting schooled" is a commonly used figure of speech which refers to learning by [an often unfortunate] experience.

9. **D** While Shakespeare uses the word *dignity*, which is generally interpreted in a positive way, the reader eventually learns that both families are alike because they *lack* dignity. Shakespeare intentionally misleads the reader by stating the *opposite* of what he means, which is the definition of verbal irony.

10. **A** The words *son* (line 1) and *sun* (line 3) are homophones, which are words that are pronounced the same but differ in meaning and possibly spelling. Hamlet is playing with the word *son*, expanding on Claudius's metaphor comparing happiness and sadness to the weather.

Denotation and Connotation
(L.8.5, L.8.5.C), page 72

Group 1: General denotation: **determined**
Ranked: **pigheaded, stubborn, dogged, determined, strong**

Group 2: General denotation: **surprised**
Ranked: **dumbfounded, shocked, astonished, surprised, amazed**

Group 3: General denotation: **attractive**
Ranked: **attractive, lovely, pretty, beautiful, stunning**

Group 4: General denotation: **interested**
Ranked: **obsessed, absorbed, focused, interested, engaged**

1. positive: **exotic**; negative: **strange**; neutral: **foreign**

2. positive: **youthful**; negative: **childish**; neutral: **young**

3. positive: **laid-back**; negative: **lazy**; neutral: **inactive**

4. positive: **interested**; negative: **nosy**; neutral: **curious**

5. **Possible answers** (included but not limited to): cried, yelled, yelped, shrieked, shouted, demanded, grumbled, muttered, hollered, lied, lectured, screamed, protested, sobbed, threatened, and growled.

6. **Possible answers** (included but not limited to): laughed, giggled, bellowed, exclaimed, chirped, affirmed, beamed, chuckled, encouraged, praised, sang, and joked.

English Language Arts Practice Test, page 74

1. **B** In addition to illustrating how upset Mildred is at the moment in which the simile is used, the comparison of Mildred to a "wax doll" suggests that she too is fake, or not "alive." This conclusion is further supported by later descriptions of Mildred's fondness for the White Clown and the TV "family," suggesting she values "fake" relationships more than real ones.

2. **D** Montag refers to Jefferson and Thoreau stating: "I don't think he knows *which* book I stole. But how do I choose a substitute? Do I turn in Mr. Jefferson? Mr. Thoreau? Which is least valuable? If I pick a substitute and Beatty does know which book I stole, he'll guess we've an entire library here!" In the context of the paragraph, Jefferson and Thoreau represent other authors of books that could be chosen as a "substitute" to the Bible.

3. See the quotations noted in the answer explanation for question 2.

4. **C** Following Montag's first question asking Mildred if the White Clown loves her, he asks if her "family"—referring to the one on the television show—loves her, as well. Montag seems to be trying to make the point that these television shows that Mildred values are insignificant compared to real human relationships. There is little to no evidence in the story to point to the analyses in choices A, B, or D.

5. **B** Montag's desire to cry immediately follows Mildred's question, "Why'd you ask a silly question like that?" Mildred didn't understand the point that Montag was trying to make: that the characters on the television shows that Mildred values are no substitute for real people who love her.

6. **Answers may vary.**

   Sample Response: The phrase "threw me my first lifeline" means that Mrs. Flowers was the first person to assist or "save" the narrator. The passage goes on to describe Mrs. Flowers' attempts at getting Marguerite to speak in school.

7. **C** The description of Mrs. Flowers having "the grace of control to appear warm in the coldest weather…," grinning with a smile "so graceful and inclusively benign," and being "one of the few gentlewomen" the narrator had ever known, along with the references to her "voile dresses," "flowered hats," and "gloves" support that Mrs. Flowers is graceful and formal, or proper.

8. **Answers will vary.** *See the quotes provided in the answer explanation for question 7.*

9. **D** The narrator's desire to thank Mrs. Flowers simply for smiling at her supports the inference that she is in awe of, or very much appreciates, Mrs. Flowers. Though choice C is a close answer and may show awe of Mrs. Flowers in *general*, because the question specifically refers to *Marguerite's* awe of Mrs. Flowers, choice D is the best answer.

10. **C** *Central (main) idea* refers to what the selection is mostly about. Unlike *theme*, the *central* or *main idea* provides more of a summary than a message. The passage describes the narrator's encounter with Mrs. Flowers, the "lady who threw [her] [her] first lifeline." The bulk of the passage proves to be about how Mrs. Flowers *assisted the narrator*, specifically, and not just solely about Mrs. Flowers (like choice B implies). Whereas choice B provides more of a message, choice C provides an accurate summary of the passage. Choices A, B, and D act as details to support the central (main) idea identified in choice C.

11. **B** "Sweet-milk fresh" is a phrase with a positive connotation. The use of the word "fresh" helps to support that the memory is new or clear in the narrator's mind.

12. **D** The title of the poem and line 9 indicate that the poem is set at night, which helps to eliminate choice A. The first stanza of the poem is written through the point of view of the Mistress (or, the cat's owner), as indicated by her reference to the "Cat" (lines 1, 4, and 8); in the second stanza, the cat is the speaker, referencing his "Mistress" (lines 9 and 13). The shift in the points of view between the stanzas creates a conversation between the Mistress and the Cat.

13. **Answers will vary.**

    Sample Response: The speaker's tone in stanza one can best be described as enticing, or persuasive, and gentle. The use of the phrases "stay by the fire," "lie still," "leaping and hissing low," "bring you a saucer of milk…so white and smooth… and sweet," and "stay with me" help to reveal this tone. The speaker is addressing the cat in a manner in which to lure him.

14. **B** In line 1, the Mistress presents the scenario of walking in the snow as a negative, remarking that it will be the cause of snow and sleet on the cat's feet. Additionally, line 8 states, "Stay with me, Cat. Outdoors the wild winds blow," suggesting that inside is much more calm and comfortable than the outdoors.

15. **C** Though the cat describes the outdoors as "dark," filled with "strange voices," "strange lore," moving creatures, and "portents abroad of magic and might," all of this seems appealing to the cat, as evidenced by his last remark to "Open the door!"

16. **C** The cat's exclamation of "Open the door!" at the end of stanza two helps to support that he is desperate to get outside.

17. **B** The Mistress's apparent desire for her cat to stay inside in stanza one helps to support that she is protective. Her tone is more gentle than demanding, as conveyed by her attempts to essentially bribe the cat.

18. **D** The Mistress's gentle tone in stanza one helps to best support that the Mistress desires that her cat stay inside. There is little to no evidence in the poem to suggest the analyses made in choices A, B, and C.

19. **A** The section titled "Origins" makes reference to the various religious ceremonies that the Hopi conduct throughout the year, supporting the inference that they are religious people.

20. **Answers will vary.** Possible textual evidence includes: "Chiefs, who were also shamans, or medicine men, governed the Hopi tribes. Groups of related families, called clans, directed their own religious ceremonies and, together, made important decisions about their village. The Hopi enjoyed religious ceremonies throughout the year, with many dances and other rituals dedicated to bringing rain for their crops. In particular, the Hopi believed in guardian spirits, called *kachinas*. Hopi men acted the part of kachinas in the tribe's dances, wearing painted masks made of wood, feathers, and other materials" (paragraphs 6 and 7).

21. **C** The first line of the article states, "Unlike most Native Americans, the Hopi people have lived in the same place for nearly a thousand years."

22. **B** The central idea of paragraph 8 is the reason for the Pueblo Rebellion of 1680. Each sentence of the paragraph serves as a supporting detail explaining either the causes or the results of the rebellion.

23. **C** *Reservation* is used three times in paragraph 9 to describe an area of land kept separate. The context clues "land" and "500-square-mile" help to reveal this meaning.

24. **Answers will vary.**

    Sample Response: The section of the article titled "Modern Life" describes the life of the Hopi today. Though the Hopi now live in more modern homes as opposed to the ones made of stone, clay, and bricks, cemented together with mud and lacking windows and doors, they still manage to "remain close to tradition." According to the section titled "Modern Life," the Hopi still live off the land as farmers and sheep ranchers. They also continue to believe in the kachina and "produce basketry, pottery, weaving, and kachina dolls." The Hopi people still live on the same land that they did almost a thousand years ago, though the size of their land has decreased.

25. **B** Lines 5–8, 15–16, and 21–24 help to reveal that the speaker is heartbroken over the death of his captain.

26. **Answers will vary.**

    Sample Response: Adjectives to describe the captain should possess a positive connotation and may include *honored*, *respected*, *loved*, *adored*, *brave*, and/or *inspiring*. Common supporting details to reference include "the people all exulting" (line 3), "my Captain" (lines 1, 7, 9, 17, 23), "For you bouquets of ribbon'd wreaths…" (line 11), "For you they call" (line 12), "eager faces" (line 12), "father" (lines 13, 18), "From fearful trip the victor ship…" (line 20), and "mournful tread" (line 22).

27. **A** The use of the words "prize," "won," "bells," "exulting," and "daring" help to convey a celebratory tone.

28. **See the answer explanation for question 27.**

29. **C** Though the speaker does reference the captain as his "father," lines 15 and 16 ("It is some dream that on the deck, / You've fallen cold and dead")—2 of the 4 lines referenced—help best to support the summary, "The speaker cannot believe the captain is dead."

30. **B** The text states that Mrs. Dubose wished "to leave this world beholden to nothing and nobody," which means about the same as choice B.

31. **D** Atticus uses the sentence to describe what courage is. In that context, knowing you're defeated but trying anyway and seeing it through seems most courageous.

32. **B** Jem's interruption serves to show that he has not understood what Atticus just said.

Following Jem's question of "Sir?" Atticus goes on to clarify Mrs. Dubose's wishes.

33. **B** Though Mrs. Dubose could be described as courageous, dignified, and stubborn, nothing in the text supports that she was disrespectful.

34. **Answers will vary.**

    Sample Response: The excerpt from *To Kill a Mockingbird* suggests that courage does not always require taking a bold or obvious risk; many times, courage can be more subtle, simply possessing the strength to keep going when it all seems pointless. The character of Mrs. Dubose helps to reveal this message by choosing to rid herself of her morphine addiction, even though she was dying and probably needed it more than ever. The passage reveals that Mrs. Dubose was in pain ("She's not suffering any more"; "Mrs. Dubose was a morphine addict… She'd have spent the rest of her life on it and died without so much agony, but she was too contrary..."), but endured it because she wanted to die "free": independent from anything and anyone. Mrs. Dubose's struggle was a painful and difficult one, but she did not give up. She died with courage, the way she wanted to.

35. **C** The statement mentioned in choice C is supported by lines 7, 15–16, 19, 21–24, 29, 30, and 32.

36. **C** Lines 1 and 2 state, "Courage isn't a brilliant dash, / A daring deed in a moment's flash;".

37. **D** The lines quoted in choices A, B, and C all suggest that courage is something long-lasting or permanent.

38. **Answers will vary.** Use the *Rubric for Informational Writing* on pages 104–105 when assessing this response. This response should identify a *specific definition of courage*, according to the passage and the poem. The identification of the passage's and the poem's common definition of courage is the claim that needs to be supported throughout the essay.

39. **D** In the sentence provided, *sleeping* is a gerund, acting as a noun to identify what the cat likes to do. Thinking of the sentence as

"My cat's favorite activity is this" more clearly indicates that *sleeping* is a thing, or noun.

40. **C** In choices A, B, and D, the subject *receives* the action. Choice C is the only sentence where the subject (*I*) *performs* the action (*sprang*).

41. **C** Choice C accurately uses a pair of commas to set off a phrase (*in a twinkling*) not essential to the meaning of the sentence.

42. **A** The sentence in choice A shows an interruption in the initial train of thought (*His eyes*). The dash also helps to emphasize "how they twinkled!" Choices B, C, and D do not use a dash correctly; in each, the break in thought or emphasis falls at an awkward part of the sentence.

43. **self-confident**

44. **elderly**

45. **Answers will vary.**

Sample Response: The pun is found in paragraph 2, when the narrator remarks, "Things seem pretty dead around here." The narrator

is playing with the word *dead*, as he or she is inside a funeral parlor.

46. **B** The sentence in question follows the clause "Immediately terrified." In this context, "[trying] to make the situation less serious or scary" is closest in meaning to, "I tried to make light of the situation."

47. **C** The earlier reference to being "terrified" helps to support that the narrator fainted upon hearing a crash and a high-pitched lament.

48. **D** The context clues "long, high-pitched," coupled with the fact that the narrator is indoors—and inside a funeral parlor no less—help best to support "wail."

49. **Your narrative should be scored using the *Rubric for Narrative Writing* provided on pages 105–106.**

50. **Your argument essay should be scored using the *Rubric for Argument Writing* provided on page 103.**

MATH

The Common Core Mathematics Standards are created to be building blocks between grade levels. The foundational skills and concepts learned in grades 6 and 7 are necessary for students to master grade 8 concepts and content. This structure allows teachers to make sure that achievement gaps are reduced and that students have the prior knowledge and skills required to continue their learning of more challenging concepts.

The Common Core standards in grades 6 and 7 allow students to continue to build a strong foundation and mathematical fluency as they expand their ability to compute rational numbers. These computational skills are applied in the domains of Geometry, Ratios and Proportional Reasoning, and Statistics and Probability. In grades 6 and 7, students are also introduced to algebraic concepts through Expressions and Equations. In grade 8, students continue to have standards in Geometry and Statistics and Probability. Their algebraic reasoning is now used for problem solving with scientific notation, linear equations, and systems of equations. The concept of Functions is introduced in 8th grade and provides a critical element of the foundational skills needed for high school mathematics.

RATIONAL AND
IRRATIONAL NUMBERS

NS.A.1 Know that numbers that are not rational are called irrational. Understand informally that every number has a decimal expansion; for rational numbers show that the decimal expansion repeats eventually, and convert to a decimal expansion which repeats eventually into a rational number.

1. Which of the following numbers is not rational?

   Ⓐ $\frac{2}{7}$

   Ⓑ $\sqrt{3}$

   Ⓒ 4

   Ⓓ $0.\overline{3}$

> To find the decimal expansion of a number, divide the numerator by the denominator.

For questions 2–4, write the decimal expansion for each number.

2. $\frac{2}{3}$ = _____

3. $\frac{2}{12}$ = _____

4. $\frac{7}{20}$ = _____

For questions 5–8, convert each decimal expansion into a rational number (fraction) in simplest form.

5. 0.362 = _____

6. 0.07 = _____

7. 0.256 = _____

8. 0.75 = _____

9. Which one of the following fractions is equivalent to $0.\overline{5}$?

Ⓐ $\dfrac{5}{10}$

Ⓑ $\dfrac{5}{9}$

Ⓒ $\dfrac{55}{100}$

Ⓓ $\dfrac{1}{2}$

10. Marcy wants to convert the repeating decimal $0.\overline{45}$ into its fractional form so that she can use it in a calculation. She remembers that she needs to start by setting up an equation. She sets up the equation and begins to solve it, but she is not sure how to complete the problem. Solve the equation below to help Marcy find the fractional equivalent of the decimal.

$$x = 0.\overline{45}$$

$$100x = 45.\overline{45}$$

$$100x - x = 45.\overline{45} - \,?$$

(Answers are on page 220.)

RATIONAL APPROXIMATIONS OF IRRATIONAL NUMBERS

NS.A.2 Use rational approximations of irrational numbers to compare the size of irrational numbers, locate them approximately on a number line diagram, and estimate the value of expressions (e.g., π^2). *For example, by truncating the decimal expansion of $\sqrt{2}$, show that $\sqrt{2}$ is between 1 and 2, then between 1.4 and 1.5, and explain how to continue to get better approximations.*

1. Estimate $\sqrt{10}$ to the nearest integer.
    - (A) 5
    - (B) 4
    - (C) 3
    - (D) 2

> You can use a number line to determine the approximate location of irrational numbers. This can help you estimate an integral value.

2. How many integers are greater than $\sqrt{25}$ and less than $\sqrt{72}$?
    - (A) 5
    - (B) 4
    - (C) 3
    - (D) 2

3. Which of the following statements is *incorrect*?
    - (A) $\sqrt{12} > 3.5$
    - (B) $\sqrt{11} > \pi$
    - (C) $\pi > \sqrt{9}$
    - (D) $\sqrt{6} < 3$

4. Determine the positive square root of the numbers below. If the number is not a perfect square, estimate the value to the nearest integer.

   A. $\sqrt{144}$ _____

   B. $\sqrt{200}$ _____

   C. $\sqrt{900}$ _____

   D. $\sqrt{10}$ _____

5. Sean estimated π to be $3.10 < \pi < 3.21$. If he uses this estimate to determine the area of a circle with a radius of 3 feet, which of the following would **not** be a reasonable value to represent the area?
   Ⓐ 28.0 ft.^{2}
   Ⓑ 28.5 ft.^{2}
   Ⓒ 28.7 ft.^{2}
   Ⓓ 27.8 ft.^{2}

6. Caitlin entered $\sqrt{5}$ into her calculator. The calculator displayed 2.236067978. Since the calculator display terminated the decimal, she concludes that $\sqrt{5}$ is a rational number. Is she correct? Explain your answer.

   _____

   _____

   _____

7. The numbers on the number line below should be in ascending order and correctly placed on the number line. Are they placed correctly? Explain your answer.

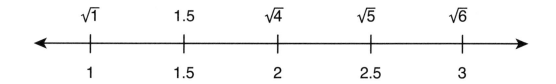

(Answers are on page 220.)

PROPERTIES OF INTEGER EXPONENTS

EE.A.1 Know and apply the properties of integer exponents to generate equivalent numerical expressions. For example, $3^2 \times 3^{-5} = 3^{-3} = \dfrac{1}{3^3} = \dfrac{1}{27}$.

1. Which one of the following expressions will result in a negative number?
   - (A) $(-2)^{-4}$
   - (B) $\left(\dfrac{1}{6}\right)^{-3}$
   - (C) $(-8)^3$
   - (D) $(2)^7$

2. Which of the following values is not equal to $\left(\dfrac{1}{5}\right)^5$?
   - (A) $\left(\dfrac{1}{5}\right)^3 \times \left(\dfrac{1}{5}\right)^2$
   - (B) $\left(\dfrac{1}{5}\right)^0 \times \left(\dfrac{1}{5}\right)^5$
   - (C) $\left(\dfrac{1}{5}\right)^{-6} \times \left(\dfrac{1}{5}\right)$
   - (D) 0.00032

$$x^a \cdot x^b = x^{a+b}$$
$$(x^a)^b = x^{ab}$$
$$\frac{x^a}{x^b} = x^{a-b}$$

3. If $2^5 \times 5^2 = 2^n \times 10^2$, what is the value of n?
   - (A) 8
   - (B) 7
   - (C) 3
   - (D) 4

4. What is the value of $(3^2)^3$?
   - (A) 729
   - (B) 216
   - (C) 512
   - (D) 18

5. What is the simplest form of $\dfrac{2^5}{4^2}$?

    Ⓐ 2^3

    Ⓑ 4^2

    Ⓒ 2^1

    Ⓓ 2^2

6. Simplify the expression $\dfrac{3^2 \times 9^3}{3^8}$, and explain why the statement below is a true statement.

$$\frac{3^2 \times 9^3}{3^8} = 1$$

7. Simplify the following expression. Write your answer in standard form, and show your work.

$$\frac{(2^2 - 1)^{12}}{3^6} \times 3^{-2} + 3^0$$

8. Helen simplifies the expression below and makes two errors. Find and explain the errors.

$$\frac{(5^3)^2}{10^2} = \frac{5^5}{100} = \frac{25}{100} = \frac{1}{4}$$

_____

_____

_____

_____

(Answers are on page 221.)

SQUARE ROOT
AND CUBE ROOT

EE.A.2 Use square root and cube root symbols to represent solutions to equations of the form $x^2 = p$ and $x^3 = p$, where p is a positive rational number. Evaluate square roots of small perfect squares and cube roots of small perfect cubes. Know that $\sqrt{2}$ is irrational.

1. A circle has an area of 64π ft.^{2} What is the radius of the circle?

   (A) 64 ft.

   (B) 8 ft.

   (C) 24 ft.

   (D) 32 ft.

   $A = \pi r^2$

2. Solve each equation for the positive value of x.

   A. $x^2 = 49$ _____

   B. $x^2 = 10^{-2}$ _____

   C. $x^2 = 1.44$ _____

   D. $x^2 - 56 = 200$ _____

3. Find the value of x in each equation.

   A. $x^3 = 27$ _____

   B. $x^3 = 8^{-1}$ _____

   C. $x^3 = 0.125$ _____

   D. $x^3 - 4 = 60$ _____

   Remember, $4^3 = 4 \times 4 \times 4 = 64$.

   Therefore, $\sqrt[3]{64} = 4$.

4. Elena wants to cover the faces of a cube with paper. The volume of the cube is 64 cm.^{3} What is the length of the sides of the square sheet of paper she will need to cover one side of the cube?

5. Simplify the following expression: $3(\sqrt[3]{27}) + 2(\sqrt{64})$.

6. A rectangle has a width of 10 feet and a length of 40 feet. What is the length of the side of a square with the same area? Show your work.

7. Is the following statement true? Explain your answer.

$$\sqrt[3]{-27} = -\sqrt{9}$$

_____

_____

_____

_____

8. Nora is making a square quilt. The area is 81 ft.^{2} She is using 3×3 inch squares of different types of fabric to make the quilt similar to the rectangular one shown below. How many squares will she need to complete the quilt? (1 foot = 12 inches)

(Answers are on page 221.)

ESTIMATING
VERY LARGE AND
VERY SMALL QUANTITIES

EE.A.3 Use numbers expressed in the form of a single digit times an integer power of 10 to estimate very large or very small quantities, and to express how many times as much one is than the other. *For example, estimate the population of the United States as 3 times 10^8 and the population of the world as 7 times 10^9, and determine that the world population is more than 20 times larger.*

1. Find the integer that makes this statement true: $20^2 = \square \times 10^2$
   - Ⓐ 3
   - Ⓑ 4
   - Ⓒ 5
   - Ⓓ 6

2. The population of the Philippine Islands is 100,618,300. Which of the following values would represent the best estimate of the population?
   - Ⓐ 10^6
   - Ⓑ 10^7
   - Ⓒ 10^8
   - Ⓓ 10^9

3. The snow leopard is on the list of endangered species. There are approximately 7,000 left in the wild. Express the number of snow leopards as a single-digit integer times a power of 10.

4. The world population is estimated to be 7 billion. The population of China is estimated to be 1,365,370,000. Approximately how many times larger is the world population compared to the population of China?

Ⓐ 2 million

Ⓑ 5×10^3

Ⓒ 5

Ⓓ 30

5. The diameter of a strand of hair is 0.00018 m. The diameter of an atom is 0.0000000001 m.

Part A. Express the diameter of a strand of hair as a single-digit integer times a power of 10.

Part B. Express the diameter of an atom as a single-digit integer times a power of 10.

Part C. Approximately, how many times larger is the diameter of the strand of hair compared to the diameter of an atom?

(Answers are on page 222.)

SCIENTIFIC NOTATION

EE.A.4 Perform operations with numbers expressed in scientific notation, including problems where both decimal and scientific notation are used. Use scientific notation and choose units of appropriate size for measurements of very large or very small quantities (e.g., use millimeters per year for seafloor spreading). Interpret scientific notation that has been generated by technology.

1. Are the following numbers written in scientific notation, yes or no? If not, state the reason.

   A. 6.03×10^3 _____

   B. 5.00×10^{-3} _____

   C. 0.65×10^8 _____

   D. 17.6×10^4 _____

2. Write each number in scientific notation.

   A. 0.000004 _____

   B. 13,200 _____

   C. 0.508 _____

   D. 137.68 _____

3. Write each number in standard form.

   A. 6.36×10^5 _____

   B. 4.05×10^{-4} _____

   C. 5.00×10^{13} _____

   D. 2.00×10^{-7} _____

A number written in scientific notation is written as the product of two factors. The first is a number that is equal to or greater than 1 and less than 10. The second factor is 10 raised to an integral power.

4. What is the value of $(3.7 \times 10^6)(2.4 \times 10^{-3})$ written in scientific notation?
    Ⓐ 6.1 $\times 10^{-18}$
    Ⓑ 8.88 $\times 10^3$
    Ⓒ 0.888 $\times 10^4$
    Ⓓ 6.1 $\times 10^3$

5. Find the sum of (4.3×10^{12}) and (9.6×10^{10}). Express your answer in scientific notation.
    Ⓐ 9.643×10^{10}
    Ⓑ 4.396×10^{10}
    Ⓒ 4.396×10^{12}
    Ⓓ 9.643×10^{12}

6. Find the difference, and express your answer in scientific notation.

    $$(5.62 \times 10^6) - (3.9 \times 10^5)$$

    Ⓐ 5.23×10^6
    Ⓑ 52.3×10^5
    Ⓒ 5.23×10^5
    Ⓓ 1.72×10^1

7. Simplify $\dfrac{(3.6 \times 10^3) + (2.8 \times 10^3)}{8 \times 10^6}$. Express your answer in scientific notation.

   (A) 8.0×10^{-2}

   (B) 0.8×10^{-3}

   (C) 8.0×10^{-4}

   (D) 8.0×10^{-3}

8. Because of their orbital paths, the distance between the Earth and Mars varies. The current average distance is 2.25×10^8 km. In 2018, scientists are anticipating their orbits will align to provide a much closer distance of 5.76×10^7 km. How much closer is this anticipated distance compared to the current average distance? Express your answer in scientific notation. Show your work.

9. California has the largest population of all the states in the United States with approximately 3.9×10^7 people. The state with the second largest population is Texas. It has a population of 2.7×10^7. How many more people live in California than in Texas? Express your answer in standard form.

10. Eva and Christina were working on their math homework together. They had to solve

the following problem: $\dfrac{6.8 \times 10^8}{2 \times 10^5}$. Eva used her calculator and said that the answer

was 3.4×10^{13}. Christina disagreed. She said that she did a quick estimate and thinks
the answer should be about 3,000.

Part A. How did Eva get her answer?

Part B. How did Christina get her estimate?

Part C. Who is correct and why?

(Answers are on page 222.)

PROPORTIONAL RELATIONSHIPS

> **EE.B.5** Graph proportional relationships, interpreting the unit rate as the slope of the graph. Compare two different proportional relationships represented in different ways. For example, compare a distance-time graph to a distance-time equation to determine which of two moving objects has greater speed.

1. Marcus reads 100 pages in $2\frac{1}{2}$ hours. What is his unit rate in pages per hour?

   Ⓐ 40 pages per hour
   Ⓒ 20 pages per hour
   Ⓑ 25 pages per hour
   Ⓓ 70 pages per hour

2. David's dad drove 174 miles in 3 hours. At this rate, which equation could be used to represent the distance (d) that he will travel in t hours?

   > A unit rate is a rate in which the second quantity in the comparison is one.

   Ⓐ $d = 3t$
   Ⓒ $d = 58t$

   Ⓑ $d = \dfrac{174}{t}$
   Ⓓ $t = 58d$

3. Manuel walks to school every day. The graph below shows Manual's distance from home over time.

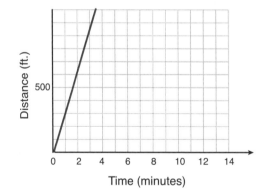

   Which of the following statements is **not** true?

   Ⓐ Manuel walks at a rate of 300 ft. per minute.
   Ⓑ The slope of the line is 300.
   Ⓒ The slope of the line is $\dfrac{1}{300}$.
   Ⓓ Manuel can walk 1,500 feet in 5 minutes.

4. Michelle is making braided bracelets to sell for a school fundraiser.

   She worked for $3\frac{1}{2}$ hours and made 140 bracelets.

   Part A. Write an equation to represent the number (n) of bracelets that can be made in a certain number of hours (h).

   Part B. Use your equation to determine the number of bracelets Michelle can make in 5 hours.

   Part C. Complete the table below using the information given in the problem.

Hours (h)	2	4		8	
# of bracelets (n)	80		240		400

5. In Baltimore, Maryland, 18.4 inches of rain fell during a storm. The storm lasted 5 hours and 45 minutes. What is the unit rate of the rainfall in inches per hour? Show your work.

6. Michael and Jose are training for the New York City Marathon. The course is 26 miles. Jose says that the equation, $d = 4.5t$, represents the distance (d) that he can run in t hours. Michael records his practice runs in a table. The table is shown below.

Hours (t)	2	$3\frac{1}{2}$	4	5	$5\frac{1}{2}$
Miles (d)	9.2	16.1	18.4	23	25.3

Who will complete the marathon first? Explain your answer.

7. A pool is filled with water at a constant rate of 420 gallons per hour.

Part A. Write an equation to represent the number of gallons, n, that can be poured over a time interval, t.

Part B. Complete the table below.

t (time in hours)	Equation	n (number of gallons)
0		
1		
2		
4		

Part C. Graph the data on a coordinate plane. Label the axes.

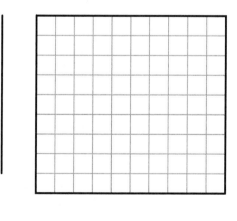

(Answers are on page 223.)

SLOPE OF A LINE

EE.B.6 Use similar triangles to explain why the slope *m* is the same between any two distinct points on a non-vertical line in the coordinate plane; derive the equation $y = mx$ for a line through the origin and the equation $y = mx + b$ for a line intercepting the vertical axis at *b*.

1. What is the slope of the line shown in the graph below?

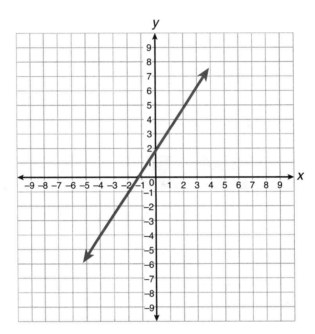

(A) $\dfrac{2}{3}$

(B) 5

(C) $\dfrac{3}{2}$

(D) $\dfrac{-3}{2}$

The slope *m* of a line is the ratio of the change in the *y*-values for a segment of the graph to the corresponding change in *x*-values.

2. Which of the following equations will produce the steepest line?

   Ⓐ $y = 3x - 2$

   Ⓑ $y = \dfrac{2}{3}x$

   Ⓒ $y = -5x$

   Ⓓ $y + 8 = 4x$

3. The triangles shown on the graph are similar. Which of the following statements, related to the slope of the line AC, is correct?

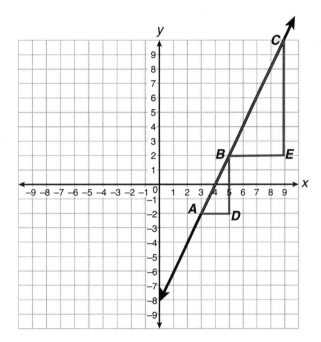

   Ⓐ The slope of $\overleftrightarrow{AC} = \dfrac{\overline{BE}}{\overline{CE}} = \dfrac{\overline{AD}}{\overline{BD}}$

   Ⓑ The slope of $\overleftrightarrow{AC} = \dfrac{\overline{AC}}{\overline{AB}} = \dfrac{\overline{BE}}{\overline{AD}}$

   Ⓒ The slope of $\overleftrightarrow{AC} = \dfrac{\overline{AB}}{\overline{BC}} = \dfrac{\overline{AD}}{\overline{BE}}$

   Ⓓ The slope of $\overleftrightarrow{AC} = \dfrac{\overline{BD}}{\overline{AD}} = \dfrac{\overline{CE}}{\overline{BE}}$

(Answers are on page 224.)

SOLVING LINEAR EQUATIONS IN ONE VARIABLE

EE.C.7.A Give examples of linear equations in one variable with one solution, infinitely many solutions, or no solutions. Show which of these possibilities is the case by successively transforming the given equation into simpler forms, until an equivalent equation of the form $x = a$, $a = a$, or $a = b$ results (where a and b are different numbers).

1. Simplify the following equations, and determine if they have one solution, infinitely many solutions, or no solution. Check the appropriate space in the table for each equation.

Equation	One Solution	Infinite Number of Solutions	No Solution
$\frac{2}{3}x = 12$			
$12x + 6 = 10x + 2x + 6$			
$3x = x + 12.7$			
$x + 3x + 3 = 4x + 2$			

2. When the equation $4x + 6 = 4x - 3$ is simplified,

   (A) $x = a$ is constant.

   (B) $x = 3$.

   (C) there is no solution.

   (D) there are an infinite number of solutions.

> If you simplify an equation and the result is a number or a variable equal to itself, the equation has an infinite number of solutions. (i.e., $x = x$)

3. Ms. Sanchez writes the following equation on the board:

$$5x + 2 = 3x + 2x + 2$$

She asks her students to each write one statement about the equation.
Four students volunteer to write their statements on the board. After a discussion,
the class agrees that one statement is incorrect. Which of the four statements
is incorrect?

- Ⓐ The equation is a true sentence.
- Ⓑ There is no solution to the equation.
- Ⓒ There are an infinite number of solutions to the equation.
- Ⓓ If you substitute the number 5 for x, both sides of the equation will be equal.

For questions 4–8, solve the equation, and check your solution.

4. $\dfrac{x}{12} = 60$

5. $2x - 8.24 = -4.6$

6. $2.6x = 3\dfrac{19}{50}$

7. $\dfrac{4}{5}x - 0.2 = 1$

8. $3x - 5 = 5x + 2$

(Answers are on page 224.)

SOLVING MULTISTEP LINEAR EQUATIONS

EE.C.7.B Solve linear equations with rational number coefficients, including equations whose solutions require expanding expressions using the distributive property and collecting like terms.

For questions 1 and 2, solve the equation by combining like terms.

1. $7x - 2x + 10 = 2.5x - 2 + 8$

2. $1.6x - x + 4 = \dfrac{2}{5}x - 8$

For questions 3 and 4, use the distributive property to help you solve the equation.

3. $12(x - 3) + 6 = -3(x + 5)$

4. $\dfrac{2}{3}(6x - 3) = 0.6(10x - 18)$

5. Franco's dad is three times his age. In 10 years, Franco's dad will be twice Franco's age plus 2. How old are Franco and his dad now? Show your work.

6. Solve and check the following equation. Show all your work.

$$5x - 2(4x + 1) = 7(2x - 3) - 15$$

7. The perimeters of the regular pentagon (all the sides are congruent) and the rectangle shown below are equal.

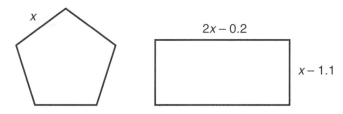

Part A. Write an equation to represent the equal perimeters.

Part B. What is the perimeter of each figure?

8. A rectangular garden has a perimeter of 15 meters. The length is twice as long as the width.

Part A. Write an equation to represent the situation given in the problem.

Part B. What is the length of the garden?

9. A square and a rectangle have the same perimeter. The width of the rectangle is 3 units less than the length of the side of the square. The length of the rectangle is 3 units more than the length of the side of the square. Let x represent the length of one side of the square.

Part A. Write an equation to represent the two equal perimeters.

Part B. Can you determine the dimensions of the two shapes? Explain your answer.

_____

_____

_____

10. Seth and Christopher are collecting baseball cards. Seth has twice as many cards as Christopher. After Christopher buys 10 more cards, they have a total of 55 cards between them. How many cards does Seth have?

(Answers are on page 226.)

SYSTEMS OF LINEAR EQUATIONS

> **EE.C.8.A** Understand that solutions to a system of two linear equations in two variables correspond to points of intersection of their graphs, because points of intersection satisfy both equations simultaneously.

1. How many lines can be drawn through one point on the coordinate plane?

   Ⓐ One line

   Ⓑ Two lines

   Ⓒ Three lines

   Ⓓ An infinite number of lines

> A system of linear equations is two or more linear equations with the same variables. A system can have one solution, no solution, or infinitely many solutions.

2. If (2, 11) is a point on the line $y = 2x + 7$, which of the following statements is *not* true?

   Ⓐ If you substitute these coordinate values into the equation, you will get a true statement.

   Ⓑ (2, 11) is the only solution to the equation.

   Ⓒ (2, 11) is one possible solution to the equation.

   Ⓓ It is possible for the graph of a different linear equation to pass through the same point.

3. If the graphs of two linear equations intersect at a point, the coordinates of that point are

   Ⓐ a common solution for both equations.

   Ⓑ a solution for only one of the equations.

   Ⓒ one of many common solutions for both equations.

   Ⓓ not a solution for either equation.

4. If you graph a system of two linear equations, which of the following possibilities *cannot* be true?

   Ⓐ The lines are parallel, and there is no solution to the system.

   Ⓑ Since there are two equations, there are two solutions to the system.

   Ⓒ The two lines intersect, and the point of intersection is the solution to the system.

   Ⓓ The two equations define the same line, and the system has infinitely many solutions.

5. Two equations in a system are shown in the graph to the right. What is the solution to the system?

- Ⓐ (–5, –1)
- Ⓑ (0, –1)
- Ⓒ (1, –2)
- Ⓓ (–2, 1)

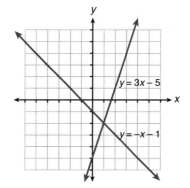

For questions 6–9, solve each system of linear equations by graphing. If there is only one solution, label the solution, and check your solution in both equations.

6. $y = 3x + 4$

$x - y = 2$

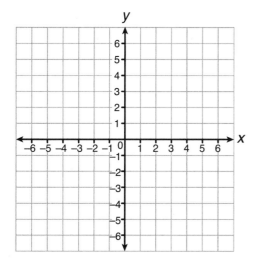

8. $y = \frac{1}{2}x - 1$

$2y = x - 10$

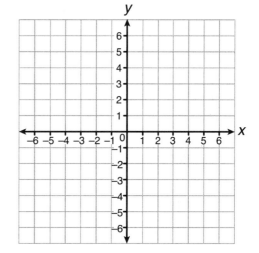

7. $y = \frac{2}{3}x - 4$

$y - x = -4$

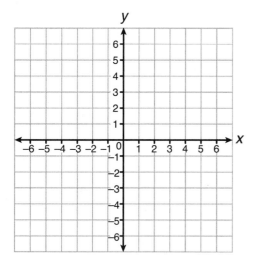

9. $y = 2x - 1$

$2y - 4x = -2$

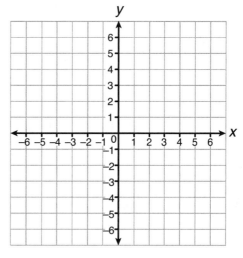

(Answers are on page 227.)

SOLVING SYSTEMS OF LINEAR EQUATIONS BY INSPECTION AND ALGEBRAICALLY

EE.C.8.B Solve systems of two linear equations in two variables algebraically, and estimate solutions by graphing the equations. Solve simple cases by inspection. *For example, 3x + 2y = 5 and 3x + 2y = 6 have no solution because 3x + 2y cannot simultaneously be 5 and 6.*

1. If the equations in a system of two linear equations have the same slope, then the system will have

   Ⓐ one solution.

   Ⓑ no solution.

   Ⓒ infinitely many solutions.

   Ⓓ no solution OR infinitely many solutions.

> To examine the slope of an equation, rewrite the equation in the form $y = mx + b$, where m represents the slope.

For questions 2–4, look at the equations in each system. What can you determine about the nature of the solution to each of the systems of linear equations? Choose A, B, C, or D.

A. The slopes of the equations are different. Therefore, there is only one solution.

B. The slopes are the same, and the *y*-intercept is different. Therefore, there is no solution.

C. The equations define the same line. Therefore, the system will have infinitely many solutions.

D. Nothing can be determined about the nature of the solution.

2. $\begin{cases} 2x - 3y = 6 \\ 4x - 6y = 12 \end{cases}$ _____

3. $\begin{cases} 2x - 17y = 8 \\ 2x - 17y = 40 \end{cases}$ _____

4. $\begin{cases} y = \dfrac{2}{3}x - 6 \\ y = 4x + 2 \end{cases}$ _____

For questions 5–7, solve the system of two equations algebraically.
Check your solution in both equations.

5. $\begin{cases} 5x + 6y = 3 \\ 2x - 6y = 11 \end{cases}$
                        Solution: (___, ___)

6. $\begin{cases} y = 4x - 11 \\ y = 7x + 4 \end{cases}$
                        Solution: (___, ___)

7. $\begin{cases} y = \dfrac{3}{5}x - 6 \\ x = 5y + 5 \end{cases}$
                        Solution: (___, ___)

For questions 8 and 9, graph each system of two linear equations. Verify your solution by solving the system algebraically. If the exact solution cannot be determined from the graph, estimate the solution. Then, find the exact solution algebraically.

8. $\begin{cases} y - 6x = -5 \\ 2y + 3x = 0 \end{cases}$

9. $\begin{cases} y = x + 2 \\ y = -\dfrac{x}{2} + 6 \end{cases}$

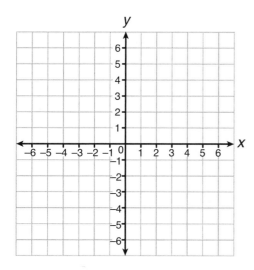

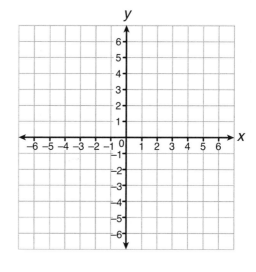

10. $\begin{cases} y = \dfrac{1}{2}x + 2 \\[2mm] y = \dfrac{3}{2}x + 1 \end{cases}$

The system above has one solution.

Part A. Is it possible to determine that there is only one solution by just looking at the equations? Explain your answer.

_____

_____

_____

_____

_____

Part B. Solve the system using any algebraic method.

Part C. Explain why you chose your method.

_____

_____

_____

_____

_____

(Answers are on page 228.)

USING SYSTEMS OF LINEAR EQUATIONS TO SOLVE PROBLEMS

EE.C.8.C Solve real-world and mathematical problems leading to two linear equations in two variables. *For example, given coordinates for two pairs of points, determine whether the line through the first pair of points intersects the line through the second pair.*

1. Line m passes through the points $(-2, 0)$ and $(2, 4)$.
   Line n passes through the points $(-3, 2)$ and $(3, -1)$.

   Part A. Do the lines intersect? Explain your answer.

   _____

   _____

   _____

   Part B. If yes, what are the coordinates of the point of intersection?

   _____

2. Line m passes through the points $(1, 3)$ and $(-3, -5)$.
   Line n passes through the points $(0, -3)$ and $(4, 5)$.

   Part A. Do the lines intersect? Explain your answer.

   _____

   _____

   _____

   Part B. If yes, what are the coordinates of the point of intersection?

   _____

For questions 3–9, write and solve a system of two linear equations.

3. The sum of two numbers is 1,068. The difference between the two numbers is 116. Find the numbers.

System: {

Answer: _____

4. One number is three times larger than another number. The sum of the two numbers is 48. Find the two numbers.

System: {

Answer: _____

5. Katie is 12 years older than her brother. Her mother says that she is five times as old as her brother. If both statements are true, how old is Katie?

System: {

Answer: _____

6. Mayfair Middle School had its annual school play to raise money for the drama club. The students sold 300 tickets and raised $1,100. The cost of tickets was $5 for adults and $3 for students. How many students attended the performance?

System: {

Answer: _____

7. Mrs. Equation wrote a 38-question test for her class. She told her students that it would be worth a total of 100 points. She also said that there would be multiple-choice questions worth 2 points each and extended-response problems worth 5 points each. She told her students that she would give them bonus points if they could figure out how many multiple-choice questions were on the test. How many multiple-choice questions are on the test?

System: $\{$

Answer: _____

8. The length of a rectangular garden plot is three times its width. Its perimeter is 344 feet. What is the length of the rectangular garden?

System: $\{$

Answer: _____

9. Alexis received $80 for her birthday. Her favorite store is having a sale. She can buy two pairs of jeans and two sweaters for $80. Or, she can buy one pair of jeans and three sweaters and still have $18 left to spend. What is the price of one pair of jeans?

System: $\{$

Answer: _____

10. Derek and Jason were on vacation and decided to rent bikes. Derek rented a bike from Rent-a-Ride. The cost was $20 plus $2 per hour. Jason rented a bike from Deals on Wheels. The cost was $10 plus $5 per hour.

Part A. Write a system of two equations to represent this situation.

System: $\left\{\vphantom{\begin{array}{c} \\ \\ \\ \end{array}}\right.$

Part B. Graph the system. Label your graph.

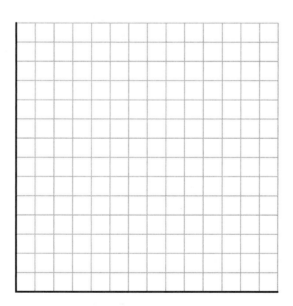

Part C. Use the graph to estimate when the cost to rent the two bikes will be the same.

Part D. If Derek and Jason rented the bikes for 5 hours, who got the better deal?

(Answers are on page 230.)

FUNCTIONS

F.A.1 Understand that a function is a rule that assigns to each input exactly one output. The graph of a function is the set of ordered pairs consisting of an input and the corresponding output.

1. A function is a rule that
   Ⓐ assigns to each output exactly one input.
   Ⓑ assigns to each input exactly one output.
   Ⓒ can always be graphed as a line.
   Ⓓ can only be represented using a table of values.

2. The equation $y = 4x - 2$ represents a function because
   Ⓐ there are an infinite number of solutions.
   Ⓑ it can be graphed on a coordinate plane.
   Ⓒ it has two variables.
   Ⓓ for every input value (x), there is only one output value (y).

3. Which set of ordered pairs does **not** represent a function?
   Ⓐ (1, 2), (3, 3), (5, 4), (3, 5)
   Ⓑ (2, 6), (3, 6), (4, 6), (5, 6)
   Ⓒ (1, 1), (2, 2), (3, 3), (4, 4)
   Ⓓ (1, 5), (8, 2), (4, 2), (9, 8)

For questions 4–6, determine if the table represents a function. Explain your answer.

4.

Input	Output
3	7
4	6
5	5
6	4
7	3

_____

_____

_____

_____

5.

x	y
2	4
3	5
2	6
3	7
2	8

_____

_____

_____

_____

6.

x	y
1	9
2	2
3	5
4	9
5	8

For questions 7–9, examine the graph. Does the graph represent a function? Explain your answer.

7.

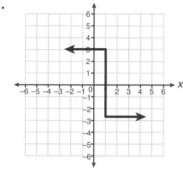

8.

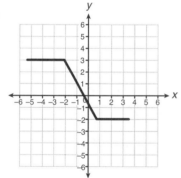

9.

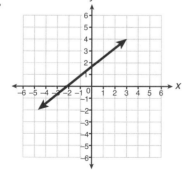

(Answers are on page 232.)

COMPARING PROPERTIES OF FUNCTIONS

> **F.A.2** Compare properties of two functions each represented in a different way (algebraically, graphically, numerically in tables, or by verbal descriptions). *For example, given a linear function represented by a table of values and a linear function represented by an algebraic expression, determine which function has the greater rate of change.*

1. Compare the two functions shown.

Function 1

x	y
1	4
2	9
3	3
4	6
5	2

Function 2

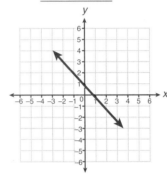

Which statement about the functions is true?

- Ⓐ Function 1 has a greater rate of change than Function 2.
- Ⓑ Function 2 has a greater rate of change than Function 1.
- Ⓒ Function 1 does not have a constant rate of change.
- Ⓓ Both functions have the same rate of change.

2. Compare the two functions shown.

Function 1

$y = 2x + 15$

Function 2

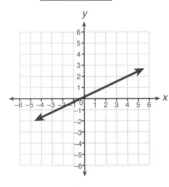

Which statement about the functions is true?

- Ⓐ Function 1 has a greater rate of change than Function 2.
- Ⓑ Function 2 has a greater rate of change than Function 1.
- Ⓒ Function 1 does not have a constant rate of change.
- Ⓓ Both functions have the same rate of change.

3. Compare the two functions shown.

Function 1

x	y
2	6
3	9
4	12
5	15
6	18

Function 2

$y = 2.7x + 3$

Which statement about the functions is true?

Ⓐ Function 1 has a greater rate of change than Function 2.

Ⓑ Function 2 has a greater rate of change than Function 1.

Ⓒ Function 1 does not have a constant rate of change.

Ⓓ Both functions have the same rate of change.

Use the information below to answer questions 4–8.

Marta is training to run in a marathon. The equation $y = 5x$ can be used to represent y, the total distance in miles that Marta has run in x hours. Her friend, Olivia, is also training. She records her time and distance for 5 days in a table.

Olivia's Table

Miles	2.4	3.6	9.6	8	4.8
Time in Minutes	30	45	120	100	60

4. At what rate (miles per hour) does Olivia run?

_____

5. Who runs at a greater constant rate?

_____

6. If the marathon is 25 miles, how long will it take Marta to complete the race at her current rate of speed?

_____

7. If they continue to run at the same rate, who will finish the marathon first?

_____

8. What will be the approximate difference in their total times?

_____   (Answers are on page 232.)

LINEAR AND NONLINEAR FUNCTIONS

F.A.3 Interpret the equation $y = mx + b$ as defining a linear function, whose graph is a straight line; give examples of functions that are not linear. *For example, the function* A $= s^2$ *giving the area of a square as a function of its side length is not linear because its graph contains the points (1, 1), (2, 4), and (3, 9), which are not on a straight line.*

1. Which of the following functions is ***not*** linear?
   - (A) $y = 5x + 6$
   - (B) $y = -4$
   - (C) $y = x^2 + 2$
   - (D) $y = x$

2. Which of the following methods ***cannot*** be used to determine if a function is linear?
   - (A) Examine the graph of the function.
   - (B) Examine the equation of the function.
   - (C) Examine two sets of ordered pairs of the function.
   - (D) Examine a table of values of the function.

3. Which equation represents a linear function?
   - (A) $y = x^2$
   - (B) $y = \dfrac{3}{4}x - 3.7$
   - (C) $y = \sqrt{x}$
   - (D) $y = x^{-4}$

> The equation $y = mx + b$ defines a linear function. The variables cannot be raised to any power greater than 1.

For questions 4–7, identify the function as linear or nonlinear. Explain your answer.

4. $y = x^3 - 2$

_____

_____

5. $y - x = 5^2$

_____

_____

6.

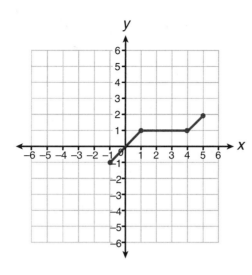

_____

_____

_____

7.

x	15	20	25	30	35
y	4	8	12	16	20

_____

_____

_____

8. In math class, students measure the diameter of circles of different sizes. They calculate the circumference of the circles and then the area, and then they graph both sets of results. Their teacher, Mr. LaSpina, observes that the two graphs represent functions, but one is linear and one is nonlinear. Which of the two graphs will represent a nonlinear relationship? Explain your answer.

_____

_____

_____

(Answers are on page 232.)

CONSTRUCTING FUNCTIONS

F.B.4 Construct a function to model a linear relationship between two quantities. Determine the rate of change and initial value of the function from a description of a relationship or from two (x, y) values, including reading these from a table or from a graph. Interpret the rate of change and initial value of a linear function in terms of the situation it models, and in terms of its graph or a table of values.

Use the following table and information to answer questions 1–3.

The table below shows the total cost for the first 6 months of services from a cable company. The company charges an installation fee and an additional monthly charge.

x (number of months)	1	2	3	4	5	6
y (total cost)	$175	$200	$225	$250	$275	$300

1. What is the monthly charge for service?
   Ⓐ $175
   Ⓑ $150
   Ⓒ $25
   Ⓓ $100

> To construct a linear function, write an equation in the form of $y = mx + b$.

2. What is the installation fee?
   Ⓐ $175
   Ⓑ $150
   Ⓒ $25
   Ⓓ $100

3. Which function represents the total cost (y) of any number of months of service (x)?
   Ⓐ $y = 175x$
   Ⓑ $y = 25x + 100$
   Ⓒ $y = 150x + 25$
   Ⓓ $y = 25x + 150$

4. The graph below represents the cost of widgets shipped by the National Widget Company. The cost is based on the total weight (lbs.).

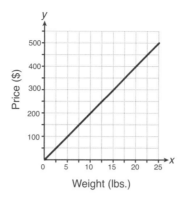

Weight (lbs.)

Part A. Construct a linear function to model the relationship between the weight (*x*) and the price (*y*).

_____

Part B. What is the rate of change of the function? Include units.

_____

5. Jason is taking a trip from Virginia to Maryland. He fills up his car's gas tank before he leaves. The graph below shows how much gas he used during his trip.

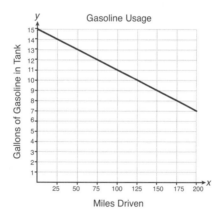

Miles Driven

Part A. Construct a function to model the linear relationship between the miles driven (*x*) and the number of gallons of gasoline in his tank (*y*).

_____

Part B. What is the rate of change of the function?

_____

Part C. What is the initial value of the function?

_____

Base your answers to questions 6–10 on the information given below.

For his 13th birthday, Adam's parents opened a saving account for him at the local bank. They made an initial deposit for him. Adam earns money mowing lawns and babysitting his younger sister. Since they opened the account, he has deposited $20 into the account each month. He is planning to continue saving at this rate to buy a new bike. At the end of four months, he has saved $130.

6. Complete the following table to show Adam's savings for the first four months.

Months (x)	Total Savings (y)
0	
1	
2	
3	
4	

7. Construct a function to model the relationship shown in the table.

8. Use the table to determine the rate of change.

_____

_____

_____

9. What does the rate of change represent in the situation described? Explain.

_____

_____

_____

10. Graph the function. Label the graph.

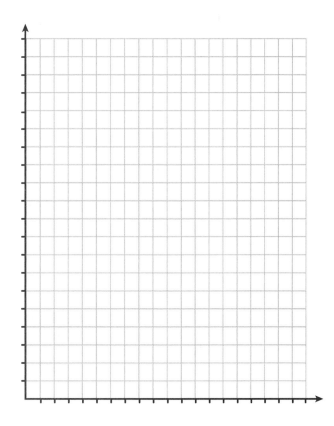

(Answers are on page 233.)

ANALYZING GRAPHS

F.B.5 Describe qualitatively the functional relationship between two quantities by analyzing a graph (e.g., where the function is increasing or decreasing, linear or nonlinear). Sketch a graph that exhibits the qualitative features of a function that has been described verbally.

1. The distance vs. time graph below could be used to describe which situation?

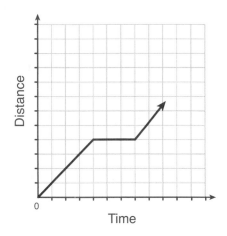

A   A train leaves the station and slowly builds up speed. After several minutes, it reaches a speed of 60 miles per hour and continues at that speed for a time and then slows down as it reaches the next station.

B   Aiden is riding his bike at a constant speed. He reaches a hill, and his speed decreases till he reaches the top. As he rides down the hill, his speed increases to his original speed.

C   Malcolm walks at a constant speed to his friend's house. He talks to his friend for a few minutes and then returns home, walking at the same speed.

D   Andrea is training for a marathon. She runs at a slow constant speed for several minutes to warm up. She then increases her speed and continues running at the faster rate.

For questions 2–4, read through each scenario, and choose the graph of the function that best matches the situation.

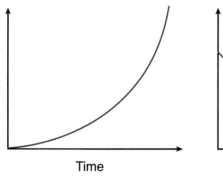

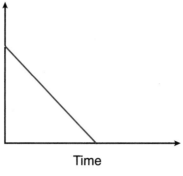

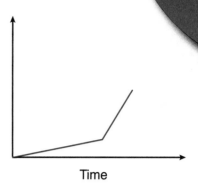

Situation A   **Situation B**   **Situation C**

2. Jessie starts to walk to school at a constant rate. She realizes that she is late and runs the last 5 blocks.

   _____

3. A pool is drained at a constant rate of 15 gallons per hour.

   _____

4. A new business starts off slowly, and then sales increase dramatically.

   _____

Use the information below to answer questions 5–7.

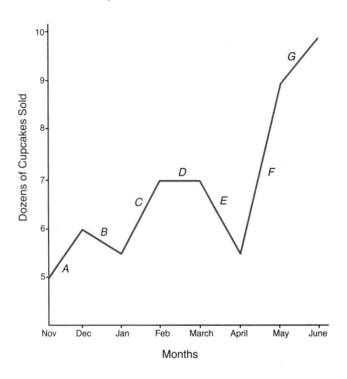

Months

Ianna started selling cupcakes at school to raise money for various charities. She recorded how many dozens she sold each month. A graph of her sales is shown below. She also made some notes about her sales. Match her comments (in questions 5–7) with the section on the graph she describes.

5. For two months, sales were exactly the same.

_____

6. After a great start, my sales dropped.

_____

7. After a drop in sales, I improved my recipe. There was a large increase in sales that continued until the end of the school year.

_____

8. Mt. Fuji is Japan's highest mountain. It is 3,776 meters high. During summer vacation, Amane visited his family in Japan and climbed the mountain with his aunt. There are 10 stations as you climb. At 8 A.M., they took a 20 minute bus from the first station to the fifth station. The distance was 2,300 meters. They hiked at a steady pace for the next 3 hours. They stopped for lunch at the eighth station, which is 3,020 meters up. After an hour, they continued at a slower pace to the top of the mountain. The total assent took 8 hours.

Sketch and label a graph that represents their 8-hour climb.

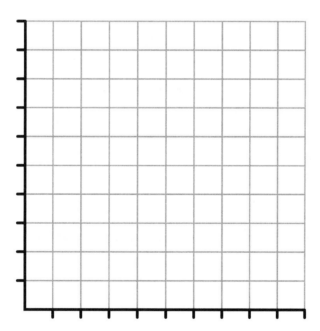

(Answers are on page 233.)

PROPERTIES OF ROTATIONS, REFLECTIONS, AND TRANSLATIONS

> **G.A.1** Verify experimentally the properties of rotations, reflections, and translations.
> **G.A.1.A** Lines are taken to lines, and line segments to line segments of the same length.
> **G.A.1.B** Angles are taken to angles of the same measure.
> **G.A.1.C** Parallel lines are taken to parallel lines.

1. When a figure is "flipped" across a line, the mirror image that is created is known as a

   > If a direction is not specified for a rotation, the rotation is counterclockwise.

   (A) rotation.

   (B) reflection.

   (C) dilation.

   (D) translation.

2. If the vertices of a figure are all slid the same distance in the same direction, the new image that is created is called a

   (A) rotation.

   (B) reflection.

   (C) dilation.

   (D) translation.

3. When a figure is turned a number of degrees around a given point, the image created is called a

   (A) rotation.

   (B) reflection.

   (C) dilation.

   (D) translation.

4. Which of the following transformations was performed on Figure *A* to produce Image *A'*?

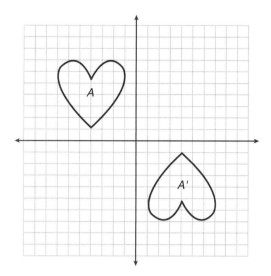

Ⓐ Translation   Ⓒ Reflection

Ⓑ Rotation   Ⓓ Refraction

5. Choose the image that could be produced after performing a translation on Figure *A*.

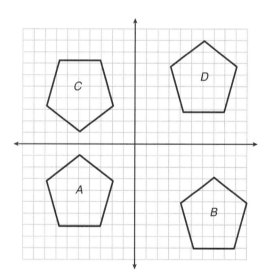

Ⓐ *B*   Ⓒ *D*

Ⓑ *C*   Ⓓ Either *B* or *D*

6. Line segment $\overline{AB}$ is reflected over the *y*-axis to form the Image $\overline{A'B'}$. Which of the following statements is always true?

Ⓐ $\overline{AB}$ is parallel to $\overline{A'B'}$.

Ⓑ The line segments are the same length.

Ⓒ The line segments are perpendicular.

Ⓓ The image is vertical.

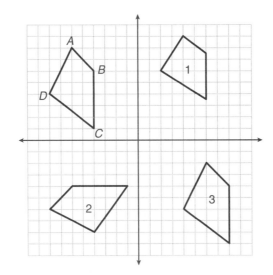

Use the graph above and the following information to answer questions 7 and 8.

Trace Figure *ABCD*, as shown above, onto a piece of paper or a transparency to help you answer questions 7 and 8.

7. Figure *ABCD* is rotated to produce a new image.

 Part A. Which of the three images shown is a rotated image of Figure *ABCD*?

 _____

 Part B. Explain how you determined your answer.

 _____

 _____

 _____

8. A translation is performed on Figure *ABCD*.

 Part A. Which of the three images shown is a translated image of *ABCD*?

 _____

 Part B. Explain how you determined your answer.

 _____

 _____

 _____

9. $\angle ABC$ is reflected across the vertical line shown to produce the Image $\angle A'B'C'$.

Part A. Draw the Image $\angle A'B'C'$ below.

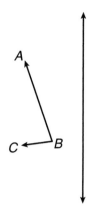

Part B. Make one observation about the two angles.

_____

_____

_____

10. Toni graphs the following two equations: $y = 3x + 2$ and $y = 3x + 4$.

Part A. Are the lines parallel? Explain your answer.

_____

_____

Part B. Next, Toni reflects the two lines over the *x*-axis. Are the reflected images of the two lines parallel?

_____

_____

Part C. What can you predict about the slopes of the two lines produced by the transformation?

_____

_____

_____

(Answers are on page 234.)

CONGRUENCE AND TRANSFORMATIONS

> **G.A.2** Understand that a two-dimensional figure is congruent to another if the second can be obtained from the first by a sequence of rotations, reflections, and translations; given two congruent figures, describe a sequence that exhibits the congruence between them.

1. Which of the following choices could **not** be used to complete this sentence? When two figures are congruent,
   - Ⓐ they are the same size and shape.
   - Ⓑ they have the same orientation.
   - Ⓒ their corresponding angles have the same measure.
   - Ⓓ their corresponding sides are the same length.

2. Figure *A* is congruent to Figure *B*. Which series of transformations map Figure *A* onto Figure *B*?
   - Ⓐ Reflection then translation
   - Ⓑ Rotation and translation
   - Ⓒ Both choice A and choice B
   - Ⓓ None of the above

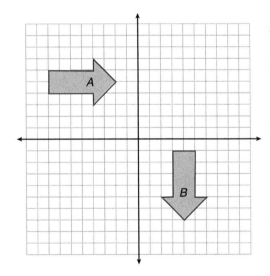

3. Identify a sequence of transformations that will transform Figure *M* into Figure *N*.

   _____

   _____

   _____

   _____

   _____

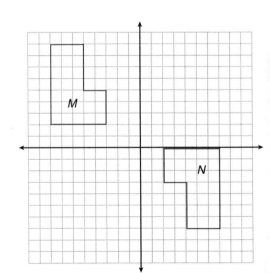

Use the following graph to answer questions 4–7.

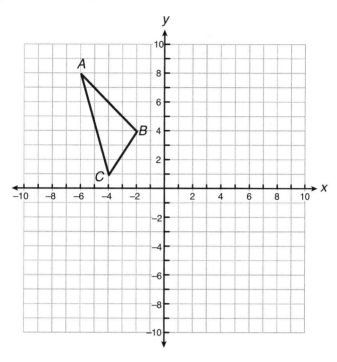

4. On the coordinate plane above, rotate △ABC 90° clockwise around the origin. Draw the image of the rotated figure, and label it A′B′C′.

5. Translate the rotated image 6 units down, and label this new Image A″B″C″.

6. Are all three triangles congruent? Explain your answer.

_____

_____

_____

7. Describe a transformation that can be performed on △A″B″C″, which will produce an image in quadrant 3 of the coordinate plane.

_____

_____

_____

_____

(Answers are on page 235.)

TRANSFORMATIONS ON THE COORDINATE PLANE

G.A.3 Describe the effect of dilations, translations, rotations, and reflections on two-dimensional figures using coordinates.

1. Which transformation will result in an image that is not congruent to the original figure?
   - Ⓐ Translation
   - Ⓑ Dilation
   - Ⓒ Rotation
   - Ⓓ Reflection

2. A dilation is performed on a figure. The new image is smaller than the original figure. This means
   - Ⓐ the scale factor is greater than one.
   - Ⓑ the scale factor is negative.
   - Ⓒ the scale factor is between zero and one.
   - Ⓓ the nature of the scale factor cannot be determined.

3. Triangle ABC is translated 5 units to the right and 2 units down on a coordinate plane. Image $\triangle A'B'C'$ is produced by the transformation. If the coordinates of point A are $(3, 6)$, what are the coordinates of A'?
   - Ⓐ $(8, 8)$
   - Ⓑ $(8, 4)$
   - Ⓒ $(1, 11)$
   - Ⓓ $(5, 1)$

4. Triangle ABC is rotated 90° counterclockwise around the origin on a coordinate plane. If the coordinates of point A are $(3, 6)$, what are the coordinates of A'?
   - Ⓐ $(6, -3)$
   - Ⓑ $(-6, 3)$
   - Ⓒ $(6, 3)$
   - Ⓓ $(-3, 6)$

5. Figure *ABCD* is dilated which produces Image *A′B′C′D′*. The center of dilation is the origin, and the scale factor is 2.5. If the coordinates of point *A* are (2, –6), what are the coordinates of point *A′*?

Ⓐ (4.5,–3.5)

Ⓑ (4.5, –8.5)

Ⓒ (5, –15)

Ⓓ (5, 15)

Use the following graph to answer questions 6 and 7.

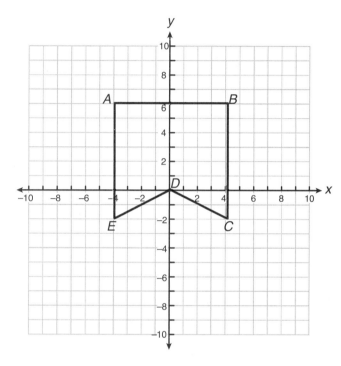

6. Transform *ABCDE* by performing a dilation centered at the origin with a scale factor of $\frac{1}{2}$. Label the image created *A′B′C′D′E′*.

7. Record the coordinates of *ABCDE* and its image, *A′B′C′D′E′*.

A(____ , ____) ⟶ A′(____ , ____)

B(____ , ____) ⟶ B′(____ , ____)

C(____ , ____) ⟶ C′(____ , ____)

D(____ , ____) ⟶ D′(____ , ____)

E(____ , ____) ⟶ E′(____ , ____)

(Answers are on page 235.)

TRANSFORMATIONS AND SIMILAR FIGURES

> **G.A.4** Understand that a two-dimensional figure is similar to another if the second can be obtained from the first by a sequence of rotations, reflections, translations, and dilations; given two similar two-dimensional figures, describe a sequence that exhibits the similarity between them.

1. Figure *A* is reflected over the *y*-axis, rotated 180°, and dilated by a factor of 3 to produce Figure *B*. Which of the following statements is true about Figure *A* and Figure *B*?

    Ⓐ The figures are congruent.

    Ⓑ The figures are mirror images of each other.

    Ⓒ The figures are similar.

    Ⓓ The measures of the angles in Figure *B* are 3 times larger than the measures of the angles in Figure *A*.

2. The triangles shown below are similar. Which of the following sequences of transformations could transform △*ABC* into △*A'B'C'*?

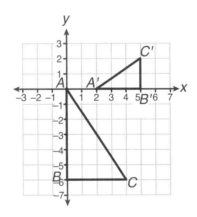

    Ⓐ Translation, rotation, and reflection

    Ⓑ Dilation, reflection, and translation

    Ⓒ Rotation, dilation, and translation

    Ⓓ Reflection, rotation, and translation

3. Quadrilateral *R* was produced by performing a sequence of transformations on Quadrilateral *X*. Based on this information, which of the following statements is **not** true?

    Ⓐ The corresponding angles of the two figures are congruent.

    Ⓑ Quadrilateral *R* and Quadrilateral *X* must be similar.

    Ⓒ Quadrilateral *R* and Quadrilateral *X* must be congruent.

    Ⓓ Corresponding sides will always have the same ratio.

Use the following graph to answer questions 4–7. Note that the figures shown are similar.

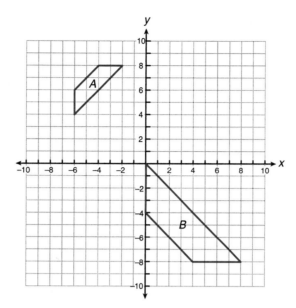

4. Describe a sequence of at least 2–3 transformations that can be used to transform Figure *A* into Figure *B*.

   (1) _____

   (2) _____

   (3) _____

5. Is this the only sequence of transformations that could produce this result? Explain.

   _____

   _____

   _____

6. Since the size of the original figure has changed, a dilation should be part of your sequence. Is there another transformation that must be a part of the sequence? Explain.

   _____

   _____

7. On the graph above, draw the figure in your sequence that would map Figure *A* onto Figure *B*. Label the figures so that they correspond to your numbered sequence in question 4.

(Answers are on page 235.)

ANGLES OF A TRIANGLE

G.A.5 Use informal arguments to establish facts about the angle sum and exterior angle of triangles, about the angles created when parallel lines are cut by a transversal, and the angle-angle criterion for similarity of triangles. *For example, arrange three copies of the same triangle so that the sum of the three angles appears to form a line, and give an argument in terms of transversals why this is so.*

Use Figure 1 to answer questions 1–6.

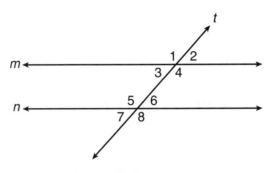

Figure 1

1. When two parallel lines are cut by a transversal, eight angles are formed as shown in Figure 1. Listed below are angle pairs that are either congruent or supplementary. Fill in the table below to identify the angle pairs. If the angles are congruent, provide the special name for the pair of angles (corresponding, vertical, alternate interior or alternate exterior).

Angle Pair	Congruent or Supplementary	If congruent, name the angle pair.
∠1 and ∠5		
∠4 and ∠6		
∠2 and ∠3		
∠3 and ∠6		
∠2 and ∠7		

The measure of ∠1 in Figure 1 is 130°. Use this information to answer questions 2–6.

2. What is the measure of ∠5? _____

3. What is the measure of ∠8? _____

4. What is the measure of ∠6? _____

5. What is the sum of the measure of ∠4 and ∠6? _____

6. What is the sum of the measure of ∠2 and ∠7? _____

> The sum of the angles in every triangle is equal to 180°.

For questions 7 and 8, find the measure of the angle indicated in the problem.

7. m∠ACD = 135°

   m∠ABC = 85°

   m∠CAB = _____

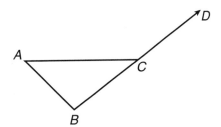

8. Find the measure of angle x. _____

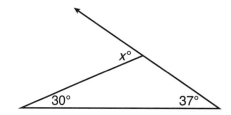

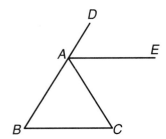

9. In the figure shown above:

$\triangle ABC$ is an equilateral triangle.
$\overline{AE}$ is parallel to $\overline{BC}$.

Find the measure of $\angle DAC$. Explain how to solve the problem.

_____

_____

_____

_____

_____

10. Line *A′C′* is drawn through triangle *ABC* to form a smaller triangle, *A′BC′*. $\overline{AC}$ is parallel to $\overline{A'C'}$. The measure of ∠*BAC* is 47°, and the measure of ∠*ABC* is 50°.

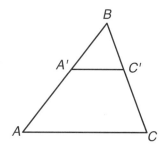

Are the two triangles similar? Explain your answer.

_____

_____

_____

_____

_____

_____

(Answers are on page 236.)

PROOF OF THE PYTHAGOREAN THEOREM

G.B.6 Explain a proof of the Pythagorean Theorem and its converse.

1. In a right triangle, the hypotenuse is
    Ⓐ the shortest side.
    Ⓑ the side opposite the right angle.
    Ⓒ the side labeled with an *h*.
    Ⓓ the largest angle.

2. A figure shows a right triangle with sides *a*, *b*, and *c*.

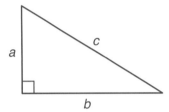

The Pythagorean Theorem states that in a right triangle, the sum of the squares of the lengths of the legs is equal to the square of the length of the hypotenuse. Which of the three sides is the hypotenuse?

_____

Use the following figure to answer questions 3–5. Note that each square represents one square unit.

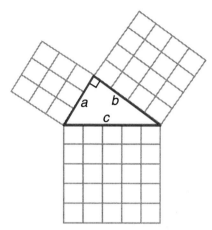

3. a^2 is represented by the square with 9 square units.

$$a^2 = 3^2 = 9$$

Find b^2. _____

4. Find c^2. _____

5. Substitute the values you obtained into the following formula to verify the theorem.

$$a^2 + b^2 = c^2$$

6. Ashanti draws a right triangle and labels its sides as 6, 8, and 12 units. Her friend, Derek, says that with those measurements it cannot be a right triangle. Who is correct? Explain your answer.

_____

_____

_____

Use the following figure to answer questions 7–10.

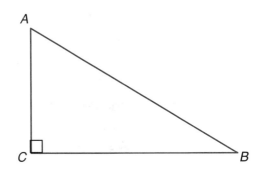

7. Using the letters *A*, *B*, and *C*, label the sides of triangle *ABC*.

8. Use a ruler to measure the side △*ABC*. (Use centimeters.)

Length of side *a* = _____

Length of side *b* = _____

Length of side *c* = _____

Substitute your measurements into the following formula to verify whether or not the triangle is a right triangle.

$$a^2 + b^2 = c^2$$

9. When you substituted and simplified, were the two sides of the equation exactly equal to each other?

_____

10. If not, what might be a reason why the values were not exactly equal?

_____

_____

_____

_____

_____

(Answers are on page 236.)

181

APPLYING THE PYTHAGOREAN THEOREM

> **G.B.7** Apply the Pythagorean Theorem to determine unknown side lengths in right triangles in real-world and mathematical problems in two and three dimensions.

For questions 1–3, use the Pythagorean Theorem to find the missing side of the right triangle. Round your answers to the nearest tenth.

1. What is the length of the side labeled x?
   - Ⓐ 15.1 in.
   - Ⓑ 31 in.
   - Ⓒ 25 in.
   - Ⓓ 28 in.

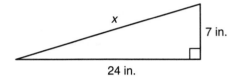

2. What is the length of the side labeled x?
   - Ⓐ 23.2 m.
   - Ⓑ 15 m.
   - Ⓒ 30 m.
   - Ⓓ 18 m.

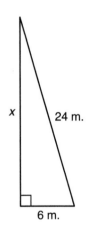

3. What is the length of the side labeled x?
   - Ⓐ 32 ft.
   - Ⓑ 5 ft.
   - Ⓒ 23 ft.
   - Ⓓ 15 ft.

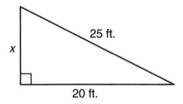

4. The isosceles triangle shown to the right has a base of 6 feet. The congruent sides are both 5 feet long. What is the height of the triangle?

5. Find the length of the diagonal $\overline{AB}$ of the rectangular prism shown below. Show your work.

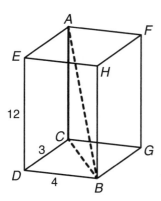

6. The cylinder shown below has a radius of 3 inches and a height of 8 inches. Find the diagonal of the cylinder. Show your work.

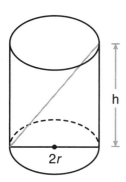

7. Ian wants to buy a big screen TV for his bedroom. The TV is 65 inches. This represents the diagonal. The height of the TV is 30 inches. The wall that Ian wants to mount the TV on is 5 feet wide. Does he have enough space, or should he buy a TV with a smaller screen? Explain your answer.

_____

_____

_____

_____

_____

(Answers are on page 237.)

THE DISTANCE BETWEEN TWO POINTS

G.B.8 Apply the Pythagorean Theorem to find the distance between two points in a coordinate system.

Use the Pythagorean Theorem to solve the problems in this section.

For questions 1 and 2, find the length of the line segment shown. Round your answers to the nearest tenth.

1. $\overline{AB}$ = _____

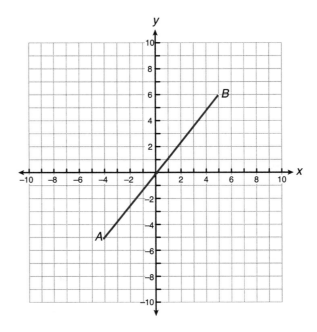

2. $\overline{RS}$ = _____

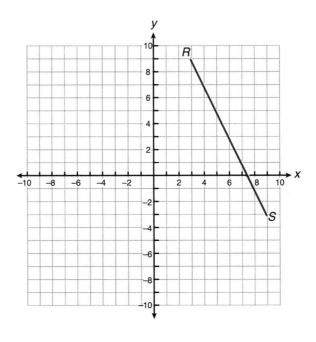

3. Which of the two line segments shown has the greater length?
Show your work.

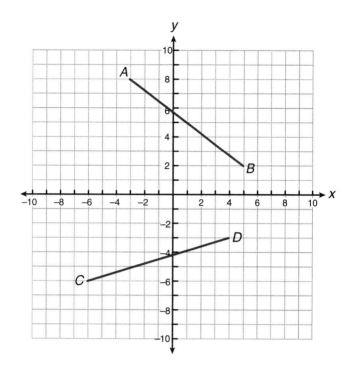

$\overline{AB}$ = _____

$\overline{CD}$ = _____

4. The coordinates of the endpoints of line segment *JH* are (–7, –6) and (–1, 2). Plot the points, and draw the line segment. Find the length of $\overline{JH}$.

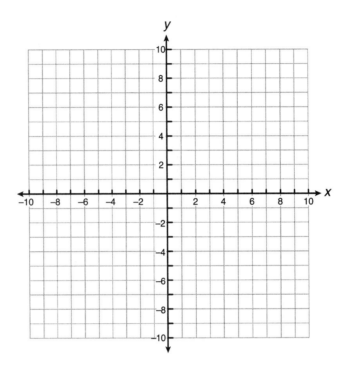

5. Find the length of diagonal *AC* for Rectangle *ABCD*. Round your answer to the nearest tenth.

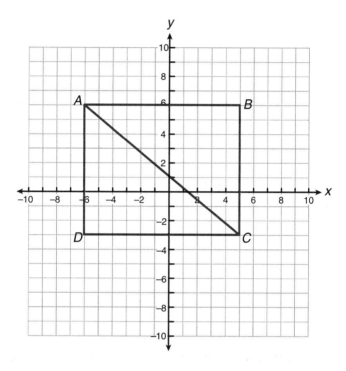

(Answers are on page 238.)

VOLUMES OF CONES, CYLINDERS, AND SPHERES

G.C.9 Know the formulas for the volumes of cones, cylinders, and spheres and use them to solve real-world and mathematical problems.

For this section, round your answers to the nearest tenth.

1. What is the volume of a soup can with a diameter of 8 cm. and a height of 10 cm.?
   - Ⓐ 2,010.6 cm.³
   - Ⓑ 502.7 cm.³
   - Ⓒ 251.3 cm.³
   - Ⓓ 201.0 cm.³

2. What is the volume of a beach ball with a diameter of 14 inches?
   - Ⓐ 1,436.8 in.³
   - Ⓑ 205.3 in.³
   - Ⓒ 11,494.0 in.³
   - Ⓓ 1,077.6 in.³

To solve these problems, you will need the following volume formulas:

$V = \pi r^2 h$ (Volume of a cylinder)

$V = \frac{1}{3}\pi r^2 h$ (Volume of a cone)

$V = \frac{4}{3}\pi r^3$ (Volume of a sphere)

3. James buys an ice cream cone, and his friend, Marissa, buys a cup of ice cream for the same price. They wonder if they are getting the same amount of ice cream. Both the cone and the cup have a diameter of 3 inches. The cup has a height of 2 inches and the cone has a height of 5 inches. Who got the better deal? Explain your answer.

_____

_____

4. Jeremy is making a model of the capital building in Washington, D.C.
    There is a dome on the top of the building. On his model, the dome has
    a radius of 3 inches. What is the volume of the dome?

5. Katie makes candles of different sizes. She needs to compare the volumes of the
    candles to determine the difference in the cost of the wax she will need. All the candles
    have a cylindrical shape. Her tallest candle is 12 inches high and the shortest is 4 inches
    high. They both have a diameter of 3 inches. What is the difference in the volume of the
    two candles?

6. Soccer balls come in different sizes. A size 5 soccer ball has a diameter of 8.9 inches.
    The diameter of a size 3 ball is 7.6 inches. What is the difference in the volumes of
    the two sizes?

(Answers are on page 239.)

CONSTRUCTING AND INTERPRETING SCATTER PLOTS

1. The following scatter plot compares the ages of a group of children with their shoe sizes. Which best describes the association?

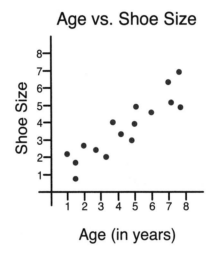

Age vs. Shoe Size

Shoe Size

Age (in years)

   Ⓐ Negative association
   Ⓑ No association
   Ⓒ Nonlinear association
   Ⓓ Positive association

2. The ordered pairs on a scatter plot are related but do not resemble a straight line. What type of association would you use to describe this data?
   Ⓐ Negative association
   Ⓑ No association
   Ⓒ Nonlinear association
   Ⓓ Positive association

Use the following graph and information to answer questions 3 and 4.

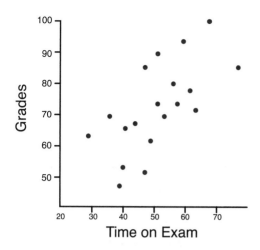

The scatter plot shown was constructed using data for the number of minutes that 8th grade students spent taking a final math exam and the grades (as percents) that these students received on the test.

3. Which of the following statements could **not** be used to describe the relationship between the time and the grades?
   Ⓐ The points indicate a positive association.
   Ⓑ The data set has no outliers.
   Ⓒ The relationship is nonlinear.
   Ⓓ The points do not cluster tightly. Therefore, there is a weak association.

4. Which statement is a reasonable interpretation of the data?
   Ⓐ If you take more time on a test, you will definitely improve your grade.
   Ⓑ Generally, the students that spend more time on the test receive a better grade.
   Ⓒ It really doesn't make a difference how long you spend taking a test.
   Ⓓ The more you study, the better your grade will be.

5. An outlier is
   Ⓐ a point or points that indicate a trend in the data.
   Ⓑ the highest point on a scatter plot.
   Ⓒ a point or points that do not follow the pattern of the rest of the data.
   Ⓓ the lowest point on a scatter plot.

Use the following information to answer questions 6–8.

The table below contains data from nine 8th grade students. It shows the daily average number of hours watching TV compared to the daily average number of hours playing sports.

TV (hours)	3	2	1	2.5	4.5	5	1	2.5	0.5
Sports (hours)	3	2	5	1	2	1	4	2	4

6. Create a scatter plot of the data on the grid below. Be sure to title your scatter plot, label each axis, and choose a scale that allows you to plot all the data.

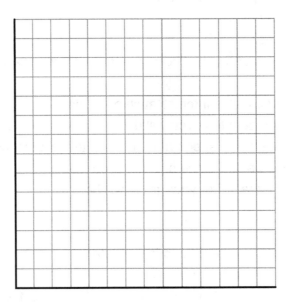

7. Based on the scatter plot, do you think that there is a relationship between watching TV and playing sports? Support your answer with observations about the data.

_____

_____

_____

8. Describe any clustering or outliers.

_____

_____

_____

(Answers are on page 240.)

LINE OF BEST FIT

SP.A.2 Know that straight lines are widely used to model relationships between two quantitative variables. For scatter plots that suggest a linear association, informally fit a straight line, and informally assess the model fit by judging the closeness of the data points to the line.

1. The line of best fit, or the trend line, for data displayed on a scatter plot should
    - Ⓐ intersect all the points on the scatter plot.
    - Ⓑ be as close to as many points as possible.
    - Ⓒ not intersect any points on the scatter plot.
    - Ⓓ intersect the first and last point on the scatter plot.

2. Jasmine makes a scatter plot of data she collected regarding attendance at school sports events from September to January. She draws a line of best fit to help her predict future attendance. Look at her graph below. What mistake did she make?

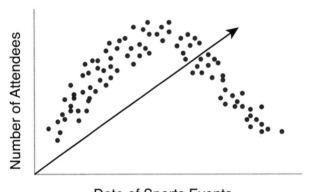

Date of Sports Events

- Ⓐ The data are curved, so her line should also curve.
- Ⓑ The data show an increase and then a decrease, but the data appear to be getting level. The line should be horizontal to indicate the average attendance.
- Ⓒ The data points do not indicate a linear association. She cannot use a line of best fit to predict future attendance.
- Ⓓ The line only intersects one point. It needs to be adjusted to be closer to more of the points in the scatter plot.

Use the following graph and information to answer questions 3 and 4.

Arm Span and Height

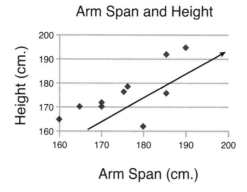

Amy recorded the height and arm span of 10 people in her family. She displayed the data in the scatter plot shown above. She drew a line of best fit and asked her math teacher if she had drawn it correctly. Her teacher said that the line did not accurately model the linear relationship of her data.

3. Make at least one observation about Amy's line, and describe how she could improve it.

_____

_____

_____

4. Use a ruler to draw a new line of best fit that would better represent the linear relationship in this scatter plot.

195

Use the following graph and information to answer questions 5–7.

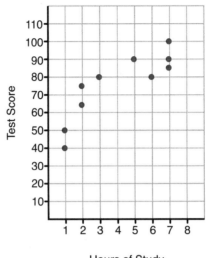

Hours of Study

The scatter plot above shows the hours studied and the test scores of 10 students in Ms. Stone's math class.

5. Choose one point on the scatter plot, and describe what it means in terms of the context.

_____

_____

_____

_____

_____

6. Based on the scatter plot, describe the relationship between test scores and hours of study.

_____

_____

_____

_____

_____

7. Draw a line of best fit for the data displayed in the scatter plot.

(Answers are on page 240.)

USING EQUATIONS OF LINEAR MODELS

SP.A.3 Use the equation of a linear model to solve problems in the context of bivariate measurement data, interpreting the slope and intercept. *For example, in a linear model for a biology experiment, interpret a slope of 1.5 cm./hr. as meaning that an additional hour of sunlight each day is associated with an additional 1.5 cm. in mature plant height.*

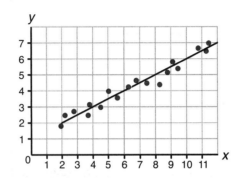

1. Which equation best approximates the trend in the scatter plot above?

   Ⓐ $y = -\dfrac{1}{2} + 2$

   Ⓑ $y = -2x + 1$

   Ⓒ $y = \dfrac{1}{2}x + 1$

   Ⓓ $y = 2x + 2$

Use the following table and information to answer questions 2–4.

Temperature (°F)	Total Sales ($)
58	220
62	330
54	190
59	340
65	410
72	520
67	410
77	620
74	540
65	450

The local ice cream shop records how much they sell and the temperature for 10 days. The data are shown in the table above. They are trying to predict sales based on the temperature.

2. These values will represent the coordinates of the points on a scatter plot.

   Part A. Which set of values will represent the independent variable (*x*)?

   Part B. Which set of values will represent the dependent variable (*y*)?

3. Construct a scatter plot of the data in the table. Label the *x*-axis and *y*-axis.

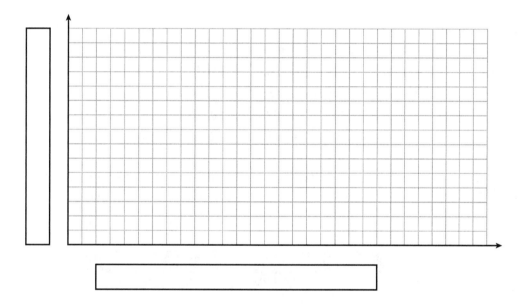

4. Draw a line of best fit for the data displayed.

(Answers are on page 241.)

USING FREQUENCY AND RELATIVE FREQUENCY TO DETERMINE PATTERNS

> **SP.A.4** Understand that patterns of association can also be seen in bivariate categorical data by displaying frequencies and relative frequencies in a two-way table. Construct and interpret a two-way table summarizing data on two categorical variables collected from the same subjects. Use relative frequencies calculated for rows or columns to describe possible association between the two variables. *For example, collect data from students in your class on whether or not they have a curfew on school nights and whether or not they have assigned chores at home. Is there evidence that those who have a curfew also tend to have chores?*

1. A two-way table can be very helpful in statistics. Some of its uses are listed below. Which of the following is *not* a use for a two-way table?
   Ⓐ A two-way table can help you organize bivariate data.
   Ⓑ A two-way table can summarize the results of a survey.
   Ⓒ A two-way table can provide coordinates for a graph.
   Ⓓ A two-way table can help in the calculation of relative frequencies.

2. The table below shows data collected from a random sample of people exiting a movie theater. They were asked their age and their movie preference. Complete the totals in the table.

Age Group	Movie Preference			Total
	Action	Drama	Comedy	
10–21	12	6	28	
22–33	18	20	20	
Total				

3. Using the data in the table for question 2, find the *row relative frequencies*, and complete the table below. Record the frequencies as decimals rounded to the nearest hundredth.

Age Group	Movie Preference			Total
	Action	Drama	Comedy	
10–21				
22–33				
Total				

4. Adam was organizing the school talent show. He thought it would be helpful to find out how many of the students that signed up to perform could play an instrument. 50 students signed up. Of the 35 girls that signed up, 28 can play an instrument. 10 of the boys also can play an instrument.

Part A. Complete the two-way table below using the information given.

	Plays Instrument	Does Not Play Instrument	Total
Boys			
Girls			
Total			

Part B. What is the total number of students that can play an instrument for the talent show?

_____

5. **Part A.** Using the data in the table for question 4, find the *row relative frequency* of the data, and complete the table below.

	Plays Instrument	Does Not Play Instrument	Total
Boys			
Girls			
Total			

Part B. Based on the relative frequency, what percent of students who enter the talent show play an instrument?

_____

To find the relative frequencies by row, write the ratio of each value to the total in that row.

Use the table and information below to answer questions 6 and 7.

	Group Class	One-on-One Trainer	Equipment	Total
Women	35	10	20	65
Men	6	12	30	48
Total	41	22	50	113

A survey was conducted at a local gym. They asked 113 of their members whether they preferred to attend a group exercise class, work out one-on-one with a trainer, or work out alone using the gym equipment. The results are shown in the table above.

6. Find the *row relative frequency* of the data, and record it as a percent rounded to the nearest tenth of a percent in the table below.

	Group Class	One-on-One Trainer	Equipment	Total
Women				
Men				
Total				

7. List three statements that you might include when summarizing this data.

1) _____

   _____

   _____

2) _____

   _____

   _____

3) _____

   _____

   _____

(Answers are on page 241.)

MATH PRACTICE TEST

My Name: _____

Today's Date: _____

Part 1

Directions: For questions 1–40, choose the best answer.

1. Which of the following numbers is not rational?

   (A) $\dfrac{2}{11}$

   (B) 5

   (C) $\sqrt{2}$

   (D) $0.\overline{345}$

2. Which one of the following fractions is equivalent to $0.\overline{27}$?

   (A) $\dfrac{2}{7}$

   (B) $\dfrac{27}{100}$

   (C) $\dfrac{27}{1000}$

   (D) $\dfrac{3}{11}$

3. Estimate $\sqrt{38}$ to the nearest integer.

   (A) 40

   (B) 8

   (C) 6

   (D) 30

4. Which one of the following expressions will result in a negative number?

   (A) -5^4

   (B) $(-3)^{10}$

   (C) 3^{-6}

   (D) $\left(\dfrac{2}{3}\right)^{-2}$

5. What is the value of $(3^2)^{-2}$?

    Ⓐ 3^4

    Ⓑ 3^0

    Ⓒ 1

    Ⓓ 3^{-4}

6. The legs of a right triangle measure 9 inches and 12 inches. What is the length of the hypotenuse?

    Ⓐ 15 inches

    Ⓑ 21 inches

    Ⓒ 12 inches

    Ⓓ 30 inches

7. A sphere has a volume of 972π ft.^{3} What is the radius of the sphere?

    Ⓐ 729 ft.

    Ⓑ   9 ft.

    Ⓒ 324 ft.

    Ⓓ   27 ft.

$$V = \frac{4}{3}\pi r^3$$

(Volume of a sphere)

8. Find the value of x in the equation, $x^3 = 27^{-1}$.

    Ⓐ 9

    Ⓑ $\dfrac{1}{3}$

    Ⓒ −3

    Ⓓ 3

9. Which value is equal to the expression, $\left(\sqrt{\dfrac{25}{49}} \times 5^{-2}\right)$, simplified?

    Ⓐ $\dfrac{1}{35}$

    Ⓑ $\dfrac{5}{7}$

    Ⓒ $\dfrac{1}{7}$

    Ⓓ $-\dfrac{1}{7}$

10. The population of Brazil is 202,033,670. Which of the following values would represent the best estimate of the population?

    Ⓐ 2×10^6

    Ⓑ 2×10^7

    Ⓒ 2×10^8

    Ⓓ 2×10^9

11. What is the value of $(7 \times 10^{-4})(2.6 \times 10^{-3})$ written in scientific notation?
  - Ⓐ 18.20×10^{12}
  - Ⓑ 1.82×10^{12}
  - Ⓒ 18.20×10^{-7}
  - Ⓓ 1.82×10^{-6}

12. Divide and write the quotient in scientific notation: $\dfrac{(5.49 \times 10^{5})}{(9 \times 10^{10})}$.
  - Ⓐ 6.100×10^{-6}
  - Ⓑ 6.100×10^{15}
  - Ⓒ 1.449×10^{-5}
  - Ⓓ -3.500×10^{-5}

13. Find the sum of (6.7×10^{8}) and (5×10^{4}). Express your answer in scientific notation.
  - Ⓐ 6.7500×10^{6}
  - Ⓑ 11.7000×10^{12}
  - Ⓒ 11.7000×10^{4}
  - Ⓓ 6.7005×10^{8}

14. Find the difference and express the answer in scientific notation: $(3.7 \times 10^{-3}) - 0.33$.
  - Ⓐ 3.370×10^{-3}
  - Ⓑ -3.263×10^{-1}
  - Ⓒ 4.000×10^{-2}
  - Ⓓ 3.263×10^{-1}

15. In February 2015, Boston's total snowfall was record breaking. One storm during the month lasted $7\frac{1}{2}$ hours with a total accumulation of 3 feet. What was the unit rate of the snowfall in inches per hour?
  - Ⓐ 2.5 inches per hour
  - Ⓑ 4.8 inches per hour
  - Ⓒ 150.0 inches per hour
  - Ⓓ 12.5 inches per hour

16. What is the slope of the line shown in the graph below?

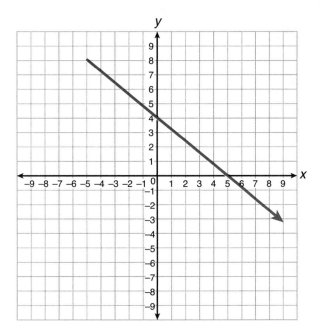

Ⓐ $\dfrac{4}{5}$

Ⓑ $-\dfrac{4}{5}$

Ⓒ $\dfrac{5}{4}$

Ⓓ $-\dfrac{5}{4}$

17. What is the solution to the equation shown?

$$2(x - 3) + 4 = 2x + 3x - 5$$

Ⓐ $-\dfrac{2}{3}$

Ⓑ $\dfrac{2}{3}$

Ⓒ -1

Ⓓ 1

18. Which of the following equations has no solution?

Ⓐ $2x = 3.25(x - 25)$

Ⓑ $2x + 4 = 2(x - 3)$

Ⓒ $6x - 3 = 2x + 4x - 3$

Ⓓ $4(x + 2) - 2x = 4x - 2$

19. The perimeter of a triangle is 40 inches. The longest side is twice the length of the shortest side plus 1. The third side is twice the shortest side minus 1. Which of the following equations could be used to find the lengths of all the sides of the triangle?

Ⓐ $(2x - 1)(2x + 1) = 40$

Ⓑ $(2x + 1) + (2x - 1) = 40$

Ⓒ $(2x + 1) + (2x - 1) + x = 40$

Ⓓ $3x = 40$

20. Lisa has two younger brothers. One brother is half her age and one is two years younger than she is. If you add all their ages together, the total is 28. Which of the following equations could you use to find Lisa's age (x)?

Ⓐ $x + 2x + \frac{1}{2}x = 28$

Ⓑ $x + \frac{1}{2}x + (x - 2) = 28$

Ⓒ $x + 2x + x = 14$

Ⓓ $3x - 2 = 28$

21. Two equations of a linear system are graphed. The lines are parallel. How would you describe the solution of this system?

Ⓐ The solution is one point that cannot be observed on the graph.

Ⓑ There are an infinite number of solutions to the system.

Ⓒ There is no solution to the system.

Ⓓ The system cannot be graphed. It must be solved algebraically.

22. When two equations in a system of linear equations intersect, which of the following statements is **not** true?

Ⓐ The point of intersection is the solution to the system.

Ⓑ The coordinates of the point are a common solution to both equations.

Ⓒ The coordinates of the point will work in only one of the equations.

Ⓓ If you solve the system algebraically, the result will be the same coordinates of the point of intersection on the graph.

23. Which set of coordinates is a solution to the system below?

$$\begin{cases} x + 2y = 12 \\ x - 2y = -6 \end{cases}$$

Ⓐ $(3, 4.5)$

Ⓑ $(2, 5)$

Ⓒ $(3, -4.5)$

Ⓓ $(5, 2)$

24. Line *n* passes through the points (0, –10) and (–2, 4). What is the equation of the line?

Ⓐ $y = -2x + 14$

Ⓑ $y = -7x + 10$

Ⓒ $y = -7x - 10$

Ⓓ $y = -10x - 7$

Slope formula

$$m = \frac{(y_2 - y_1)}{(x_2 - x_1)}$$

25. What is the slope of a line that passes through the points (2, 2) and (–4, –3)?

Ⓐ $m = \dfrac{1}{2}$

Ⓑ $m = \dfrac{5}{6}$

Ⓒ $m = \dfrac{6}{5}$

Ⓓ $m = -\dfrac{5}{6}$

26. Triangle *ABC* is located in quadrant 2 on the coordinate plane and is reflected over the *y*-axis, The Image *A′B′C′* is then reflected over the *x*-axis, producing the final image, *A″B″C″*. Which of the following rotations, if performed on the original figure, would have the same result?

Ⓐ 90° counterclockwise rotation

Ⓑ 90° clockwise rotation

Ⓒ 180° rotation

Ⓓ 360° rotation

27. A triangle is drawn on the coordinate plane. The coordinates of its vertices are all negative. The figure is rotated 90°, and then the new image is reflected over the *x*-axis. In what quadrant will you find the final image?

Ⓐ Quadrant 1

Ⓑ Quadrant 2

Ⓒ Quadrant 3

Ⓓ Quadrant 4

28. A triangle with the coordinates (1, –3), (4, –1), and (6, –5) is reflected over the *x*-axis. What are the coordinates of the image produced by the reflection?

Ⓐ (–1, –3), (–4, –1), (–6, –5)

Ⓑ (–3, 1), (–1, 4), (–5, 6)

Ⓒ (3, 1), (1, 4), (5, 6)

Ⓓ (1, 3), (4, 1), (6, 5)

29. Which set of ordered pairs does *not* represent a function?

Ⓐ (1, 7), (3, 8), (4, 2), (5, 9)

Ⓑ (1, 2), (2, 2), (2, 4), (4, 6)

Ⓒ (1, 5), (2, 5), (3, 5), (4, 5)

Ⓓ (2, 6), (3, 7), (4, 6), (5, 7)

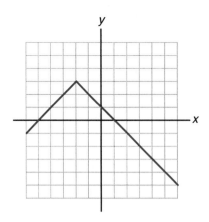

30. Which sentence best describes the graph shown above?
    Ⓐ The graph represents a linear function.
    Ⓑ The graph represents a nonlinear function.
    Ⓒ The graph does not represent a function.
    Ⓓ There is not enough information to determine if the graph represents a function.

31. Which equation represents a linear function?
    Ⓐ $y = 2\sqrt{x}$
    Ⓑ $y = x^3 + 7$
    Ⓒ $y = \dfrac{3}{4}x - 3$
    Ⓓ $x^2 + y^2 = 4$

32. Compare the two functions shown.

    Function 1

    $y = 3x - 5$

    Function 2

    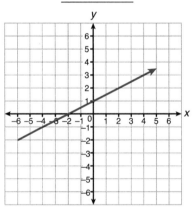

    Which statement about the functions is true?
    Ⓐ Function 1 has a greater rate of change than Function 2.
    Ⓑ Function 2 has a greater rate of change than Function 1.
    Ⓒ Function 1 does not have a constant rate of change.
    Ⓓ Both functions have the same rate of change.

Use the graph and the information below to answer questions 33 and 34.

Strike Bowling Alley's Price

Strike Bowling Alley charges a fee for shoe rentals plus an additional charge of $3 per game. The relationship of total cost (in dollars) to the number of games played is shown in the graph above.

33. What does the slope of the graph represent?
   Ⓐ The cost of shoes per game
   Ⓑ The additional cost per game
   Ⓒ The additional cost per hour
   Ⓓ The additional cost per person

34. Which function represents the total cost (y) of any number of games (x) played by one person?
   Ⓐ $y = 3x$
   Ⓑ $y = \frac{1}{3}x + 5$
   Ⓒ $y = 3x + 5$
   Ⓓ $y = 5x + 3$

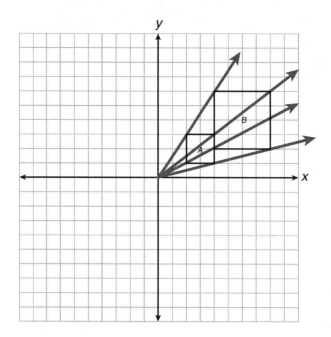

35. Figure *B* is an image produced by a dilation of Figure *A*. Which of the following statements is ***not*** true?
    Ⓐ The scale factor is 2.
    Ⓑ The origin is the center of dilation.
    Ⓒ The figures are congruent.
    Ⓓ The figures are similar.

36. A rectangular garden has a diagonal path. The dimensions of the garden are 3 feet by 6 feet. What is the approximate length of the diagonal path? (Estimate to the nearest integer.)
    Ⓐ 5 feet
    Ⓑ 6 feet
    Ⓒ 7 feet
    Ⓓ 27 feet

37. What is the exact volume of a sphere with a diameter of 6 inches?
    Ⓐ 288.0π in.³
    Ⓑ 36.0π in.³
    Ⓒ 27.0π in.³
    Ⓓ 113.1π in.³

$$V = \frac{4}{3}\pi r^3$$

(Volume of a sphere)

Use the figure and information below to answer questions 38–40.

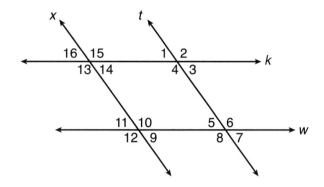

Line *k* is parallel to line *w*. Line *x* is parallel to line *t*. m∠16 = 50°.

38. Which pair of angles are corresponding angles?
    Ⓐ ∠11 and ∠2
    Ⓑ ∠2 and ∠8
    Ⓒ ∠11 and ∠16
    Ⓓ ∠3 and ∠5

39. Which pair of angles are alternate interior angles?
    Ⓐ ∠2 and ∠12
    Ⓑ ∠7 and ∠16
    Ⓒ ∠2 and ∠4
    Ⓓ ∠13 and ∠10

40. Find the sum of ∠1 and ∠7.
    Ⓐ 100°
    Ⓑ 180°
    Ⓒ 160°
    Ⓓ 360°

Part 2

Directions: For questions 41–50, show your work wherever possible.

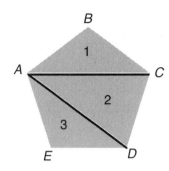

41. The figure above is a regular pentagon (all sides and interior angles are congruent). The diagonals drawn divide the figure into three triangles (1, 2, and 3). Of the three triangles, are any congruent? Explain your answer.

_____

_____

_____

_____

42. Alexis graphed the system of equations below, but she forgot to label the lines with the equations and label her solution. Label each line with its equation, and label the solution.

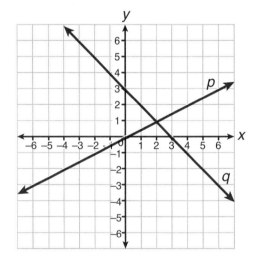

Check the solution in each equation.

43. Alexis graphs another system and says that there is no solution to the system because the lines do not intersect. Below is a picture of her graph. Do you agree with Alexis? Explain your answer.

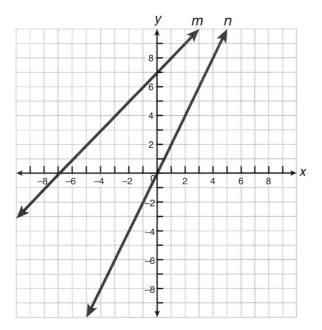

_____

_____

_____

_____

44. We can check Alexis's theory by solving the system algebraically. Determine the equations of each line, and solve the system algebraically. If there is a solution, check the solution in both equations.

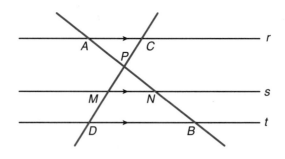

45. The lines *r*, *s*, and *t* in the figure shown above are parallel.
The measure of $\angle CAP = 35°$.

Part A. Based on the information given, are $\triangle CPA$ and $\triangle DPB$ similar?

_____

Part B. Explain your answer.

_____

_____

_____

_____

46. A manufacturer is shipping glass spheres in a box with a cylindrical shape.
The sphere fits perfectly.

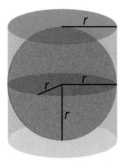

$V = \pi r^2 h$
(Volume of a cylinder)

$V = \dfrac{4}{3} \pi r^3$
(Volume of a sphere)

They need to calculate the remaining volume to determine how much packaging material must be added to protect the spheres. The radius of the sphere is 3 inches. What is the volume of the remaining space inside the cylinder? Show your work.

47. The figure shown below consists of a cone mounted on top of a cylinder with the same radius. Find the volume of the entire figure. Show all your work. Express your answer in terms of π.

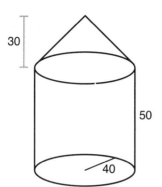

$V = \pi r^2 h$
(Volume of a cylinder)

$V = \dfrac{1}{3} \pi r^2 h$
(Volume of a cone)

48. In science class, students are studying phases of matter. They learned that during a phase change, the temperature does not change. For their lab, Carol and her partner took temperature readings and recorded their observations. They plotted their data as shown in the graph below.

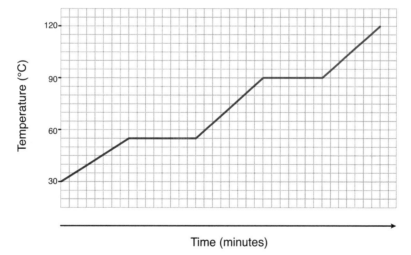

Describe what might have occurred during their experiment based on the data plotted.

_____

_____

_____

_____

49. Jennie surveyed middle school and high school students. She asked how many of them go out on school nights and recorded her totals in the table shown.

	Do you go out on school nights?	
	YES	NO
Middle School	45	55
High School	30	10

She concluded that middle school students are 1.5 times more likely to go out on school nights than high school students. Do you agree with Jennie? Make a row relative frequency table, and use it to support your answer.

_____

_____

_____

_____

_____

_____

50. The Adams family is planning a week-long vacation to Florida to visit family and go to an amusement park! They would like to rent a mid-size car while they are visiting. They compare two rental companies: Rent-O-Car and Budget Karz. Rent-O-Car charges $10 per day. Budget Karz charges an initial fee of $30 and an additional $5 per day.

Part A. Write an equation for each of the car rentals representing the total cost (y) for the number of days (x) that they rent the car.

_____

_____

_____

_____

Part B. Will there be a time when their rentals will cost the same amount? How did you determine your answer? If yes, after how many days?

_____

_____

_____

_____

Part C. If they rented the car for one week, which rental should they choose? Explain your answer.

_____

_____

_____

_____

(Answers are on page 242.)

MATH ANSWERS EXPLAINED

THE NUMBER SYSTEM

Rational and Irrational Numbers (NS.A.1), page 116

1. **B** Since 3 is not a perfect square, the square root of 3 is irrational.

2. **0.66... or 0.$\overline{6}$**

3. **0.1666... or 0.1$\overline{6}$**

4. **0.35**

5. $0.362 = \dfrac{362}{1000} = \dfrac{\mathbf{181}}{\mathbf{500}}$

6. $0.07 = \dfrac{\mathbf{7}}{\mathbf{100}}$

7. $0.256 = \dfrac{256}{1000} = \dfrac{\mathbf{32}}{\mathbf{125}}$

8. $0.75 = \dfrac{75}{100} = \dfrac{\mathbf{3}}{\mathbf{4}}$

9. **B** If you find the decimal expansion of the fraction, you will get the repeating decimal 0.55...

10.
$$x = 0.\overline{45}$$
$$100x = 45.\overline{45}$$
$$100x - x = 45.\overline{45} - 0.\overline{45}$$
$$99x = 45$$
$$\frac{99}{99}x = \frac{45}{99}$$
$$x = \frac{45}{99} = \frac{\mathbf{5}}{\mathbf{11}}$$

Rational Approximations of Irrational Numbers (NS.A.2), page 118

1. **C** $\sqrt{10}$ is between $\sqrt{9}$ and $\sqrt{16}$. Therefore, it is between 3 and 4. Since it is much closer to $\sqrt{9}$, 3 is the best estimate.

2. **C** To determine how many integers are greater than $\sqrt{25}$ and less than $\sqrt{72}$, you must find the square roots of all the perfect squares between the two radicals. They are 36, 49, and 64. The next perfect square would be 81, which is greater than 72. Therefore, 6 ($\sqrt{36}$), 7 ($\sqrt{49}$), and 8 ($\sqrt{64}$) would be the 3 integers.

3. **A** If you place $\sqrt{9}$ through $\sqrt{16}$ on a number line, you will be able to make some observations.

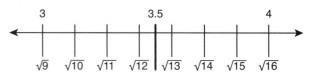

Note: The distances between the irrational numbers on the number line are not equidistant. You can see that 3.5 will be somewhere between $\sqrt{12}$ and $\sqrt{13}$. Therefore, $\sqrt{12}$ < 3.5.

4. A. **12**
   B. **14** (Estimate)
   C. **30**
   D. **3** (Estimate)

5. **D** 27.8 ft.^{2} is not reasonable given the range of the estimate given. The area of a circle can be found using the formula, $A = \pi r^2$. If the radius is 3 feet, then $A = \pi(3)^2 = 9\pi$. If we rearrange the equation by solving for π, we have $\pi = \dfrac{A}{9}$. Now you can substitute each of the choices in for the area.

   A. $\pi = \dfrac{A}{9}$, $\pi \approx \dfrac{28.0}{9} = 3.111...$

   B. $\pi = \dfrac{A}{9}$, $\pi \approx \dfrac{28.5}{9} = 3.1666...$

   All are within the range

   C. $\pi = \dfrac{A}{9}$, $\pi \approx \dfrac{28.7}{9} = 3.1888...$

   D. $\pi = \dfrac{A}{9}$, $\pi \approx \dfrac{27.8}{9} = 3.0888...$ ← Not in range

6. **No, Caitlin is not correct.** Since 5 is not a perfect square, the square root of 5 is irrational. It cannot be written as the ratio of two integers. The value displayed on the calculator is rounded and can be used to estimate the value of $\sqrt{5}$.

7. **No, they are not all placed correctly.** Most of the numbers are placed correctly in ascending order. However, $\sqrt{5}$ and $\sqrt{6}$ are both less than 2.5 and should be placed between 2 and 2.5 on the number line.

EXPRESSIONS AND EQUATIONS

Properties of Integer Exponents (EE.A.1), page 120

1. **C** $(-8)^3 = (-8)(-8)(-8) = -512$

    A. $(-2)^{-4} = \left(\dfrac{1}{-2}\right)^4 = \dfrac{1}{16}$

    B. $\left(\dfrac{1}{6}\right)^{-3} = 6^3 = 216$

    D. $(2)^7 = 128$

2. **C** $\left(\dfrac{1}{5}\right)^{-6} \times \left(\dfrac{1}{5}\right) = \left(\dfrac{1}{5}\right)^{-6+1} + 1 = \left(\dfrac{1}{5}\right)^{-5}$

    Using the properties of exponents, when you multiply like bases, you add the exponents. Therefore, all the choices, except choice C, are equal to $\left(\dfrac{1}{5}\right)^5$ or $\dfrac{1}{3125}$, which is equal to 0.00032.

3. **C**
    $2^5 \times 5^2 = 2^n \times 10^2$ (Factor $10 = 2 \times 5$)
    $\qquad = 2^n \times (2 \times 5)^2$
    $\qquad = 2^n \times 2^2 \times 5^2$
    $\qquad = (2^n \times 2^2) \times 5^2$
    $\qquad = 2^{n+2} \times 5^2$

    Now, the expressions are in similar form, and we can see that $n + 2 = 5$. Therefore, $n = 3$.

4. **A** $(3^2)^3 = 3^6 = 3 \times 3 \times 3 \times 3 \times 3 \times 3 = 729$

5. **C** $\dfrac{2^5}{4^2} = \dfrac{2^5}{(2^2)^2} = \dfrac{2^5}{2^4} = 2^{5-4} = 2^1$

6. **If you simplify this expression using the properties of exponents, you can see that this expression is equal to 1:**

    $\dfrac{3^2 \times 9^3}{3^8} = \dfrac{3^2 \times (3^2)^3}{3^8} = \dfrac{3^2 \times 3^6}{3^8} = \dfrac{3^8}{3^8} = 3^0 = 1$

7. **82** Using the order of operations and the properties of integer exponents, simplify the expression until it is in its simplest form.

    $$\dfrac{(2^2 - 1)^{12}}{3^6} \times 3^{-2} + 3^0$$

    $$\dfrac{(4 - 1)^{12}}{3^6} \times 3^{-2} + 3^0$$

    $$\dfrac{3^{12}}{3^6} \times \dfrac{1}{3^2} + 3^0$$

    $$\dfrac{3^{12}}{3^8} + 1 = 3^4 + 1 = 81 + 1 = 82$$

8. **Answers will vary.** Answers may include: The first error that Helen made was that she simplified the expression $(5^3)^2$. She incorrectly added the exponents and rewrote it as 5^5: $(5^3)^2 = 5^3 \times 5^3 = 5^6$. The second error that Helen made was that she simplified 5^5 as 25, but $5^5 = 5 \times 5 \times 5 \times 5 \times 5 = 3,125$.

Square Root and Cube Root (EE.A.2), page 122

1. **B** Start with the formula for the area of a circle, and substitute in the area given. Then solve for r:
    $$A = \pi r^2$$
    $$64\pi = \pi r^2$$
    Divide both sides of the equation by π.
    $$\dfrac{64\pi}{\pi} = \dfrac{\pi r^2}{\pi}$$
    $$64 = r^2$$
    $$\sqrt{64} = \sqrt{r^2}$$
    $$8 = r$$

2. A. $x = 7$

    B. $x = \dfrac{1}{10}$

    C. $x = 1.2$

    D. $x = 16$

3. A. $x = 3$

    B. $x = \dfrac{1}{2}$

    C. $x = 0.5$

    D. $x = 4$

4. **4 cm.** The length of the sides of the square will be 4 cm. Since you are given the volume of the cube, start with the formula for volume, and substitute in the given volume. $V = e^3$ (e is the edge of the cube, which is the same as the length of the side of the square.)
    $$V = e^3$$
    $$64 = e^3$$
    $$\sqrt[3]{64} = \sqrt[3]{e^3}$$
    Since $4 \times 4 \times 4 = 64$, $\sqrt[3]{64} = 4$
    $$4 = e$$

5. **25**
    $$3(\sqrt[3]{27}) + 2(\sqrt{64}) =$$
    $$3(3) + 2(8) = 9 + 16 = 25$$

6. **The length of each side of the square is 20 ft.**

First, you must find the area of the rectangle:

$A_r = L \times W$ (Area of a rectangle)
$A_r = (40)(10)$
$A_r = 400$ ft.^{2}

Now, you will be able to use the area to determine the length of the side of the square with the same area.

$A_s = s^2$ (Area of a square)
$400 = s^2$ (Substitute the value found into the formula)
$\sqrt{400} = \sqrt{s^2}$ (Find the square root of both sides of the equation)
$20 = s$

7. **Yes** Since $(-3)(-3)(-3) = -27$, $\sqrt[3]{-27} = -3$ and $-\sqrt{9} = -1(\sqrt{9}) = -1(3) = -3$. Therefore, the two expressions are equal.

8. Nora will need **1,296 squares**. One method of solving this problem:

First convert the square feet into square inches. Since each square foot will contain 144 square inches (12×12), multiply 81 ft.^{2} by 144.

$$81 \times 144 = 11,664 \text{ in.}^2$$

Next, since each square is 3×3 inches, we can determine that there are 9 in.^{2} in each small square. Last, divide the total area by 9 to determine how many squares will be needed.

$$11,664 \div 9 = 1,296$$

Estimating Very Large and Very Small Quantities (EE.A.3), page 124

1. **B**
$20^2 = 20 \times 20 = 400$
$400 = 4 \times 100 = 4 \times 10^2$

2. **C** $10^8 = 100,000,000$, which is the value that is closest to the actual value.

3. **7×10^3** $7,000 = 7 \times 1,000 = 7 \times 10^3$

4. **C** In order to determine how many times larger the world population is, you should set up a division problem. In this solution, we will use scientific notation to make the computations easier. Also, since this problem is asking for an estimate, the values may be rounded.

$$\frac{\text{world population}}{\text{population of China}} \quad \text{(Set up for the division)}$$

$$\frac{7 \text{ billion}}{1,365,370,000} = \frac{7 \times 10^9}{1.4 \times 10^9}$$

(Use rounded value for estimate)

$$\frac{7}{1.4} \times \frac{10^9}{10^9} = 5 \times 10^0 = 5 \times 1 = 5$$

5. **Part A: 2×10^{-4} m.** The actual value is 1.8×10^{-4} m., but since you are asked to express the value as a single-digit integer times a power of 10, you must round 1.8 to the nearest integer.

Part B: 1×10^{-10} m.

Part C: 2,000,000 times larger The diameter of the strand of hair is approximately 2 million times larger. If you round the diameter of the hair, you can use 2×10^{-4} m. to make the calculations easier.

$$\frac{2 \times 10^{-4}}{1 \times 10^{-10}} = \frac{2}{1} \times \frac{10^{-4}}{10^{-10}} = 2 \times 10^{-4-(-10)}$$

$$= 2 \times 10^{-4+10} = 2 \times 10^6$$
$$= 2,000,000$$

Scientific Notation (EE.A.4), page 126

1. A. **Yes**
   B. **Yes**
   C. **No** The first factor is less than 1.
   D. **No** The first factor is greater than 10.

2. A. **4×10^{-6}**
   B. **1.32×10^4**
   C. **5.08×10^{-1}**
   D. **1.3768×10^2**

3. A. **636,000**
   B. **0.000405**
   C. **50,000,000,000,000**
   D. **0.0000002**

4. **B** Simplify using the commutative property:

$$(3.7 \times 10^6)(2.4 \times 10^{-3})$$
$$(3.7 \times 2.4)(10^6 \times 10^{-3})$$
$$8.88 \times 10^3$$

5. **C** When adding numbers written in scientific notation, we want both of the numbers to have the 10 raised to the same power.

$$(4.3 \times 10^{12}) + (9.6 \times 10^{10}) =$$
$$(4.3 \times 10^{12}) + (0.096 \times 10^{12})$$

Using the distributive property:

$$(4.3 + 0.096) \times 10^{12} = 4.396 \times 10^{12}$$

6. **A** Similar to question 5, rewrite the problem.

$$(5.62 \times 10^6) - (3.9 \times 10^5) = (5.62 \times 10^6) - (0.39 \times 10^6)$$
$$(5.62 - 0.39) \times 10^6 = 5.23 \times 10^6$$

7. **C**

$$\frac{(3.6 \times 10^3) + (2.8 \times 10^3)}{8 \times 10^6}$$

To add numbers written in scientific notation, use the distributive property. The numbers must both be written using the same power of 10. Then, add the coefficients and keep the power of 10.

$$\frac{6.4 \times 10^3}{8 \times 10^6} = \frac{6.4}{8} \times \frac{10^3}{10^6} = 0.8 \times 10^{-3}$$

Now, rewrite the answer in scientific notation: 8×10^{-4}

8. The distance will be **1.674×10^8**.
   You must first determine that you are looking for the difference between the average distance and the anticipated distance. To subtract numbers that are written in scientific notation, we need to write both numbers using the same power of ten. It does not really matter whether you use 10^8 or 10^7. Usually, it is easier with the larger exponent, so that is what is shown here.

   $(2.25 \times 10^8) - (5.76 \times 10^7)$
   (Rewrite the second number using 10^8)
   $(2.25 \times 10^8) - (0.576 \times 10^8)$
   (Distributive property)
   $(2.25 - 0.576) \times 10^8$
   (Subtract coefficients)
   1.674×10^8

9. **12 million more people live in California.**
   To find how many more people live in California, you must subtract:

   $$(3.9 \times 10^7) - (2.7 \times 10^7)$$

   Since the exponents are the same, you can use the distributive property and then subtract.
   $(3.9 - 2.7) \times 10^7 = 1.2 \times 10^7 = 12,000,000$

10. **Part A: Eva entered $6.8 \times 10^8 \div 2 \times 10^5$ in her calculator.**
    Part B: Answers may vary. One possible method:
    Christina simplified the problem to estimate.

    $$\frac{6}{2} \times \frac{10^8}{10^5} = 3 \times 10^3 = 3,000$$

    Part C: Christina is correct. Eva forgot to use parentheses when she entered the

problem. It should have been entered as: $(6.8 \times 10^8) \div (2 \times 10^5)$. Without the parentheses, the calculator follows the order of operations. Therefore, operations would be completed from left to right, since there is only multiplication and division.

Proportional Relationships (EE.B.5), page 130

1. **A**

$$\frac{100}{2\frac{1}{2}} = \frac{x}{1}$$

$$2.5x = 100$$
$$x = 40$$

2. **C** To find the rate,

$$r = \frac{174 \text{ miles}}{3 \text{ hours}} = \frac{58 \text{ miles}}{1 \text{ hour}} = 58 \text{ miles/hour}$$

Using the formula $d = rt$, you can substitute in the rate. The result is $d = 58t$.

3. **C** The graph depicts the unit rate of 300 ft./min., (choice A), which is also the slope of the line (choice B). Therefore, choice C is not true.

4. **Part A:** $n = 40h$

$$\frac{\text{Number of bracelets}}{\text{Hours worked}} = \frac{140}{3\frac{1}{2}} = 40 \text{ bracelets per hour}$$

Part B: 200 bracelets
$n = 40h$
$n = 40(5)$
$n = 200$

Part C:

Hours (h)	2	4	6	8	10
# of bracelets (n)	80	160	240	320	400

5. **3.2 inches/hour** First, since you need the unit rate in inches per hour, rewrite the time in hours and fractions of an hour.

$$5 \text{ hrs. and } 45 \text{ min.} = 5\frac{3}{4} \text{ hrs.}$$

Now you can divide to find the unit rate.

$$\frac{18.4 \text{ inches}}{5\frac{3}{4} \text{ hours}} = \frac{x \text{ inches}}{1 \text{ hour}}$$

$$5.75x = 18.4$$
$$x = 3.2$$

6. **Michael will complete the marathon before Jose.**

   Explanations will vary. One possible explanation:

   From Jose's equation, we can tell by the slope that he is running at a rate of 4.5 miles/hour. From the table, you can determine that Michael is running at a rate of 4.6 miles/hour. Since $d = rt$, you can use $t = \dfrac{d}{r}$ to determine the approximate time each one will take to complete the marathon.

   Michael: $t = \dfrac{26 \text{ miles}}{4.6} \approx 5.7$ hours

   Jose: $t = \dfrac{26 \text{ miles}}{4.5} \approx 5.8$ hours

   Therefore, Michael will complete the marathon first.

7. **Part A:** $n = 420t$

   Part B:

t (time in hours)	Equation: $n = 420t$	n (number of gallons)
0	$n = 420(0)$	0
1	$n = 420(1)$	420
2	$n = 420(2)$	840
4	$n = 420(4)$	1,680

   Part C:

   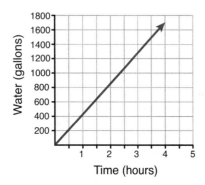

Slope of a Line (EE.B.6), page 134

1. **C** Slope $(m) = \dfrac{\text{Change in the } y\text{-value}}{\text{Change in the } x\text{-value}} = \dfrac{3}{2}$

2. **C** The equation with the slope that has the greatest absolute value will produce the steepest line. $\left| -5 \right| = 5$.

   A. $\left| 3 \right| = 3$

   B. $\left| \dfrac{2}{3} \right| = \dfrac{2}{3}$

C. $\left| -5 \right| = 5$ (Greatest absolute value)

D. $\left| 4 \right| = 4$

3. **D** This answer states that the slope of the line $\overleftrightarrow{AC}$ is equal to the slopes of the line segments from the similar right triangles that lie on the line.

Solving Linear Equations in One Variable (EE.C.7.A), page 136

1.

Equation	One Solution	Infinite Number of Solutions	No Solution
$\dfrac{2}{3}x = 12$	X		
$12x + 6 = 10x + 2x + 6$		X	
$3x = x + 12.7$	X		
$x + 3x + 3 = 4x + 2$			X

$\dfrac{2}{3}x = 12$

Multiply both sides of the equation by the reciprocal.

$$\dfrac{3}{2} \times \dfrac{2}{3}x = 12 \times \dfrac{3}{2}$$

$x = 18$ (one solution)

$12x + 6 = 10x + 2x + 6$

Combine like terms on the right side of the equation, and continue to simplify.

$$12x + 6 = 12x + 6$$
$$12x + 6 - 6 = 12x + 6 - 6$$
$$12x = 12x$$
$$\dfrac{12x}{12} = \dfrac{12x}{12}$$

$x = x$ (infinite number of solutions)

$3x = x + 12.7$

Combine like terms on the left side of the equation, and continue to simplify.

$$3x - x = x - x + 12.7$$
$$2x = 12.7$$
$$\dfrac{2x}{2} = \dfrac{12.7}{2}$$

$x = 6.35$ (one solution)

$$x + 3x + 3 = 4x + 2$$

Combine like terms on the left side, and continue to simplify.

$$4x + 3 = 4x + 2$$
$$4x - 4x + 3 = 4x - 4x + 2$$
$$3 \neq 2 \text{ (false statement——}$$
$$\text{no solution)}$$

2. **C** When you simplify the equation by subtracting $4x$ from both sides, the result is a false statement. Therefore, there is no solution.

$$4x + 6 = 4x - 3$$
$$4x - 4x + 6 = 4x - 4x - 3$$
$$6 \neq -3$$

3. **B**

$$5x + 2 = 3x + 2x + 2$$

Combine like terms on the right side. Continue to simplify, as shown.

$$5x + 2 = 5x + 2$$
$$5x + 2 - 2 = 5x + 2 - 2$$
$$5x = 5x$$
$$\frac{5x}{5} = \frac{5x}{5}$$
$$x = x$$

Choices A, C, and D are all true. When you simplify the equation, although the statement is true (choice A), there is no *one* solution. There are an infinite number of solutions (choice C). This means that any number, including 5 (choice D), will result in a true statement.

4. $x = 720$

$$\frac{x}{12} = 60$$
$$12 \times \frac{x}{12} = 60 \times 12$$
$$x = 720$$

Check:
$$\frac{x}{12} = 60$$
$$\frac{720}{12} = 60$$
$$60 = 60$$

5. $x = 1.82$

$$2x - 8.24 = -4.6$$
$$2x - 8.24 + 8.24 = -4.6 + 8.24$$
$$2x = 3.64$$
$$\frac{2x}{2} = \frac{3.64}{2}$$
$$x = 1.82$$

Check:
$$2x - 8.24 = -4.6$$
$$2(1.82) - 8.24 = -4.6$$
$$3.64 - 8.24 = -4.6$$
$$-4.6 = -4.6$$

6. $x = 1.3$

$$2.6x = 3\frac{19}{50}$$
$$\frac{2.6x}{2.6} = \frac{3\frac{19}{50}}{2.6}$$
$$x = 1.3$$

Check:
$$2.6x = 3\frac{19}{50}$$
$$2.6(1.3) = 3\frac{19}{50}$$
$$3.38 = 3\frac{19}{50}$$

Note: $3\frac{19}{50} = 3\frac{38}{100} = 3.38$

7. $x = 1.5$

$$\frac{4}{5}x - 0.2 = 1$$
$$\frac{4}{5}x - 0.2 + 0.2 = 1 + 0.2$$
$$\frac{4}{5}x = 1.2$$
$$\frac{5}{4} \times \frac{4}{5}x = 1.2 \times \frac{5}{4}$$
$$x = 1.5$$

Check:
$$\frac{4}{5}x - 0.2 = 1$$
$$\frac{4}{5}(1.5) - 0.2 = 1$$
$$1.2 - 0.2 = 1$$
$$1 = 1$$

8. $x = -\frac{7}{2}$

$$3x - 5 = 5x + 2$$
$$3x - 5 + 5 = 5x + 2 + 5$$
$$3x = 5x + 7$$
$$3x - 5x = 5x - 5x + 7$$
$$-2x = 7$$
$$x = -\frac{7}{2}$$

225

Check:
$$3x - 5 = 5x + 2$$
$$3\left(-\frac{7}{2}\right) - 5 = 5\left(-\frac{7}{2}\right) + 2$$
$$-10\frac{1}{2} - 5 = -17\frac{1}{2} + 2$$
$$-15\frac{1}{2} = -15\frac{1}{2}$$

Solving Multistep Linear Equations (EE.C.7.B), page 138

1. **$x = -1.6$**
$$7x - 2x + 10 = 2.5x - 2 + 8$$
$$5x + 10 = 2.5x + 6$$
$$5x + 10 - 10 = 2.5x + 6 - 10$$
$$5x = 2.5x - 4$$
$$5x - 2.5x = 2.5x - 2.5x - 4$$
$$2.5x = -4$$
$$\frac{2.5x}{2.5} = \frac{-4}{2.5}$$
$$x = -1.6$$

2. **$x = -60$**
$$1.6x - x + 4 = \frac{2}{5}x - 8$$
$$0.6x + 4 = \frac{2}{5}x - 8$$
$$0.6x + 4 - 4 = \frac{2}{5}x - 8 - 4$$
$$0.6x = \frac{2}{5}x - 12$$
$$0.6x - \frac{2}{5}x = \frac{2}{5}x - \frac{2}{5}x - 12$$
$$\frac{6}{10}x - \frac{2}{5}x = -12$$
$$\frac{6}{10}x - \frac{4}{10}x = -12$$
$$\frac{1}{5}x = -12$$
$$5 \times \frac{1}{5}x = -12 \times 5$$
$$x = -60$$

3. **$x = 1$**
$$12(x - 3) + 6 = -3(x + 5)$$
$$12x - 36 + 6 = -3x - 15$$
$$12x - 30 = -3x - 15$$
$$12x - 30 + 3x = -3x + 3x - 15$$
$$15x - 30 = -15$$
$$15x - 30 + 30 = -15 + 30$$
$$15x = 15$$
$$x = 1$$

4. **$x = 4.4$**
$$\frac{2}{3}(6x - 3) = 0.6(10x - 18)$$
$$\frac{2}{3}(6x) + \frac{2}{3}(-3) = 0.6(10x) + 0.6(-18)$$
$$4x - 2 = 6x - 10.8$$
$$4x - 6x - 2 = 6x - 6x - 10.8$$
$$-2x - 2 = -10.8$$
$$-2x - 2 + 2 = -10.8 + 2$$
$$-2x = -8.8$$
$$x = 4.4$$

5. **Franco is 12 and his dad is 36.** One possible method follows.

   Let x = Franco's current age, and let $3x$ represent his dad's current age. We can now write an equation that can use two different expressions to represent his dad's age in 10 years: 2 times Franco's age in 10 years plus 2 = his dad's age now plus 10

   $$2(x + 10) + 2 = 3x + 10$$
   $$2x + 20 + 2 = 3x + 10$$
   $$2x + 22 = 3x + 10$$
   $$2x - 2x + 22 = 3x - 2x + 10$$
   $$22 = x + 10$$
   $$22 - 10 = x + 10 - 10$$
   $$12 = x$$

   Franco is 12 years old. His dad is 3(12) or 36 years old.

6. **$x = 2$**
$$5x - 2(4x + 1) = 7(2x - 3) - 15$$
$$5x - 8x - 2 = 14x - 21 - 15$$
$$\text{(Distributive Property)}$$
$$-3x - 2 = 14x - 36$$
$$-3x + 3x - 2 = 14x + 3x - 36$$
$$-2 = 17x - 36$$
$$-2 + 36 = 17x - 36 + 36$$
$$34 = 17x$$
$$2 = x$$

7. **Part A: $5x = 2(2x - 0.2) + 2(x - 1.1)$**
   Part B: The perimeter of each figure is 13 units.
$$5x = 2(2x - 0.2) + 2(x - 1.1)$$
$$5x = 4x - 0.4 + 2x - 2.2$$
$$5x = 6x - 2.6$$
$$5x - 6x = 6x - 6x - 2.6$$
$$-1x = -2.6$$
$$\frac{-1x}{-1} = \frac{-2.6}{-1}$$
$$x = 2.6$$

Substitute the value for x into each expression, and find the perimeter of both figures.

Pentagon: $5(2.6) = 13$

Rectangle: $2(2 \times 2.6 - 0.2) + 2(2.6 - 1.1)$
$2(5.2 - 0.2) + 2(1.5)$
$2(5) + 3 = 10 + 3 = 13$

8. **Part A:** $w + w + 2w + 2w = 15$
Part B: The garden has a length of 5 meters.

$w + w + 2w + 2w = 15$
$6w = 15$
$w = 2.5$
Length $= 2w = 2(2.5) = 5$ meters

9. **Part A:** $4x = 2(x - 3) + 2(x + 3)$
$4x = 2(x - 3) + 2(x + 3)$
$4x = 2x - 6 + 2x + 6$
$4x = 4x$
$x = x$

Part B: No When you simplify the equation, there is no *one* solution. There are many solutions that will work for this situation.

10. **Seth has 30 cards.** There are various ways to solve the problem. One method is to set up an equation. Let $x =$ the number of cards that Christopher has. Then, let $2x =$ Seth's cards. After Christopher buys 10 more, they have a total of 55 cards.

$2x + x + 10 = 55$
$3x + 10 = 55$
$3x = 45$
$x = 15$

The number of cards that Seth has is $2x$ or $2(15)$, which is 30 cards.

Systems of Linear Equations (EE.C.8.A), page 140

1. **D** An infinite number of lines can be drawn through any point on a coordinate plane.

2. **B** (2, 11) is one of many points on the line; therefore, it is one of many solutions. Since it is a solution, choices A and C are both true statements. As stated in question 1, an infinite number of lines can pass through that point. Therefore, choice D is also a true statement.

3. **A** When two lines intersect, the point of intersection is a point that is on both the lines. Therefore, the coordinates of that point, when substituted into each equation, will result in true or correct statements. Choice C may seem correct at first. Although both equations will have an infinite number of solutions, there is only one common solution.

4. **B** This is the only statement that cannot be true. When you graph a system of two linear equations, the result is two lines. Those lines can be parallel (no solution), intersect at a point (one solution), or lie on top of each other (share infinitely many solutions). There will never be two points of intersection for two straight lines.

5. **C** (1, –2) are the correct coordinates of the point of intersection.

6. **Solution: (–3, –5)**

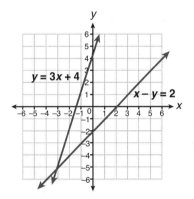

Point of Intersection = (–3, –5)

It is easier to graph the equation $x - y = 2$ if you rewrite it in $y = mx + b$ form, $(y = x - 2)$.
Check:

$y = 3x + 4$ $x - y = 2$
$-5 = 3(-3) + 4$ $(-3) - (-5) = 2$
$-5 = -9 + 4$ $-3 + 5 = 2$
$-5 = -5$ $2 = 2$

7. **Solution: (0, –4)**

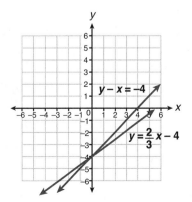

Point of Intersection = (0, –4)

Check:

$$y = \frac{2}{3}x - 4 \qquad\qquad y - x = -4$$

$$-4 = \frac{2}{3}(0) - 4 \qquad\qquad -4 - 0 = -4$$

$$-4 = -4 \qquad\qquad\qquad -4 = -4$$

8. **No Solution**

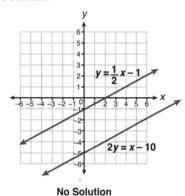

No Solution

Parallel lines

$$y = \frac{1}{2}x - 1$$

You can rewrite $2y = x - 10$ as $y = \frac{1}{2}x - 5$. (Same slope)

9. **Both equations graph as the same line.**

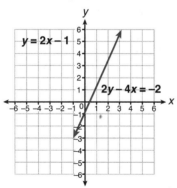

Infinitely Many Solutions

$y = 2x - 1$

$2y - 4x = -2$ (Rewrite in $y = mx + b$ form)

$2y = 4x - 2$ (Add $4x$ to both sides of the equation)

$y = 2x - 1$ (Divide both sides by 2)

Solving Systems of Linear Equations by Inspection and Algebraically (EE.C.8.B), page 142

1. **D** When two equations have the same slope, there are two possibilities. If the y-intercepts are different, then the lines are parallel. In that case, there would be no solution to the system. The equations could also represent the same line. If they graph as the same line, the system would have infinitely many solutions.

2. **C** If you divide every term in the second equation ($4x - 6y = 12$) by 2, you are left with the equivalent equation, $2x - 3y = 6$. This is the same equation as the first. Therefore, they will graph as the same line. The system will have infinitely many solutions.

3. **B** Both equations have a slope of $\frac{2}{17}$.

   However, the y-intercepts are different. Therefore, the lines will be parallel and not intersect. Also, the system has no solution because $2x - 17y$ cannot simultaneously be equal to 8 and 40.

4. **A** The slopes of the equations are different. The lines will intersect at a point, which is the one common solution for both equations.

   Note: For questions 5–7, there are many ways to solve these systems algebraically. Sample methods are presented below.

5. **Solution:** $\left(2, -\frac{7}{6}\right)$

   $$5x + 6y = 3$$
   $$2x - 6y = 11$$

   > Notice that the terms $6y$ and $-6y$ are opposites. Therefore, when they are added together, they have a sum of zero.

   If you add the two equations in the system, the y-term is eliminated, and you can solve for x.

   $$7x = 14$$
   $$x = 2$$

   Then, substitute the value for x into one of the equations and solve for y.

   $$5x + 6y = 3$$
   $$5(2) + 6y = 3$$
   $$10 + 6y = 3$$
   $$10 - 10 + 6y = 3 - 10$$
   $$6y = -7$$
   $$y = -\frac{7}{6}$$

6. **Solution:** $(-5, -31)$

   $$\begin{cases} y = 4x - 11 \\ y = 7x + 4 \end{cases}$$

   > Since both equations in the system are equal to y, we can write a new equation and solve for x.

$$4x - 11 = 7x + 4$$
$$4x - 11 + 11 = 7x + 4 + 11$$
$$4x = 7x + 15$$
$$4x - 7x = 7x - 7x + 15$$
$$-3x = 15$$
$$x = -5$$

Substitute and solve for y:
$$y = 4x - 11$$
$$y = 4(-5) - 11$$
$$y = -20 - 11$$
$$y = -31$$

7. **Solution: (12.5, 1.5)**

$$\begin{cases} y = \dfrac{3}{5}x - 6 \\ x = 5y + 5 \end{cases}$$

> In this system, we could use the substitution method that we used previously. Since both equations are set equal to one variable, you have a choice. Here, the expression for y from the first equation is substituted into the second equation. Then we can solve for x.

$$x = 5y + 5$$
$$x = 5\left(\dfrac{3}{5}x - 6\right) + 5$$
$$x = 3x - 30 + 5$$
$$x = 3x - 25$$
$$x - 3x = 3x - 3x - 25$$
$$-2x = -25$$
$$x = 12.5$$

Substitute and solve for y:
$$y = \dfrac{3}{5}x - 6$$
$$y = \dfrac{3}{5}(12.5) - 6$$
$$y = 7.5 - 6$$
$$y = 1.5$$

For questions 8 and 9, estimates are not given but your estimate should be reasonably close to the actual solution.

8. **Solution:** $\left(\dfrac{2}{3}, -1\right)$

$$\begin{cases} y - 6x = -5 \\ 2y + 3x = 0 \end{cases}$$

One possible algebraic solution:
$$y - 6x = -5 \text{ or } y = 6x - 5$$

Substitute the expression for y into the other equation.

$$2y + 3x = 0$$
$$2(6x - 5) + 3x = 0$$
$$12x - 10 + 3x = 0$$
$$15x - 10 + 10 = 0 + 10$$
$$15x = 10$$
$$\dfrac{15x}{15} = \dfrac{10}{15}$$
$$x = \dfrac{2}{3}$$

Substitute the x-value into one of the original equations and solve for y.

$$y - 6x = -5$$
$$y - 6\left(\dfrac{2}{3}\right) = -5$$
$$y - 4 = -5$$
$$y - 4 + 4 = -5 + 4$$
$$y = -1$$

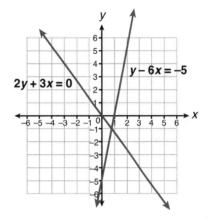

9. **Solution:** $\left(2\dfrac{2}{3}, 4\dfrac{2}{3}\right)$

$$\begin{cases} y = x + 2 \\ y = -\dfrac{x}{2} + 6 \end{cases}$$

Algebraic Solution: Since both equations have expressions equal to y, you can write a new equation with the expressions equal to each other. Then solve for x.

$$x + 2 = -\dfrac{x}{2} + 6 \quad \text{or} \quad x + 2 = -\dfrac{1}{2}x + 6$$
$$x + \dfrac{1}{2}x + 2 = -\dfrac{1}{2}x + \dfrac{1}{2}x + 6$$
$$\dfrac{3}{2}x + 2 = 6$$
$$\dfrac{3}{2}x + 2 - 2 = 6 - 2$$
$$\dfrac{3}{2}x = 4$$
$$\dfrac{2}{3}\left(\dfrac{3}{2}x\right) = \dfrac{2}{3}(4)$$
$$x = \dfrac{8}{3} = 2\dfrac{2}{3}$$

229

Solve for y:

$$y = x + 2$$

$$y = 2\frac{2}{3} + 2$$

$$y = 4\frac{2}{3}$$

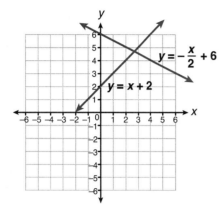

10. **Part A: Yes** You can determine that there will be only one solution. The equations are in $y = mx + b$ form. You can see that the slopes are different; therefore, the lines will intersect at one point.

Part B: Solution: $\left(1, 2\frac{1}{2}\right)$ One method that might be chosen is to set the two expressions, which are equal to y, equal to each other. Then solve for x.

$$\frac{1}{2}x + 2 = \frac{3}{2}x + 1$$

$$\frac{1}{2}x - \frac{3}{2}x + 2 = \frac{3}{2}x - \frac{3}{2}x + 1$$

$$-1x + 2 = 1$$

$$-1x + 2 - 2 = 1 - 2$$

$$-1x = -1$$

$$x = 1$$

Solve for y:

$$y = \frac{1}{2}x + 2$$

$$y = \frac{1}{2}(1) + 2$$

$$y = \frac{1}{2} + 2$$

$$y = 2\frac{1}{2}$$

Part C: Answers will vary.

1. **Part A: Yes** The lines intersect. If we are given two points, we can determine the slope of a line. The slopes are different. Therefore, the lines will intersect. Using an alternate method, we can plot the points and draw the two lines to see if they intersect. As shown below, the lines do intersect.

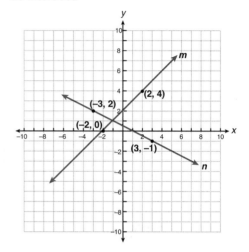

Part B: The coordinates of the point of intersection are **(−1, 1)**.

2. **Part A: No** The lines will not intersect. Using the same slope formula, we can determine that both lines have a slope of 2.

Line m: (1, 3) and (−3, −5)

$$m = \frac{(y_2 - y_1)}{(x_2 - x_1)}$$

$$m = \frac{(-5 - 3)}{(-3 - 1)}$$

$$m = \frac{-8}{-4} = 2$$

Line n: (0, −3) and (4, 5)

$$m = \frac{(y_2 - y_1)}{(x_2 - x_1)}$$

$$m = \frac{(5 - -3)}{(4 - 0)}$$

$$m = \frac{8}{4} = 2$$

Since both lines have the same slope, they are either the same line or parallel lines. In order to determine if the lines are parallel, we need to either graph the lines or determine the equations of the lines. To determine the equations, start with the standard form of a linear equation,

$y = mx + b$, and substitute in the slope ($m = 2$) and the coordinates of one of the points on the line. Then you will be able to determine the y-intercept (b).

Line m: (1, 3) and (–3, –5)

Using point (1,3):

$$y = mx + b$$
$$3 = 2(1) + b$$
$$3 = 2 + b$$
$$b = 1$$

Equation of line m is $y = 2x + 1$

Line n: (0, –3) and (4, 5)

Using point (0, –3):

$$y = mx + b$$
$$-3 = (2)(0) + b$$
$$-3 = 0 + b$$
$$-3 = b$$

Equation of line n is $y = 2x - 3$

Since the y-intercepts are different (and the slopes are the same), the lines are parallel and do not intersect.

Part B: There is no point of intersection.

For questions 3–9, the equations and variables used in the solutions represent only one way to solve each problem. There are many valid equations and variables that can be used to solve these problems.

3. Let x represent one number, and let y represent the other number.

   System: $\begin{cases} x + y = 1{,}068 \\ x - y = 116 \end{cases}$

   Answer: **The numbers are 476 and 592.**

4. Let x represent one number, and let y represent the other number.

   System: $\begin{cases} y = 3x \\ x + y = 48 \end{cases}$

   Answer: **The numbers are 12 and 36.**

5. Let k represent Katie's age, and let b represent her brother's age.

   System: $\begin{cases} k = b + 12 \\ k = 5b \end{cases}$

   Answer: **Katie is 15 years old.** (Her brother is 3.)

6. Let x represent the number of adult tickets, and let y represent the number of student tickets.

   System: $\begin{cases} x + y = 300 & \text{(Total number of tickets)} \\ 5x + 3y = 1{,}100 & \text{(Total dollar value of tickets sold)} \end{cases}$

   Answer: **200 students attended the performance.**

7. Let x represent the number of multiple-choice questions, and let y represent the number of extended-response problems.

   System: $\begin{cases} x + y = 38 & \text{(Total number of test questions)} \\ 2x + 5y = 100 & \text{(Total number of points for the test)} \end{cases}$

   Answer: **There are 30 multiple-choice questions on the test.**

8. Let l represent the length of the rectangular garden, and let w represent the width.

   System: $\begin{cases} 2l + 2w = 344 & \text{(Perimeter)} \\ l = 3w \end{cases}$

   Answer: **The length of the garden is 129 feet.**

9. Let j represent the price of one pair of jeans, and let s represent the price of one sweater.

   System: $\begin{cases} 2j + 2s = 80 \\ j + 3s = 62 \end{cases}$

   Answer: **The price of one pair of jeans is $29.**

10. Let y represent the total cost, and let x represent the number of hours.

    Part A:

    System: $\begin{cases} y = 2x + 20 & \text{(Derek—Rent-a-Ride)} \\ y = 5x + 10 & \text{(Jason—Deals on Wheels)} \end{cases}$

    Part B:

    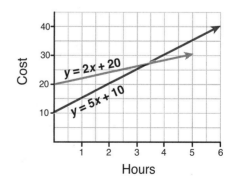

    Part C: A good estimate would be at $3\frac{1}{2}$ hours.

    Part D: Derek got the better deal. His total cost was $30. Jason had to pay $35.

FUNCTIONS

Functions (F.A.1), page 150

1. **B** A function is a rule that assigns to each input exactly one output.

2. **D** Choices A, B, and C are all true statements. However, the only reason why the equation represents a function is because for every input value (x), there is only one output value (y).

3. **A** In choice A, there are two sets of coordinates, (3, 3) and (3, 5), with the same input (x) but different outputs (y). Therefore, this set does not represent a function.

4. **Yes** For each input, there is only one output.

5. **No** When $x = 2$, there are three different y-values given. Also, when $x = 3$, there are two different values given for the corresponding y-value. Therefore, the coordinates listed do not represent a function.

6. **Yes** For each input (x), there is only one output (y).

7. **No** For the input value $x = 1$, there is more than one corresponding y-value.

8. **Yes** For each input (x), there is only one output (y). If you hold a straightedge or a pencil vertically, and slide it along the x-axis, it can help you determine if there is more than one y-value paired with any x-value. (This is sometimes called the vertical line test.)

9. **Yes** For each input (x), there is only one output (y).

Comparing Properties of Functions (F.A.2), page 152

1. **C** Function 1 does not have a constant rate of change. The rate of change is a ratio that compares the amount of change in the y-values to the amount of change in the x-values. The x-values show a steady increase of one, but the corresponding y-values show no pattern.

2. **A** Function 1 has a greater rate of change than Function 2. The rate of change for Function 1 is 2 ($y = 2x + 15$). When the equation is in $y = mx + b$ form, you can determine the rate of change by looking at the slope (m). For Function 2, we must look at the graph. We can see that for every 1 unit the y-value increases, there is an increase of 2 units in the x-value. So, the rate of change is $\frac{1}{2}$.

3. **A** Function 1 has a greater rate of change than Function 2. The rate of change for Function 1 is 3. The rate of change for Function 2 is 2.7.

4. **Olivia runs at a rate of 4.8 miles per hour.** You must convert the minutes to hours in order to find the miles per hour. If we add a row and write the time in hours, it may be helpful.

Miles (y)	2.4	3.6	9.6	8	4.8
Time in minutes	30	45	120	100	60
Time in hours (x)	$\frac{1}{2}$	$\frac{3}{4}$	2	$1\frac{2}{3}$	1

Now you can see that the

miles per hour = $\frac{\text{miles}}{\text{hours}} = \frac{4.8}{1} = 4.8$.

Check this by dividing any value for miles in the table by the corresponding time in hours. The result will be the same since Olivia is running at a constant rate.

5. **Marta runs at a greater constant rate.** By looking at the equation ($y = 5x$), you can see that she runs at a constant rate of 5 miles per hour.

6. **It will take Marta 5 hours.** Since the distance is 25 miles, we can substitute 25 for y in the equation and solve for x (number of hours).

$$y = 5x$$
$$25 = 5x$$
$$5 = x$$

7. **Marta will finish first.** Olivia is running at 4.8 miles per hour.

$$\frac{25}{4.8} = 5.2 \text{ hours}$$

To convert the remaining 0.2 hours:

5.2 hours × 60 minutes = 312 minutes

There are 300 minutes in 5 hours, so it will take Olivia more than 5 hours (approximately 5 hours and 12 minutes).

8. The approximate difference is **12 minutes**.

Linear and Nonlinear Functions (F.A.3), page 154

1. **C** A linear equation can be written in the form $y = mx + b$. Since the x-variable is squared, the equation cannot represent a linear function.

2. **C** If you think of a graph, two sets of ordered pairs will give you two points. The two points

will result in a straight line, which is only a segment of the graph of the function. You could not assume that the function was linear.

3. **B** $y = \frac{3}{4}x - 3.7$ represents a linear function in the form $y = mx + b$.

4. **Nonlinear** In a linear equation, no variable is raised to a power other than 1.

5. **Linear** The equation can be written in the form $y = mx + b$.

   $y - x = 5^2$
   $y - x = 25$ (Add x to both sides of the equation)
   $y = x + 25$

6. **Nonlinear** The graph of a linear function is a straight line.

7. **Linear** Since the rate of change (or slope) is constant $\left(\dfrac{\text{Change in } y}{\text{Change in } x} = \dfrac{4}{5}\right)$, the graph of these coordinates will result in a straight line.

8. **The graph of the area will be nonlinear.** Since $A = \pi r^2$, the squared term will result in a nonlinear graph. The graph of the circumference is linear since the formula is $C = \pi d$.

Constructing Functions (F.B.4), page 156

1. **C** $25 is the monthly service charge. If you look at the y-values, you will notice an increase of $25 each month.

2. **B** The installation fee can be determined by subtracting the monthly service charge from the first month's total cost ($175 − $25 = $150).

3. **D** From the table, we can see that there is a constant rate of change. Therefore, the function is linear and we can use the form: $y = mx + b$. The rate of change (m) is 25, and the initial value (b) is 150.

4. **Part A:** $y = 20x$ Since the initial value is zero, we can determine the rate of change or slope by choosing any point and determining the ratio of y to x. For example, look at the point (15, 300). The rate of change is $\dfrac{300}{15} = \dfrac{20}{1}$.

   Part B: The rate of change is $20 per pound.

5. **Part A:** $y = -\dfrac{1}{25}x + 15$

   Part B: $-\dfrac{1}{25}$ There is a decrease of one gallon in the tank for every 25 miles driven.

   Part C: The initial value is 15 gallons.

6. The easiest way to set up the table is to start at the bottom. We know he has $130 by the fourth month. Then work backwards, subtracting $20 each month.

Months (x)	Total Savings (y)
0	$50
1	$70
2	$90
3	$110
4	$130

7. $y = 20x + 50$

8. **The rate of change is 20.** As determined in the answer to question 7, the m value in the equation $y = 20x + 50$ is 20.

9. **The rate of change represents the monthly deposit of $20.**

10.

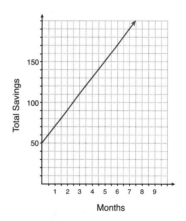

Analyzing Graphs (F.B.5), page 160

1. **C** The first part of the graph indicates a constant rate of distance over time. The second segment of the graph is a horizontal line. This means that as the time is increasing, the distance remains the same or there is no movement. Choice C is the only situation that describes a stop when Malcolm talks to his friend.

2. **Situation C** The y-axis represents the distance. The graph indicates a slow, constant rate at the

start of the time period. The sudden increase in the distance covered in a short amount of time (when Jessie starts to run) is represented by the increase in the slope of the line.

3. **Situation B** A pool draining at a constant rate would be represented by a linear function with a negative slope, as shown in Situation B. The function is decreasing. The y-axis would represent the number of gallons in the pool.

4. **Situation A** Although the sales at the start of the time period are increasing, they are not increasing at a constant rate. The graph in Situation A shows a nonlinear function with an increase that starts off slowly and then dramatically increases. The amount of sales would be represented by the y-axis.

5. **D** The horizontal line indicates that there was no change in the amount sold.

6. **B** The graph shows an initial rise (A) followed by a drop (B).

7. **F** In April, there is a drop (E) followed by a big increase in sales.

8. Since the stations are not the same distance apart, using the actual height provides a more accurate sketch of Amane's climb.

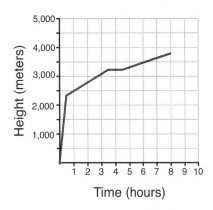

GEOMETRY

Properties of Rotations, Reflections, and Translations (G.A.1, G.A.1.A, G.A.1.B, G.A.1.C), page 164

1. **B** Reflecting a figure across a line "flips" the figure over the line to produce a mirror image.

2. **D** A translation is a transformation that slides every point of a figure the same distance in the same direction to produce a congruent image.

3. **A** A rotation is a transformation that turns every point of a given figure the same number of degrees around a fixed point to produce a rotated congruent image.

4. **B** Since the orientation of the figure is reversed, the image could not have been produced by a translation. There is no single reflection that would produce Image A'. A rotation of Figure A 180° around the origin will result in Image A'.

5. **D** Either B or D could be produced by sliding Figure A to produce either image.

6. **B** This is the only statement that will be true for *all* line segments regardless of length or position.

7. **Part A: Image 2**
   Part B: If you rotate *ABCD* 90° counterclockwise around the origin, it will produce Image 2.

8. **Part A: Image 3**

   Part B: If you translate *ABCD* 11 units to the right and 11 units down, it will produce the image shown as Image 3. When you place the traced figure over Image 3, you can see that they are the same size and shape.

9. **Part A: Your drawing should look like the drawing shown here.**

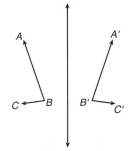

Part B: Answers will vary. Some possible observations are:
   - The angles have the same measure.
   - Point B and Point B' are the same distance from the line of reflection.
   - The angles look like mirror images.

10. **Part A: Yes** The lines are parallel because they have the same slope.
    Part B: Yes When parallel lines are reflected over a line (in this case it is the x-axis), the reflected lines are also parallel.

Part C: Answers will vary. Some possible predictions are:

- The slopes of the reflected lines will be different from the original lines.
- The slopes of the reflected lines will be negative.
- The reflected lines will both have the same slope since they are parallel.

Congruence and Transformations (G.A.2), page 168

1. **B** When a figure is rotated or reflected, the orientation will change, but the image will be congruent (same size, shape, and corresponding angles and sides).

2. **B** By observing the orientation of Figure *B*, you can see that the figure has been turned. Therefore, a rotation must be included in a possible series of transformations to produce Figure *B*. The figure appears to have been rotated 90° clockwise and then translated 9 units down. If Figure *A* were reflected, there is no line of reflection that would result in a figure with the same orientation as Figure *B*.

3. **Answers will vary.** Some possible answers are:
- Rotation and translation
- Reflection over the *x*-axis, reflection over the *y*-axis, and translation

4. **See graph below.**

5. **See graph below.**

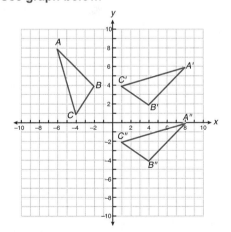

6. **Yes** Since the images are the result of a series of transformations (a rotation and a translation), all the figures are congruent.

7. **Answers will vary.** One possible answer is that you could translate Triangle *A″B″C″* 8 units to the left.

Transformations on the Coordinate Plane (G.A.3), page 170

1. **B** Two figures are congruent if their size and shape are the same. When a dilation is performed on a figure, the new image is either smaller or larger than the original figure depending on the scale factor.

2. **C** When a figure is reduced in size by a dilation, the scale factor is a fraction between zero and one.

3. **B** When the figure is moved 5 units to the right, 5 is added to the *x*-coordinate. When it is moved 2 units down, 2 is subtracted from the *y*-coordinate: $(x + 5, y - 2)$.

4. **B** When a figure is rotated counterclockwise 90°, the coordinates are switched and the first coordinate of the new point is negated: $(x, y) \rightarrow (-y, x)$.

5. **C** Both coordinates are multiplied by the factor of 2.5.

6. **See graph below.**

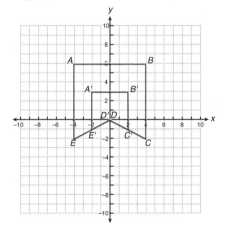

7.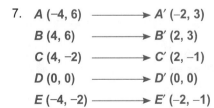

$A (-4, 6) \longrightarrow A' (-2, 3)$

$B (4, 6) \longrightarrow B' (2, 3)$

$C (4, -2) \longrightarrow C' (2, -1)$

$D (0, 0) \longrightarrow D' (0, 0)$

$E (-4, -2) \longrightarrow E' (-2, -1)$

Transformations and Similar Figures (G.A.4), page 172

1. **C** The angles are congruent, but one figure is 3 times larger than the other.

2. **C** Since the sizes of the triangles are different, we know that a dilation had to occur. The different orientation indicates a rotation.

Choice C is the only choice with both of these transformations.

3. **C** Since the sequence might include a dilation, we cannot assume that the figures will be congruent. You may be tempted to choose choice D, but remember, if the figure is not dilated, the ratio of corresponding sides will be 1:1. Therefore, choice D is a true statement.

4. **Answers will vary.** Here is one possible solution:
    (1) Reflection over the *x*-axis.
    (2) Translation (*x* + 6, *y* + 4).
    (3) Dilation by a scale factor of 2.

5. **No** There are many sequences that would have the same final result.

6. **Answers will vary.** Since the orientation of the figure has changed, a rotation or reflection had to occur.

7. **See graph below.**

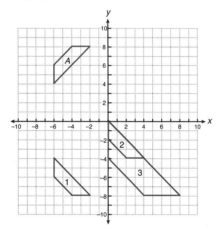

Angles of a Triangle (G.A.5), page 174

1.

Angle Pair	Congruent or Supplementary	If congruent, name the angle pair.
∠1 and ∠5	Congruent	Corresponding angles
∠4 and ∠6	Supplementary	
∠2 and ∠3	Congruent	Vertical angles
∠3 and ∠6	Congruent	Alternate interior angles
∠2 and ∠7	Congruent	Alternate exterior angles

2. **130°**
3. **130°**
4. **50°**
5. **180°**
6. **100°**
7. m∠*CAB* = 50°
    m∠*ACD* = 135°
    m∠*ACB* = 180 − 135 = 45°
    m∠*ABC* = 85°
    180 − (85 + 45) = 180 − 130 = 50

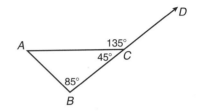

8. **x = 67°** The exterior angle of a triangle is equal to the sum of the measures of the two nonadjacent interior angles.

9. **m∠*DAC* = 120°** Explanations will vary. One explanation: Since Triangle *ABC* is equilateral, all the interior angles are equal and are 60°. ∠*DAC* and ∠*BAC* are supplementary and have a sum of 180°. 180 − 60 = 120.

10. **Yes** Since line *A′C′* is parallel to *AC*, ∠*BA′C′* and ∠*BAC* are corresponding angles and are congruent. (∠*BC′A′* and ∠*BCA* are also corresponding angles.) ∠*B* is common to both triangles and congruent to itself. Once again, if two pairs of angles in two triangles are congruent, then the triangles are similar.

Proof of the Pythagorean Theorem (G.B.6), page 178

1. **B** The side opposite the right angle is the hypotenuse.

2. **Side *c* is the hypotenuse.** It is opposite the right angle.

3. $b^2 = 4^2 = 16$

4. $c^2 = 5^2 = 25$

5. $a^2 + b^2 = c^2$
    9 + 16 = 25
    25 = 25

6. **Derek is correct.** You can check to verify that it is a right triangle by using the Pythagorean Theorem, $a^2 + b^2 = c^2$

$$6^2 + 8^2 = 12^2$$
$$36 + 64 = 144$$
$$100 \neq 144$$

7. **The conventional method is to label the side opposite the angle with the corresponding lowercase letter.** It is important to label the hypotenuse as c.

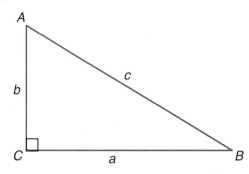

8. Measurement variations are expected but should be approximately the values shown.

Length of side a = **5.6 cm.**
Length of side b = **3.3 cm.**
Length of side c = **6.5 cm.**

$$a^2 + b^2 = c^2$$
$$(5.6)^2 + (3.3)^2 = (6.5)^2$$
$$31.36 + 10.89 = 42.25$$
$$42.25 = 42.25$$

9. **No** If the values are rounded to the nearest whole number, however, they will be equal. (Although this is a right triangle, it is unlikely, when we take direct measurements, that the values will be exact.)

10. **Answers will vary.** Our measurements are not exact. Therefore, there will be an expected difference in the values.

Applying the Pythagorean Theorem (G.B.7), page 182

1. **C**

$$a^2 + b^2 = c^2$$
$$7^2 + 24^2 = x^2$$
$$49 + 576 = x^2$$
$$625 = x^2$$
$$\sqrt{625} = \sqrt{x^2}$$
$$25 = x$$

2. **A**

$$a^2 + b^2 = c^2$$
$$x^2 + 6^2 = 24^2$$
$$x^2 + 36 = 576$$
$$x^2 + 36 - 36 = 576 - 36$$
$$x^2 = 540$$
$$\sqrt{x^2} = \sqrt{540}$$
$$x \approx 23.2$$

3. **D**

$$a^2 + b^2 = c^2$$
$$20^2 + x^2 = 25^2$$
$$400 + x^2 = 625$$
$$400 - 400 + x^2 = 625 - 400$$
$$x^2 = 225$$
$$\sqrt{x^2} = \sqrt{225}$$
$$x = 15$$

4. **The height of the triangle is 4 feet.** If we view the isosceles triangle as two congruent right triangles, we can use the Pythagorean Theorem to find the height. The congruent sides are 5 feet long. That means that the length of the hypotenuse of the shaded triangle is 5 ft. One of the legs would be half the base or 3 ft. (Note that the b in the illustration represents the base of the isosceles triangle.)

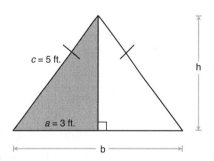

Using the Pythagorean Theorem,

$$a^2 + b^2 = c^2$$
$$3^2 + x^2 = 5^2$$
$$9 + x^2 = 25$$
$$9 - 9 + x^2 = 25 - 9$$
$$x^2 = 16$$
$$x = 4$$

The right triangle in this problem is a 3, 4, 5 triangle. This is known as a Pythagorean triple. Pythagorean triples are integer solutions to the Pythagorean Theorem. There are an infinite number of these triples. Some are easily recognized, like the 3, 4, 5 right triangle. You may want to investigate this topic!

5. **The length of the diagonal is 13.** To solve this problem, we need to use the Pythagorean Theorem twice. If you look at the base of the rectangular prism, you can see the right triangle *CDB*, which has been highlighted. This is a 3, 4, 5 triangle as mentioned in the previous problem. So, we know that the length of the diagonal *CB* is 5. You can see that the diagonal of *CDB* is also the leg of the "invisible" right triangle *ABC*. So, the legs of the right triangle *ABC* are $\overline{AC}$ and $\overline{CB}$. Their lengths are 12 and 5, respectively. $\overline{AB}$ is the hypotenuse. If we use the Pythagorean Theorem, we can determine that the length is 13.

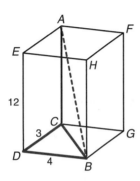

$$a^2 + b^2 = c^2$$
$$5^2 + 12^2 = c^2$$
$$25 + 144 = c^2$$
$$169 = c^2$$
$$\sqrt{169} = \sqrt{c^2}$$
$$13 = c$$

6. **The diagonal is 10 inches.** Visualize a right triangle. The diameter ($2r = 2(3) = 6$ inches) and the height (8 inches) of the cylinder are the legs of the triangle. The diagonal is the hypotenuse. Again, we can use the Pythagorean Theorem!

$$a^2 + b^2 = c^2$$
$$6^2 + 8^2 = c^2$$
$$36 + 64 = c^2$$
$$100 = c^2$$
$$\sqrt{100} = \sqrt{c^2}$$
$$10 = c$$

7. **Yes, Ian has enough space.** If you draw and label a picture, it will make it easy to solve this problem. We need to determine the length of the TV. So, we will use the Pythagorean Theorem.

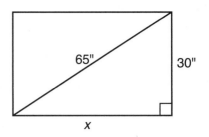

$$a^2 + b^2 = c^2$$
$$x^2 + 30^2 = 65^2$$
$$x^2 + 900 = 4{,}225$$
$$x^2 + 900 - 900 = 4{,}225 - 900$$
$$x^2 = 3{,}325$$
$$\sqrt{x^2} = \sqrt{3{,}325}$$

$$x \approx 57.7 \text{ inches}$$

Ian's wall is 5 ft., or 60 inches (5×12), wide. It will be tight, but the TV will fit!

The Distance between Two Points (G.B.8), page 184

1. **14.2 units** To solve this problem using the Pythagorean Theorem, you must construct a right triangle. Extend a verical line down from point *B* and a horizontal line to the right of point *A* until they intersect to form a right angle (as shown).

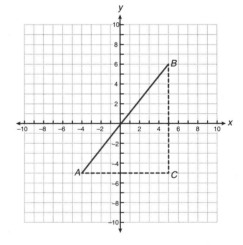

Now you can determine the length of the legs of the triangle using the coordinate grid. The length of $\overline{AC}$ is 9 units. The length of $\overline{BC}$ is 11 units. Substitute the values into the equation and solve for *c*.

$$a^2 + b^2 = c^2$$
$$11^2 + 9^2 = c^2$$
$$121 + 81 = c^2$$
$$202 = c^2$$
$$\sqrt{202} = \sqrt{c^2}$$
$$14.2 \approx c$$

2. **13.4 units** Use the same method as shown in question 1 to construct a right triangle with $\overline{RS}$ as the hypotenuse.

$$a^2 + b^2 = c^2$$
$$12^2 + 6^2 = c^2$$
$$144 + 36 = c^2$$
$$180 = c^2$$
$$\sqrt{180} = \sqrt{c^2}$$
$$13.4 \approx c$$

3. $\overline{AB}$ = 10 units
$\overline{CD}$ = 10.4 units (rounded to the nearest tenth)
$\overline{CD}$ **has the greater length.**

4. **The length of $\overline{JH}$ is 10 units.**

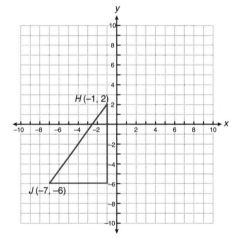

$$a^2 + b^2 = c^2$$
$$8^2 + 6^2 = c^2$$
$$64 + 36 = c^2$$
$$100 = c^2$$
$$\sqrt{100} = \sqrt{c^2}$$
$$10 = c$$

5. **The length of the diagonal AC is 14.2 units** (rounded to the nearest tenth).

$$a^2 + b^2 = c^2$$
$$11^2 + 9^2 = c^2$$
$$121 + 81 = c^2$$
$$202 = c^2$$
$$\sqrt{202} = \sqrt{c^2}$$
$$14.2 \approx c$$

Volumes of Cones, Cylinders, and Spheres (G.C.9), page 188

> All the volume formulas in this section require the radius of the solid. If you are given the diameter, divide by 2 to get the radius.
> $$r = d \div 2$$

1. **B**
$$V = \pi r^2 h$$
$$V = \pi(4)^2(10)$$
$$V = \pi(16)(10)$$
$$V = 160\pi \approx 502.7$$

2. **A**
$$V = \frac{4}{3}\pi r^3$$
$$V = \frac{4}{3}\pi(7)^3$$
$$V = \frac{4}{3}\pi(343) = 457\frac{1}{3}\pi$$
$$V \approx 1{,}436.8$$

3. **Marissa got the better deal.** We need to calculate the volume of the cone and the cup (cylinder) and compare the volumes.

Volume of Marissa's cup:
$$V = \pi r^2 h$$
$$V = \pi(1.5)^2(2)$$
$$V \approx 14.1 \text{ in.}^3$$

Volume of James' cone:
$$V = \frac{1}{3}\pi r^2 h$$
$$V = \frac{1}{3}\pi(1.5)^2(5)$$
$$V \approx 11.8 \text{ in.}^3$$

The cup contains more ice cream.

4. **The volume of the dome is 56.5 in.^{3}** To find the volume of the dome, you can use the formula for the volume of a sphere and divide it by 2.

$$V = \left(\frac{4}{3}\pi r^3\right) \div 2$$
$$V = \left(\frac{4}{3}\pi(3)^3\right) \div 2$$
$$V = (36\pi) \div 2 = 18\pi \approx 56.5 \text{ in.}^3$$

5. The difference in the volume of the candles is approximately **56.5 in.^{3}**

We need to calculate the volumes of the two candles and compare their volumes.

Large candle:
$$V = \pi r^2 h$$
$$V = \pi(1.5)^2(12)$$
$$V = 27\pi$$

Small candle:
$$V = \pi r^2 h$$
$$V = \pi(1.5)^2(4)$$
$$V = 9\pi$$

Since the larger candle is 3 times the height, the volume is 3 times greater. The difference is $27\pi - 9\pi = 18\pi \approx 56.5$ in.^{3}

6. The difference in the two volumes is approximately **139.3 in.^{3}**

Size 5 soccer ball:	Size 3 soccer ball:
$d = 8.9$ in.	$d = 7.6$ in.
$r = 4.45$ in.	$r = 3.8$ in.
$V = \frac{4}{3}\pi r^3$	$V = \frac{4}{3}\pi r^3$
$V = \frac{4}{3}\pi(4.45)^3$	$V = \frac{4}{3}\pi(3.8)^3$
$V \approx 369.1$ in.^{3}	$V = 229.8$ in.^{3}

$$369.1 - 229.8 = 139.3 \text{ in.}^3$$

STATISTICS AND PROBABILITY

Constructing and Interpreting Scatter Plots (SP.A.1), page 190

1. **D** The points generally increase from left to right.

2. **C** What is being described is a cluster of points that may form some kind of a curved pattern, but the pattern does not resemble a straight line.

3. **C** The statement "The relationship is nonlinear" is not true. All the points cluster roughly along a line that slants up from left to right with no outliers. The association is weak, positive, and linear.

4. **B** Based on this scatter plot, the students that spent more time on the test received a better grade.

5. **C** An outlier is a point or points that do not follow the pattern of the rest of the data.

6. **See graph below.**

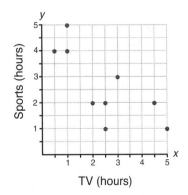

TV (hours)

7. **Yes** Generally, the more TV you watch, the less time you spend playing sports. Note: If you have Sports on the x-axis and TV on the y-axis, the scatter plot will still show a negative relationship.

8. **The points roughly cluster around a line that slants downward from left to right.**

Line of Best Fit (SP.A.2), page 194

1. **B** The line of best fit should be as close to as many points as possible.

2. **C** The data points do not indicate a linear association. She cannot use a line of best fit to predict future attendance.

3. **Answers will vary.** One possible answer: Ideally, the line of best fit should be drawn with about as many points above the line as there are below the line. It should be as close to as many points as possible. Amy could improve it by shifting it upward.

4. See **gray arrow** on the graph below.

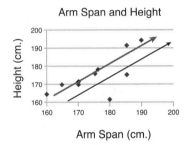

Arm Span and Height

5. **Answer will vary.** One possible answer: (5, 90). One student studied for 5 hours and received a 90% on the test.

6. **The more a student studied, the better his or her grade was on the test.**

7. **Answers will vary.** See the graph below for one possible line. Your line should be in a similar position.

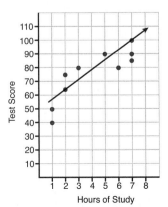

Hours of Study

Using Equations of Linear Models (SP.A.3), page 198

1. **C** The slope is positive $\frac{1}{2}$, and the line, if extended, would intersect the y-axis at 1.

2. **Part A:** The independent variable (x) is the **temperature**.

   Part B: The dependent variable (y) is the **Total Sales**.

3. See graph.

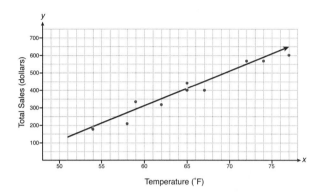

4. **Answers will vary.** See sample line on the graph for question 3.

Using Frequency and Relative Frequency to Determine Patterns (SP.A.4), page 200

1. **C** A two-way table cannot provide coordinates for graphing. A two-way table is a frequency table that displays categorical data.

2. See table below.

Movie Preference				
Age Group	Action	Drama	Comedy	Total
10–21	12	6	28	46
22–33	18	20	20	58
Total	30	26	48	104

3. See table below.

Movie Preference				
Age Group	Action	Drama	Comedy	Total
10–21	$\left(\frac{12}{46}\right) \approx 0.26$	$\left(\frac{6}{46}\right) \approx 0.13$	$\left(\frac{28}{46}\right) \approx 0.61$	1.00
22–33	$\left(\frac{18}{58}\right) \approx 0.31$	$\left(\frac{20}{58}\right) \approx 0.34$	$\left(\frac{20}{58}\right) \approx 0.34$	0.99
Total	$\left(\frac{30}{104}\right) \approx$ 0.29	$\left(\frac{26}{104}\right) \approx$ 0.25	$\left(\frac{48}{104}\right) \approx$ 0.46	1.00

4. **Part A:** See table below.

	Plays Instrument	Does Not Play Instrument	Total
Boys	10	5	15
Girls	28	7	35
Total	38	12	50

   Part B: 38 students

5. **Part A:** See table below.

	Plays Instrument	Does Not Play Instrument	Total
Boys	0.67	0.33	1.0
Girls	0.80	0.20	1.0
Total	0.76	0.24	1.0

   Part B: 76% of the students who entered the talent show can play an instrument.

6. See table below.

	Group Class	One-on-One Trainer	Equipment	Total
Women	53.8%	15.4%	30.8%	100%
Men	12.5%	25.0%	62.5%	100%
Total	36.3%	19.5%	44.2%	100%

7. **Answers will vary.** Some possible answers include:
   - Most of the women prefer group classes.
   - Most of the men prefer to work out alone on gym equipment.
   - Almost half of the members surveyed prefer to work out on the gym equipment.
   - Approximately 20% of the members surveyed prefer to work out with a trainer.

MATH PRACTICE TEST, page 204

Part 1

1. **C** This is the only choice that cannot be expressed as the ratio of two integers. Since 2 is not a perfect square, the square root of 2 is irrational.

2. **D**
$$x = 0.\overline{27}$$
$$100x = 27.\overline{27}$$
$$100x - x = 27.\overline{27} - 0.\overline{27}$$
$$99x = 27$$
$$\frac{99}{99}x = \frac{27}{99}$$
$$x = \frac{27}{99} = \frac{3}{11}$$

3. **C** 38 is not a perfect square so $\sqrt{38}$ is between 6 and 7. If you look at the two perfect squares that 38 is between (36 and 49), you can see that the value is closer to 36.

4. **A** $(-1)(5)(5)(5)(5) = -625$

5. **D** Multiply the exponents $(3^2)^{-2} = 3^{-4}$

6. **A** Use the Pythagorean Theorem to find the hypotenuse (c) of the right triangle.
$$a^2 + b^2 = c^2$$
$$9^2 + 12^2 = c^2$$
$$81 + 144 = c^2$$
$$225 = c^2$$
$$15 = c$$

7. **B** Substitute the volume into the volume formula and solve for r.
$$V = \frac{4}{3}\pi r^3$$
$$972\pi = \frac{4}{3}\pi r^3$$
$$\frac{972\pi}{\pi} = \frac{\frac{4}{3}\pi r^3}{\pi}$$
$$972 = \frac{4}{3}r^3$$
$$\frac{3}{4}972 = \left(\frac{3}{4}\right)\left(\frac{4}{3}\right)r^3$$
$$729 = r^3$$
$$\sqrt[3]{729} = \sqrt[3]{r^3}$$
$$9 = r$$

8. **B**
$$x^3 = 27^{-1}$$
$$x^3 = \frac{1}{27}$$
$$x^3 = \frac{1}{3^3}$$
$$\sqrt[3]{x^3} = \sqrt[3]{\frac{1}{3^3}}$$
$$x = \frac{1}{3}$$

9. **A**
$$\sqrt{\frac{25}{49}} \times 5^{-2} = \frac{\sqrt{25}}{\sqrt{49}} \times \frac{1}{5^2} = \frac{5}{7} \times \frac{1}{25} = \frac{5}{175} = \frac{1}{35}$$

10. **C** 202,033,670 rounded to the nearest hundred-million is $200{,}000{,}000 = 2 \times 10^8$.

11. **D** Use the commutative property to rewrite the problem:
$$(7 \times 10^{-4})(2.6 \times 10^{-3})$$
$$(7 \times 2.6)(10^{-4} \times 10^{-3})$$
$$18.2 \times 10^{-7}$$

This is choice C, which is the correct product, BUT it is not written in scientific notation. In order for the first factor to be a number between 1 and 10, divide the first factor by 10 and multiply the second factor by ten. The result is 1.82×10^{-6}, choice D.

12. **A** You can rewrite the problem as two separate division problems. This will make it easier to solve.
$$\frac{5.49 \times 10^5}{9 \times 10^{10}}$$
$$\frac{5.49}{9} \times \frac{10^5}{10^{10}}$$
$$0.61 \times 10^{-5} = 6.1 \times 10^{-6}$$

13. **D** In order to add numbers written in scientific notation, both numbers must have 10 raised to the same power. It is easier to use the greater power.
$$(6.7 \times 10^8) + (5 \times 10^4)$$
$$= (6.7 \times 10^8) + (0.0005 \times 10^8)$$
$$= (6.7 + 0.0005) \times 10^8$$
$$= 6.7005 \times 10^8$$

14. **B** For subtraction, use the same method used for addition.
$$(3.7 \times 10^{-3}) - 0.33$$

First, rewrite the second number in scientific notation.

$$(3.7 \times 10^{-3}) - (3.3 \times 10^{-1})$$

Since -1 is the greater exponent, rewrite 3.7×10^{-3}

$$(0.037 \times 10^{-1}) - (3.3 \times 10^{-1})$$
$$= (0.037 - 3.3) \times 10^{-1}$$
$$= -3.263 \times 10^{-1}$$

An alternate method: Write both numbers in standard form and subtract. Then, rewrite the difference in scientific notation.

15. **B**

3 feet fell in $7\frac{1}{2}$ hours

You must convert the feet to inches. Remember, there are 12 inches in 1 foot.

$$\frac{3 \text{ feet}}{7.5 \text{ hours}} = \frac{36 \text{ inches}}{7.5 \text{ hours}} = \frac{4.8 \text{ inches}}{1 \text{ hour}}$$

16. **B**

$$\frac{\text{Change in } y}{\text{Change in } x} = \frac{-4}{+5}$$

17. **D**

$$2(x - 3) + 4 = 2x + 3x - 5$$
$$2x - 6 + 4 = 5x - 5$$
$$2x - 2 = 5x - 5$$
$$2x - 5x - 2 = 5x - 5x - 5$$
$$-3x - 2 = -5$$
$$-3x - 2 + 2 = -5 + 2$$
$$-3x = -3$$
$$\frac{-3x}{-3} = \frac{-3}{-3}$$
$$x = 1$$

18. **B** When you try to solve this equation, the result is an inequality. This means that there is no solution. If you distribute the expression on the right side of the equation, you should be able to see that there will be no solution.

$$2x + 4 \neq 2x - 6$$

19. **C** Let x = the shortest side
   $2x + 1$ = the longest side
   $2x - 1$ = the third side
The perimeter is the sum of all the sides. Therefore, we can write the equation as:

$$(2x + 1) + (2x - 1) + x = 40.$$

20. **B** Let x = Lisa's age
   $\frac{1}{2}x$ = the age of one brother
   $x - 2$ = the age of the second brother

The total of all three ages is 28:

$$x + \frac{1}{2}x + (x - 2) = 28$$

21. **C** There is no solution to the system. Since the lines are parallel, they do not intersect.

22. **C** The statement "The coordinates of the point will work in only one of the equations" is not true. When two lines intersect, the coordinates of the point of intersection will work in both equations. The point is on both lines.

23. **A** The easiest way to solve this system is to add the equations and solve for x.

$$x + 2y = 12$$
$$\underline{x - 2y = -6}$$
$$2x = 6$$
$$\frac{2x}{2} = \frac{6}{2}$$
$$x = 3$$

Next, substitute the value for x into one of the equations. Then solve for y.

$$x + 2y = 12$$
$$3 + 2y = 12$$
$$3 - 3 + 2y = 12 - 3$$
$$2y = 9$$
$$\frac{2y}{2} = \frac{9}{2}$$
$$y = 4.5$$

24. **C** To write the equation of a line, you need to know the y-intercept (b) and the slope (m). Since the line passes through the point $(0, -10)$, we know the y-intercept.

$$y = mx + b$$
$$y = mx - 10$$

Since we are given a second set of coordinates $(-2, 4)$, we can substitute them into the equation to solve for m.

$$4 = m(-2) - 10$$
$$4 + 10 = -2m - 10 + 10$$
$$14 = -2m$$
$$\frac{14}{-2} = \frac{-2m}{-2}$$
$$-7 = m$$

Now we have the slope and the y-intercept, and we can write the equation.

$$y = -7x - 10$$

25. **B** We can use the coordinates to determine

the $\dfrac{\text{change in } y}{\text{change in } x}$.

$$m = \dfrac{-3 - 2}{-4 - 2}$$

$$m = \dfrac{-5}{-6} = \dfrac{5}{6}$$

26. **C** A rotation of 180° will produce an image located in the exact same position in quadrant 4 as Triangle $A''B''C''$.

27. **A** Since the coordinates of the figure are all negative, the figure is in Quadrant 3. The 90° rotation produces an image in Quadrant 4. Remember, unless specified, a rotation is counterclockwise. After a reflection over the x-axis, the final image is in Quadrant 1.

28. **D** When a figure is reflected over the x-axis, the y-coordinate will have the opposite sign of the original set of coordinates.

29. **B** The second and third sets of coordinates have an input of 2 with two different outputs (2 and 4). A function has only one output for every input. Therefore, this set cannot represent a function.

30. **B** By definition, a function is a rule that assigns a single output (y-value) for every input (x-value). Using the vertical line test, we can see that the graph depicts a function. Since the graph is not a straight line, the function is nonlinear.

31. **C** This is the only equation in the form $y = mx + b$.

32. **A** Function 1 has a greater rate of change than Function 2. The slope of Function 1 is 3. The slope of the second function is $\dfrac{1}{2}$.

33. **B** The graph has a slope of 3, which represents the additional charge of $3 per game.

34. **C** The 3x represents the additional charge per game, and the 5 represents the initial shoe rental fee.

35. **C** Two figures are congruent if their size and shape are the same. When a dilation was performed on Figure A, the new image, Figure B, is larger than the original figure and therefore not the same size.

36. **C** First draw a diagram of the garden. The diagonal forms two triangles. Since the shape is rectangular, the angles are 90°. The diagonal is the hypotenuse of both triangles, so we can use the Pythagorean Theorem to find the length of the path.

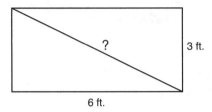

$$a^2 + b^2 = c^2$$
$$3^2 + 6^2 = c^2$$
$$9 + 36 = c^2$$
$$45 = c^2$$
$$\sqrt{45} = \sqrt{c^2}$$
$$6.7 \approx c$$

Rounded to the nearest integer, the answer is 7 feet.

37. **B** $d = 6$ inches $r = 3$ inches

$$V = \dfrac{4}{3}\pi r^3$$
$$V = \dfrac{4}{3}\pi(3)^3$$
$$V = 4((3)^2)\pi$$
$$V = 4(9)\pi$$
$$V = 36\pi$$

38. **C** When parallel lines (line k and line w) are cut by a transversal (line x), eight angles are formed. The four, lower angles are exact copies of the four top angles. Corresponding angles are angles that are in the same position and are congruent. Angle 16 is the acute angle on the top left. Angle 11 is the corresponding angle, which is in the same position in the lower group.

39. **D** Both angles are inside the parallel lines and on opposite sides of the transversal.

40. **A** Both angles are acute and congruent to ∠16. Therefore, they are both 50° and their sum is 100°.

Part 2

41. **Yes** △1 and △3 are congruent. ∠ABC and ∠AED are congruent as stated in the problem. A rotation of either figure would result in a congruent image over the other.

244

42.

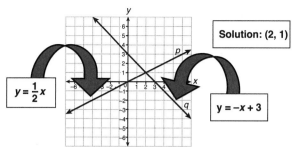

Solution: (2, 1)

$y = \frac{1}{2}x$

$y = -x + 3$

43. **No** Although the lines don't intersect on the graph, you can see that if they were extended, they would eventually intersect. You may also notice that the slopes are different. Therefore, the lines must intersect. You can determine the equation for each line by determining the y-intercept (b) and the slope (m) from the graph.

For line m:
$y = mx + b$
$y = (1)x + 7$
$y = x + 7$

For line n:
$y = mx + b$
$y = \left(\frac{2}{1}\right)x + 0$
$y = 2x$

$$\begin{cases} y = x + 7 \\ y = 2x \end{cases}$$

44. You can set the two expressions, that are equal to y, equal to each other. Then solve for x.

$$x + 7 = 2x$$
$$x - x + 7 = 2x - x$$
$$7 = x$$

Substitute the value for x into one of the equations, and solve for y.

$$y = x + 7$$
$$y = 7 + 7 = 14$$
$$x = 7 \text{ and } y = 14$$

Solution: **(7, 14)**

45. **Part A: Yes**

Part B: $\angle APC$ and $\angle DPB$ are vertical angles, and they are congruent. $\angle CAP$ and $\angle PBD$ are alternate interior angles, and they are also congruent. Since two of the corresponding angles in each triangle are congruent, the triangles must be similar.

46. The volume of the remaining space is 18π in.^{3} or approximately **56.5 in.^{3}** To solve this problem, you must find the volume of the sphere and the cylinder. Next, you must subtract the volume of the sphere from the volume of the cylinder.

> Since the sphere fits perfectly into the cylinder, the height of the cylinder is equal to the diameter of the sphere ($d = 2r$).

Volume of Sphere:
$r = 3$ inches
$h = 6$ inches
$V = \frac{4}{3}\pi r^3$
$V = \frac{4}{3}\pi(3)^3$
$V = (4)(9)\pi$
$V = 36\pi$ in.^{3}

Volume of Cylinder:
$r = 3$ inches
$h = 6$ inches
$V = \pi r^2 h$
$V = \pi(3)^2(6)$
$V = \pi(9)(6)$
$V = 54\pi$ in.^{3}

It is more accurate (and easier!) to leave the values in terms of pi. If you round, do it as the last step in you solution.

Volume of cylinder – Volume of sphere
= 54π in.^{3} – 36π in.^{3} = 18π in.^{3}

The volume of the remaining space is 18π in.$^3 \approx 56.5$ in.^{3}

47. This problem is similar to question 46. You must find the volume of each shape separately, but, in this problem, the volumes need to be added together to find the volume of the total solid shape.

Volume of a cone:
$V = \frac{1}{3}\pi r^2 h$
$V = \frac{1}{3}\pi(40)^2(30)$
$V = \pi(40)^2(10)$
$V = 16{,}000\pi$ units^3

Volume of a cylinder:
$V = \pi r^2 h$
$V = \pi(40)^2(50)$
$V = 80{,}000\pi$ units^3

Volume of the cone + Volume of the cylinder
= $16{,}000\pi$ units^3 + $80{,}000\pi$ units^3
= $96{,}000\pi$ units^3

The total volume is **$96{,}000\pi$ units^3**.

48. **Answers will vary.** The only label we have for the x-axis is that the time is in minutes. Some observations that might be included are:

- Initially, the temperature increased at a constant rate.
- There were two intervals when the temperature of the substance remained constant. This occurred at 55° and at 90°.

- Since the temperature did not change during these intervals, this may indicate a phase change.
- The graph shows an increasing nonlinear functional relationship.

49. **Row Relative Frequency Table:**

	Do you go out on school nights?		
	YES	NO	Total
Middle School	0.45 (45%)	0.55 (55%)	1.00 (100%)
High School	0.75 (75%)	0.25 (25%)	1.00 (100%)
	0.54 (54%)	0.46 (46%)	1.00 (100%)

No, Jennie is not correct. When we look at the frequency table, we can compare the percentage of each group that goes out on school nights. When we compare the 45% of the middle school students to the 75% of the high school students, we can see that more high school students go out. It is actually more than 1.5 times more likely that high school students will go out as opposed to middle school students going out $\left(\dfrac{75}{45} = 1\dfrac{2}{3}\right)$.

50. **Part A:** Rent-O-Car $\quad y = 10x$
Budget Karz $\quad\quad y = 5x + 30$

Part B: Yes. If you solve the system, the solution will represent the point when the cost and time are the same. (You could graph the equations.) If we set the expressions (that are equal to y) equal to each other, we can solve for x.

$$10x = 5x + 30$$
$$10x - 5x = 5x - 5x + 30$$
$$5x = 30$$
$$x = 6$$

Substitute $x = 6$ into one of the equations, and solve for y.

$$y = 10x$$
$$y = 10(6)$$
$$y = 60$$

Solution: **(6, 60) The solution means that after 6 days (x), both rentals would cost the same amount, $60 ($y$).**

Part C: To find the cost to rent the car for one week, substitute 7 for x in each question.

Rent-O-Car:	Budget Karz:
$y = 10x$	$y = 5x + 30$
$y = 10(7)$	$y = 5(7) + 30$
$y = 70$	$y = 35 + 30 = 65$

If they are renting a car for the whole week, they should choose Budget Karz. The cost will be $5 less than at Rent-O-Car.

APPENDIX A

ENGLISH LANGUAGE ARTS STANDARDS

Reading: Literature
CCSS.ELA-Literacy.RL.8.1 Cite the textual evidence that most strongly supports an analysis of what the text says explicitly as well as inferences drawn from the text.
CCSS.ELA-Literacy.RL.8.2 Determine a theme or central idea of a text and analyze its development over the course of the text, including its relationship to the characters, setting, and plot; provide an objective summary of the text.
CCSS.ELA-Literacy.RL.8.3 Analyze how particular lines of dialogue or incidents in a story or drama propel the action, reveal aspects of a character, or provoke a decision.
CCSS.ELA-Literacy.RL.8.4 Determine the meaning of words and phrases as they are used in a text, including figurative and connotative meanings; analyze the impact of specific word choices on meaning and tone, including analogies or allusions to other texts.
CCSS.ELA-Literacy.RL.8.5 Compare and contrast the structure of two or more texts and analyze how the differing structure of each text contributes to its meaning and style.
CCSS.ELA-Literacy.RL.8.6 Analyze how differences in the points of view of the characters and the audience or reader (e.g., created through the use of dramatic irony) create such effects as suspense or humor.
CCSS.ELA-Literacy.RL.8.7 Analyze the extent to which a filmed or live production of a story or drama stays faithful to or departs from the text or script, evaluating the choices made by the director or actors.
CCSS.ELA-Literacy.RL.8.8 (RL.8.8 not applicable to literature)
CCSS.ELA-Literacy.RL.8.9 Analyze how a modern work of fiction draws on themes, patterns of events, or character types from myths, traditional stories, or religious works such as the Bible, including describing how the material is rendered new.
CCSS.ELA-Literacy.RL.8.10 By the end of the year, read and comprehend literature, including stories, dramas, and poems, at the high end of grades 6–8 text complexity band independently and proficiently.

Reading: Informational Text
CCSS.ELA-Literacy.RI.8.1 Cite the textual evidence that most strongly supports an analysis of what the text says explicitly as well as inferences drawn from the text.
CCSS.ELA-Literacy.RI.8.2 Determine a central idea of a text and analyze its development over the course of the text, including its relationship to supporting ideas; provide an objective summary of the text.
CCSS.ELA-Literacy.RI.8.3 Analyze how a text makes connections among and distinctions between individuals, ideas, or events (e.g., through comparisons, analogies, or categories).
CCSS.ELA-Literacy.RI.8.4 Determine the meaning of words and phrases as they are used in a text, including figurative, connotative, and technical meanings; analyze the impact of specific word choices on meaning and tone, including analogies or allusions to other texts.
CCSS.ELA-Literacy.RI.8.5 Analyze in detail the structure of a specific paragraph in a text, including the role of particular sentences in developing and refining a key concept.
CCSS.ELA-Literacy.RI.8.6 Determine an author's point of view or purpose in a text and analyze how the author acknowledges and responds to conflicting evidence or viewpoints.
CCSS.ELA-Literacy.RI.8.7 Evaluate the advantages and disadvantages of using different mediums (e.g., print or digital text, video, multimedia) to present a particular topic or idea.

CCSS.ELA-Literacy.RI.8.8 Delineate and evaluate the argument and specific claims in a text, assessing whether the reasoning is sound and the evidence is relevant and sufficient; recognize when irrelevant evidence is introduced.

CCSS.ELA-Literacy.RI.8.9 Analyze a case in which two or more texts provide conflicting information on the same topic and identify where the texts disagree on matters of fact or interpretation.

CCSS.ELA-Literacy.RI.8.10 By the end of the year, read and comprehend literary nonfiction at the high end of the grades 6–8 text complexity band independently and proficiently.

Writing

CCSS.ELA-Literacy.W.8.1 Write arguments to support claims with clear reasons and relevant evidence.

CCSS.ELA-Literacy.W.8.1.A Introduce claim(s), acknowledge and distinguish the claim(s) from alternate or opposing claims, and organize the reasons and evidence logically.

CCSS.ELA-Literacy.W.8.1.B Support claim(s) with logical reasoning and relevant evidence, using accurate, credible sources and demonstrating an understanding of the topic or text.

CCSS.ELA-Literacy.W.8.1.C Use words, phrases, and clauses to create cohesion and clarify the relationships among claim(s), counterclaims, reasons, and evidence.

CCSS.ELA-Literacy.W.8.1.D Establish and maintain a formal style.

CCSS.ELA-Literacy.W.8.1.E Provide a concluding statement or section that follows from and supports the argument presented.

CCSS.ELA-Literacy.W.8.2 Write informative/explanatory texts to examine a topic and convey ideas, concepts, and information through the selection, organization, and analysis of relevant content.

CCSS.ELA-Literacy.W.8.2.A Introduce a topic clearly, previewing what is to follow; organize ideas, concepts, and information into broader categories; include formatting (e.g., headings), graphics (e.g., charts, tables), and multimedia when useful to aiding comprehension.

CCSS.ELA-Literacy.W.8.2.B Develop the topic with relevant, well-chosen facts, definitions, concrete details, quotations, or other information and examples.

CCSS.ELA-Literacy.W.8.2.C Use appropriate and varied transitions to create cohesion and clarify the relationships among ideas and concepts.

CCSS.ELA-Literacy.W.8.2.D Use precise language and domain-specific vocabulary to inform about or explain the topic.

CCSS.ELA-Literacy.W.8.2.E Establish and maintain a formal style.

CCSS.ELA-Literacy.W.8.2.F Provide a concluding statement or section that follows from and supports the information or explanation presented.

CCSS.ELA-Literacy.W.8.3 Write narratives to develop real or imagined experiences or events using effective technique, relevant descriptive details, and well-structured event sequences.

CCSS.ELA-Literacy.W.8.3.A Engage and orient the reader by establishing a context and point of view and introducing a narrator and/or characters; organize an event sequence that unfolds naturally and logically.

CCSS.ELA-Literacy.W.8.3.B Use narrative techniques, such as dialogue, pacing, description, and reflection, to develop experiences, events, and/or characters.

CCSS.ELA-Literacy.W.8.3.C Use a variety of transition words, phrases, and clauses to convey sequence, signal shifts from one time frame or setting to another, and show the relationships among experiences and events.

CCSS.ELA-Literacy.W.8.3.D Use precise words and phrases, relevant descriptive details, and sensory language to capture the action and convey experiences and events.

CCSS.ELA-Literacy.W.8.3.E Provide a conclusion that follows from and reflects on the narrated experiences or events.

CCSS.ELA-Literacy.W.8.4 Produce clear and coherent writing in which the development, organization, and style are appropriate to task, purpose, and audience. (Grade-specific expectations for writing types are defined in standards 1–3 above.)

CCSS.ELA-Literacy.W.8.5 With some guidance and support from peers and adults, develop and strengthen writing as needed by planning, revising, editing, rewriting, or trying a new approach, focusing on how well purpose and audience have been addressed. (Editing for conventions should demonstrate command of Language standards 1–3 up to and including grade 8.)

CCSS.ELA-Literacy.W.8.6 Use technology, including the Internet, to produce and publish writing and present the relationships between information and ideas efficiently as well as to interact and collaborate with others.

CCSS.ELA-Literacy.W.8.7 Conduct short research projects to answer a question (including a self-generated question), drawing on several sources and generating additional related, focused questions that allow for multiple avenues of exploration.

CCSS.ELA-Literacy.W.8.8 Gather relevant information from multiple print and digital sources, using search terms effectively; assess the credibility and accuracy of each source; and quote or paraphrase the data and conclusions of others while avoiding plagiarism and following a standard format for citation.

CCSS.ELA-Literacy.W.8.9 Draw evidence from literary or informational texts to support analysis, reflection, and research.

> CCSS.ELA-Literacy. 8.9.A Apply *grade 8 Reading standards* to literature (e.g., "Analyze how a modern work of fiction draws on themes, patterns of events, or character types from myths, traditional stories, or religious works such as the Bible, including describing how the material is rendered new").
>
> CCSS.ELA-Literacy.8.9.B Apply *grade 8 Reading standards* to literary nonfiction (e.g., "Delineate and evaluate the argument and specific claims in a text, assessing whether the reasoning is sound and the evidence is relevant and sufficient; recognize when irrelevant evidence is introduced").

CCSS.ELA-Literacy.W.8.10 Write routinely over extended time frames (time for research, reflection, and revision) and shorter time frames (a single sitting or a day or two) for a range of discipline-specific tasks, purposes, and audiences.

Speaking and Listening

CCSS.ELA-Literacy.SL.8.1 Engage effectively in a range of collaborative discussions (one-on-one, in groups, and teacher-led) with diverse partners on grade 8 topics, texts, and issues, building on others' ideas and expressing their own clearly.

> CCSS.ELA-Literacy.SL.8.1.A Come to discussions prepared, having read or researched material under study; explicitly draw on that preparation by referring to evidence on the topic, text, or issue to probe and reflect on ideas under discussion.
>
> CCSS.ELA-Literacy.SL.8.1.B Follow rules for collegial discussions and decision-making, track progress toward specific goals and deadlines, and define individual roles as needed.
>
> CCSS.ELA-Literacy.SL.8.1.C Pose questions that connect the ideas of several speakers and respond to others' questions and comments with relevant evidence, observations, and ideas.
>
> CCSS.ELA-Literacy.SL.8.1.D Acknowledge new information expressed by others, and, when warranted, qualify or justify their own views in light of the evidence presented.

CCSS.ELA-Literacy.SL.8.2 Analyze the purpose of information presented in diverse media and formats (e.g., visually, quantitatively, orally) and evaluate the motives (e.g., social, commercial, political) behind its presentation.

CCSS.ELA-Literacy.SL.8.3 Delineate a speaker's argument and specific claims, evaluating the soundness of the reasoning and relevance and sufficiency of the evidence and identifying when irrelevant evidence is introduced.

CCSS.ELA-Literacy.SL.8.4 Present claims and findings, emphasizing salient points in a focused, coherent manner with relevant evidence, sound valid reasoning, and well-chosen details; use appropriate eye contact, adequate volume, and clear pronunciation.

CCSS.ELA-Literacy.SL.8.5 Integrate multimedia and visual displays into presentations to clarify information, strengthen claims and evidence, and add interest.

CCSS.ELA-Literacy.SL.8.6 Adapt speech to a variety of contexts and tasks, demonstrating command of formal English when indicated or appropriate. (See grade 8 Language standards 1 and 3 for specific expectations.)

Language

CCSS.ELA-Literacy.L.8.1 Demonstrate command of the conventions of standard English grammar and usage when writing or speaking.

    CCSS.ELA-Literacy.L.8.1.A Explain the function of verbals (gerunds, participles, infinitives) in general and their function in particular sentences.

    CCSS.ELA-Literacy.L.8.1.B Form and use verbs in the active and passive voice.

    CCSS.ELA-Literacy.L.8.1.C Form and use verbs in the indicative, imperative, interrogative, conditional, and subjunctive mood.

    CCSS.ELA-Literacy.L.8.1.D Recognize and correct inappropriate shifts in verb voice and mood.

CCSS.ELA-Literacy.L.8.2 Demonstrate command of the conventions of standard English capitalization, punctuation, and spelling when writing.

    CCSS.ELA-Literacy.L.8.2.A Use punctuation (comma, ellipsis, dash) to indicate a pause or break.

    CCSS.ELA-Literacy.L.8.2.B Use an ellipsis to indicate an omission.

    CCSS.ELA-Literacy.L.8.2.C Spell correctly.

CCSS.ELA-Literacy.L.8.3 Use knowledge of language and its conventions when writing, speaking, reading, or listening.

    CCSS.ELA-Literacy.L.8.3.A Use verbs in the active and passive voice and in the conditional and subjunctive mood to achieve particular effects (e.g., emphasizing the actor or the action; expressing uncertainty or describing a state contrary to fact).

CCSS.ELA-Literacy.L.8.4 Determine or clarify the meaning of unknown and multiple- meaning words or phrases based on *grade 8 reading and content*, choosing flexibly from a range of strategies.

    CCSS.ELA-Literacy.L.8.4.A Use context (e.g., the overall meaning of a sentence or paragraph; a word's position or function in a sentence) as a clue to the meaning of a word or phrase.

    CCSS.ELA-Literacy.L.8.4.B Use common, grade-appropriate Greek or Latin affixes and roots as clues to the meaning of a word (e.g., *precede, recede, secede*).

    CCSS.ELA-Literacy.L.8.4.C Consult general and specialized reference materials (e.g., dictionaries, glossaries, thesauruses), both print and digital, to find the pronunciation of a word or determine or clarify its precise meaning or its part of speech.

    CCSS.ELA-Literacy.L.8.4.D Verify the preliminary determination of the meaning of a word or phrase (e.g., by checking the inferred meaning in context or in a dictionary).

CCSS.ELA-Literacy.L.8.5 Demonstrate understanding of figurative language, word relationships, and nuances in word meanings.

    CSS.ELA-Literacy.L.8.5.A Interpret figures of speech (e.g., verbal irony, puns) in context.

    CCSS.ELA-Literacy.L.8.5.B Use the relationship between particular words to better understand each of the words.

    CCSS.ELA-Literacy.L.8.5.C Distinguish among the connotations (associations) of words with similar denotations (definitions) (e.g., *bullheaded, willful, firm, persistent, resolute*).

CCSS.ELA-Literacy.L.8.6 Acquire and use accurately grade-appropriate general academic and domain-specific words and phrases; gather vocabulary knowledge when considering a word or phrase important to comprehension or expression.

APPENDIX B
MATH STANDARDS

The Number System
CCSS.Math.Content. 8.NS.A.1 Know that numbers that are not rational are called irrational. Understand informally that every number has a decimal expansion; for rational numbers show that the decimal expansion repeats eventually, and convert a decimal expansion which repeats eventually into a rational number.
CCSS.Math.Content.8.NS.A.2 Use rational approximations of irrational numbers to compare the size of irrational numbers, locate them approximately on a number line diagram, and estimate the value of expressions (e.g., π^2). *For example, by truncating the decimal expansion of $\sqrt{2}$, show that $\sqrt{2}$ is between 1 and 2, then between 1.4 and 1.5, and explain how to continue on to get better approximations.*

Expressions and Equations
CCSS.Math.Content.8.EE.A.1 Know and apply the properties of integer exponents to generate equivalent numerical expressions. For example, $3^2 \times 3^{-5} = 3^{-3} = \left(\dfrac{1}{3}\right)^3 = \dfrac{1}{27}$.
CCSS.Math.Content.8.EE.A.2 Use square root and cube root symbols to represent solutions to equations of the form $x^2 = p$ and $x^3 = p$, where p is a positive rational number. Evaluate square roots of small perfect squares and cube roots of small perfect cubes. Know that $\sqrt{2}$ is irrational.
CCSS.Math.Content.8.EE.A.3 Use numbers expressed in the form of a single digit times an integer power of 10 to estimate very large or very small quantities, and to express how many times as much one is than the other. *For example, estimate the population of the United States as 3 times 10^8 and the population of the world as 7 times 10^9, and determine that the world population is more than 20 times larger.*
CCSS.Math.Content.8.EE.A.4 Perform operations with numbers expressed in scientific notation, including problems where both decimal and scientific notation are used. Use scientific notation and choose units of appropriate size for measurements of very large or very small quantities (e.g., use millimeters per year for seafloor spreading). Interpret scientific notation that has been generated by technology.
CCSS.Math.Content.8.EE.B.5 Graph proportional relationships, interpreting the unit rate as the slope of the graph. Compare two different proportional relationships represented in different ways. For example, compare a distance-time graph to a distance-time equation to determine which of two moving objects has greater speed.
CCSS.Math.Content.8.EE.B.6 Use similar triangles to explain why the slope m is the same between any two distinct points on a non-vertical line in the coordinate plane; derive the equation $y = mx$ for a line through the origin and the equation $y = mx + b$ for a line intercepting the vertical axis at b.

CCSS.Math.Content.8.EE.C.7 Solve linear equations in one variable.
    CCSS.Math.Content.8.EE.C.7.A Give examples of linear equations in one variable with one solution, infinitely many solutions, or no solutions. Show which of these possibilities is the case by successively transforming the given equation into simpler forms, until an equivalent equation of the form $x = a$, $a = a$, or $a = b$ results (where a and b are different numbers).
    CCSS.Math.Content.8.EE.C.7.B Solve linear equations with rational number coefficients, including equations whose solutions require expanding expressions using the distributive property and collecting like terms.

CCSS.Math.Content.8.EE.C.8 Analyze and solve pairs of simultaneous linear equations.

> **CCSS.Math.Content.8.EE.C.8.A** Understand that solutions to a system of two linear equations in two variables correspond to points of intersection of their graphs, because points of intersection satisfy both equations simultaneously.
>
> **CCSS.Math.Content.8.EE.C.8.B** Solve systems of two linear equations in two variables algebraically, and estimate solutions by graphing the equations. Solve simple cases by inspection. *For example, 3x + 2y = 5 and 3x + 2y = 6 have no solution because 3x + 2y cannot simultaneously be 5 and 6.*
>
> **CCSS.Math.Content.8.EE.C.8.C** Solve real-world and mathematical problems leading to two linear equations in two variables. *For example, given coordinates for two pairs of points, determine whether the line through the first pair of points intersects the line through the second pair.*

Functions

CCSS.Math.Content.8.F.A.1 Understand that a function is a rule that assigns to each input exactly one output. The graph of a function is the set of ordered pairs consisting of an input and the corresponding output.[1] [1] Function notation is not required for Grade 8.

CCSS.Math.Content.8.F.A.2 Compare properties of two functions each represented in a different way (algebraically, graphically, numerically in tables, or by verbal descriptions). *For example, given a linear function represented by a table of values and a linear function represented by an algebraic expression, determine which function has the greater rate of change.*

CCSS.Math.Content.8.F.A.3 Interpret the equation $y = mx + b$ as defining a linear function, whose graph is a straight line; give examples of functions that are not linear. *For example, the function $A = s^2$ giving the area of a square as a function of its side length is not linear because its graph contains the points (1,1), (2,4) and (3,9), which are not on a straight line.*

CCSS.Math.Content.8.F.B.4 Construct a function to model a linear relationship between two quantities. Determine the rate of change and initial value of the function from a description of a relationship or from two (x, y) values, including reading these from a table or from a graph. Interpret the rate of change and initial value of a linear function in terms of the situation it models, and in terms of its graph or a table of values.

CCSS.Math.Content.8.F.B.5 Describe qualitatively the functional relationship between two quantities by analyzing a graph (e.g., where the function is increasing or decreasing, linear or nonlinear). Sketch a graph that exhibits the qualitative features of a function that has been described verbally.

Geometry

CCSS.Math.Content.8.G.A.1 Verify experimentally the properties of rotations, reflections, and translations:

> **CCSS.Math.Content.8.G.A.1.A** Lines are taken to lines, and line segments to line segments of the same length.
>
> **CCSS.Math.Content.8.G.A.1.B** Angles are taken to angles of the same measure.
>
> **CCSS.Math.Content.8.G.A.1.C** Parallel lines are taken to parallel lines.

CCSS.Math.Content.8.G.A.2 Understand that a two-dimensional figure is congruent to another if the second can be obtained from the first by a sequence of rotations, reflections, and translations; given two congruent figures, describe a sequence that exhibits the congruence between them.

CCSS.Math.Content.8.G.A.3 Describe the effect of dilations, translations, rotations, and reflections on two-dimensional figures using coordinates.

CCSS.Math.Content.8.G.A.4 Understand that a two-dimensional figure is similar to another if the second can be obtained from the first by a sequence of rotations, reflections, translations, and dilations; given two similar two-dimensional figures, describe a sequence that exhibits the similarity between them.

CCSS.Math.Content.8.G.A.5 Use informal arguments to establish facts about the angle sum and exterior angle of triangles, about the angles created when parallel lines are cut by a transversal, and the angle-angle criterion for similarity of triangles. *For example, arrange three copies of the same triangle so that the sum of the three angles appears to form a line, and give an argument in terms of transversals why this is so.*

CCSS.Math.Content.8.G.B.6 Explain a proof of the Pythagorean Theorem and its converse.

CCSS.Math.Content.8.G.B.7 Apply the Pythagorean Theorem to determine unknown side lengths in right triangles in real-world and mathematical problems in two and three dimensions.

CCSS.Math.Content.8.G.B.8 Apply the Pythagorean Theorem to find the distance between two points in a coordinate system.

CCSS.Math.Content.8.G.C.9 Know the formulas for the volumes of cones, cylinders, and spheres and use them to solve real-world and mathematical problems.

Statistics and Probability

CCSS.Math.Content.8.SP.A.1 Construct and interpret scatter plots for bivariate measurement data to investigate patterns of association between two quantities. Describe patterns such as clustering, outliers, positive or negative association, linear association, and nonlinear association.

CCSS.Math.Content.8.SP.A.2 Know that straight lines are widely used to model relationships between two quantitative variables. For scatter plots that suggest a linear association, informally fit a straight line, and informally assess the model fit by judging the closeness of the data points to the line.

CCSS.Math.Content.8.SP.A.3 Use the equation of a linear model to solve problems in the context of bivariate measurement data, interpreting the slope and intercept. *For example, in a linear model for a biology experiment, interpret a slope of 1.5 cm/hr as meaning that an additional hour of sunlight each day is associated with an additional 1.5 cm in mature plant height.*

CCSS.Math.Content.8.SP.A.4 Understand that patterns of association can also be seen in bivariate categorical data by displaying frequencies and relative frequencies in a two-way table. Construct and interpret a two-way table summarizing data on two categorical variables collected from the same subjects. Use relative frequencies calculated for rows or columns to describe possible association between the two variables. *For example, collect data from students in your class on whether or not they have a curfew on school nights and whether or not they have assigned chores at home. Is there evidence that those who have a curfew also tend to have chores?*